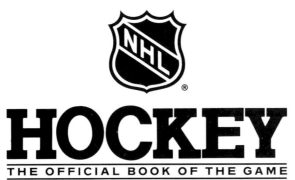

HOCKEY

THE OFFICIAL BOOK OF THE GAME

★ ★ ★ ★ ★ ★ ★

HOCKEY

THE OFFICIAL BOOK OF THE GAME

MALLARD
PRESS

MALLARD PRESS
An imprint of BDD Promotional Book Company, Inc.
666 Fifth Avenue,
New York, N.Y. 10103

"Mallard Press and its accompanying design and logo
are trademarks of BDD Promotional Book Company,
Inc."

Copyright © National Hockey League Services, Inc.
and Dan Diamond and Associates, Inc., 1990

First published in the United States of America
in 1990 by The Mallard Press
by arrangement with The Hamlyn Publishing Group
Limited, a division of Reed International Books,
Michelin House, 81 Fulham Road, London SW3 6RB,
England

ISBN 0-792-45283-6
8 7 6 5 4 3 2 1

Printed and bound in Hong Kong

**Photographic
Acknowledgements**
All of the photographs in this book were obtained
from NHL Services, Inc., the Hockey Hall of Fame and
Museum and Bruce Bennett Studios.

INTRODUCTION

Welcome to the first edition of *NHL Hockey: The Official Book of the Game.*

This book brings together more than 500 descriptions of the people, teams, events, anecdotes and technical terms that make up what is undisputedly the world's fastest game. Arranged from A to Z, *NHL Hockey: The Official Book of the Game* is easy to use. It describes the achievements of the game's all-time great players, coaches and managers, and provides background on early leagues.

It looks at junior, college and youth hockey in the United States and Canada and focuses on the brightest stars of today's NHL.

International, European and Olympic hockey are also covered, with special entries for each major hockey nation and international tournament. As Scandinavian, Czech and Soviet players further make their mark in the NHL, international hockey – whether involving club or national teams – cannot help but continue to improve the sport.

This book is published at a time of great growth in hockey. NHL rosters are dotted with gifted star players from North America and Europe and, beginning in 1991-92, a further expansion will see new teams enter the League.

But with this growth comes a desire to observe and enjoy hockey from the perspective of the game's rich history. Two milestones are fast approaching: the 75th anniversary season of the NHL will be celebrated in 1991-92 and the centennial of the Stanley Cup in 1992-93. As well, 1992 will also see an entirely new and greatly expanded Hockey Hall of Fame which will open its doors in downtown Toronto.

The writers of *NHL Hockey: The Official Book of the Game,* bring more than a century of combined hockey knowledge and love of the game to the pages in this book. Their goal is to connect the excitement of today's hockey with the sport's storied past and the promise of its exciting future.

Hoping this book and the game of hockey bring you much pleasure in the years to come...

National Hockey League 1990

Abel, Sid

b. Melville, Saskatchewan, 22 February 1918.
Hall of Fame: 1969

Sid Abel began his NHL career in 1938 with the Detroit Red Wings and spent nine full seasons and parts of three others in a Detroit uniform. He was an all-star, a Hart Trophy winner, and captain of the Wings at 24, establishing himself as one of the league's great centers on Detroit's Production Line with Gordie Howe and Ted Lindsay. Abel scored 189 goals in the NHL, including a personal high of 34 in 1949-50. He left Detroit in 1952 to become playing coach of the Chicago Blackhawks, leading that team to its first playoff berth in nine seasons. Sid left Chicago after two seasons, but returned to coaching midway through 1957-58 with Detroit. He became general manager in 1962, succeeding Jack Adams. In his 10½ years behind the Wings' bench, Abel's teams won a league championship and made the Stanley Cup playoffs seven times.

Adams, Charles

b. Newport, Vermont, 18 October 1876; d. 1947.
Hall of Fame: Builder, 1960

Charles Adams worked with Art Ross to establish the Boston Bruins, the first U.S.-based NHL franchise. The Bruins played their first game and the first NHL game in the United States on 1 December 1924, a 2-1 victory over the Canadiens. In 1926, Adams purchased the entire Western Canada League for $300,000, securing for the Bruins stars such as Eddie Shore, Harry Oliver, Mickey MacKay and Duke Keats while numerous other fine players were made available to Detroit, Chicago and New York. As a result of this player-wealth, the NHL blossomed into a big-time operation. In 1927, he issued financial guarantees that resulted in the construction of the Boston Garden, where the Bruins still play.

Adams, Jack

b. Fort William, Ontario, 14 June 1895; d. 1 May 1968. Hall of Fame: 1959

Center Jack Adams was a fine player and one of hockey's greatest executive talents. Before joining Detroit in 1927 as manager-coach, he played as an amateur in the Northern Michigan Senior League as well as in Peterborough and Sarnia, Ontario. His pro career began with the Toronto Arenas in 1918. Like many early stars, Adams played for numerous teams. He won the scoring title in the Pacific Coast Hockey Association with 24 goals in 24 games with Vancouver and later played for Toronto St. Pats and for the Ottawa Senators, Stanley Cup winners in 1926-27. As coach and manager of the Red Wings, Adams developed the hockey farm system and built winning teams. His Detroit clubs won 12 regular-season championships, and seven Stanley Cups. His greatest personal satisfaction came from the development of Gordie Howe. He was president of the Central Pro League from 1962 to 1968.

Adams, Weston Sr.

b. 9 August 1904; d. 19 March 1973. Hall of Fame: Builder, 1972

The son of Boston Bruins' founder Charles Adams, Weston Adams, Sr. was continuously and intimately associated with the Boston Bruins throughout his life. He became president of the club in 1936, relinquishing this office during World War II when the Bruins merged with the Boston Garden Arena Corporation. When the Bruins' fortunes flagged in the early 1960s, he set out an intensive recruiting program and personally scouted all over North America. He became president of the Bruins in 1964, remaining in office until 1969 when he retired in favor of his son, Weston, Jr. He was responsible for the now-common practice of removing the goaltender for an extra attacker on a delayed penalty call.

Ahearne, Bunny

b. County Wexford, Ireland, 19 November 1900; d. 11 April 1985. Hall of Fame: Builder, 1977

Bunny Ahearne became secretary of the British Ice Hockey Association in 1933 and retained that position for 40 years. He managed the British Nationals, a team bolstered by Canadians of British parentage which won the 1936 Olympic gold medal. He became IIHF president in 1957, and held key positions until his retirement in 1975. During the Ahearne years, the IIHF championship became a leading international sports event. He negotiated lucrative broadcast rights sales and pioneered rink-board advertising decades before its first appearance in North American rinks.

Allan Cup

The Allan Cup is awarded to the senior A hockey champion of Canada and the U.S. It was donated by steamship magnate Sir Montagu Allan in 1908. Since 1928, it has been awarded by the Canadian Amateur Hockey Association to the best Canadian or American amateur hockey team at the senior A level. The only American team to win the award was the Spokane (Washington) Jets, winners in 1970 and 1972. Until the early 1960s, the Allan Cup winner represented Canada in international competition.

All-Star Game

Before the NHL officially sanctioned an annual all-star contest, three unofficial benefit games were held. The first was the Ace Bailey game, held in 1934 for Toronto player Ace Bailey who had been injured when checked from behind by Boston's Eddie Shore. This game saw the Toronto Maple Leafs play the NHL's all-stars. The Howie Morenz benefit game was played in 1937 to raise money for Morenz's family after the star player's untimely death. This game saw a combined Montreal Maroons and Canadiens squad play the NHL stars. The Babe Siebert game was played in 1939 to raise money for Seibert's family after the Montreal player's death by drowning the previous summer. This game saw the Canadiens play the league's all-stars. The first official NHL all-star game was played in Maple Leaf Gardens in 1947. It featured the Stanley Cup champion Toronto Maple Leafs against the NHL's all-stars. The game was well-received and though the format has been modified through the years the all-star game continues in the NHL today as an annual midseason match between the Wales and Campbell Conference all-star teams.

All-Star Team

NHL all-star teams were first selected in the 1930-31 season when the following players were named: First team – Charlie Gardiner, Chicago; Eddie Shore, Boston; 'King' Clancy, Toronto;

Opposite: Jack Adams' success as a coach and manager inspired the NHL to introduce the Jack Adams Award in 1974 to honor the League's coach of the year. Jacques Demers of the Detroit Red Wings is the only man to have won the award twice, capturing the honor in 1987 and again in 1988.

Howie Morenz, Canadiens; Bill Cook, Rangers; Aurel Joliet, Canadiens; Lester Patrick, Rangers, coach. Second team – 'Tiny' Thompson, Boston; Sylvio Mantha, Canadiens; 'Ching' Johnson, New York; Frank Boucher, New York; 'Dit' Clapper, Boston; 'Bun' Cook, New York; Dick Irvin, Chicago, coach. Over the years an assortment of methods were employed to select the all-stars. Voting for the team currently is conducted by members of the Professional Hockey Writers'

Association at the end of each season. Coaches are no longer selected as part of the annual all-star teams.

Amateur Hockey Association of the United States (AHAUS)

The Amateur Hockey Association of the United States was born out of a dispute between professional hockey's leaders and those who

Campbell Conference all-stars, left to right, Dave Ellett, Mark Messier, Joey Mullen and Joe Nieuwendyk celebrate a goal during the Campbell's 9–5 win in the 40th Annual All-Star Game played 7 February 1989 in Edmonton. The Campbell Conference has won only three all-star games since the current format was established in 1975.

headed America's venerable Amateur Athletic Union (AAU). The leading force behind AHAUS's development was Tommy Lockhart, who ran both the New York Rovers hockey club and the Eastern Amateur Hockey League in which the Rovers played. AHAUS developed as an outgrowth of the Eastern League and soon controlled much of amateur hockey in the United States. When it came time to choose Olympic teams, AHAUS collided with the AAU and the bodies battled for through the 1930s and 1940s with AHAUS eventually emerging as the game's governing body in the U.S. Today, the organization is headed by former NHL coach Bob Johnson and is based in Colorado. AHAUS, also known as USA Hockey, is involved in numerous activities, from the organizing of the Olympic team to the publication of technical hockey manuals.

American Hockey League (AHL)

The American Hockey League is one of the two top minor pro leagues in North America. It evolved from three leagues – the Canadian Professional League, the International League, and the Canadian-American League. The Canadian Professional and the Can-Am leagues began in 1926-27, with the former giving way to the International League after three years. Later,

the Can-Am League was also absorbed by the International League, forming the American Hockey League in 1936-37. At the start, the American Hockey League was made up of Buffalo, Cleveland, Pittsburgh, and Syracuse in a western division and Philadelphia, Springfield, New Haven, and Providence in the east. The league thrived after World War II, despite the occasional loss of a franchise. Some AHL franchises moved on to the NHL or the World Hockey Association, including Buffalo, Philadelphia, Washington, and St. Louis. Change continued, both in number and location of franchises. The league continued through the 1980s and by the start of the 1989-90 season, there were fourteen cities divided into two divisions: Adirondack, Baltimore, Binghamton, Hershey, Newmarket, Rochester, and Utica in the Southern Division and Halifax, Maine, Moncton, New Haven, Cape Breton, Sherbrooke, and Springfield in the Northern Division. The AHL's top prize is the Calder Cup.

Anniversary Celebrations

The NHL will celebrate two anniversaries in the early 1990s. 1991-92 will be the 75th season of National Hockey League play and the 1993 playoffs will mark the centennial of the Stanley Cup.

The Wales Conference all-stars pose for the camera prior to the 1986 All-Star Game, held in Hartford. Although the fans choose the starting line-ups for both the Wales and Campbell Conference teams for the mid-season classic, representatives from each NHL team are selected by the coaches.

Apps, Syl (Sr.)

b. Paris, Ontario, 18 January 1915.
Hall of Fame: 1961

Center Syl Apps was an inspirational leader of the Toronto Maple Leafs. His entire pro career was spent with Toronto, most of it as team captain. He joined the Leafs in 1936 and became the first winner of the Calder Trophy, awarded by NHL president Frank Calder to the top rookie in the league. Apps earned five all-star team selections in seven seasons before joining the Canadian Army during World War II. He also won the Lady Byng Trophy, for the most gentlemanly player, in 1941-42. After the war, Apps returned to the Leafs, scoring an average of 25 goals in each of the next three seasons. Upon his retirement after the 1947-48 campaign, his career goals total stood at 201 [n] an average of 20 per season. He led the Leafs to three Stanley Cups. Apps was a gifted all-round athlete, finishing sixth in the pole vault at the 1936 Olympic Games. His son, Syl, Jr., played in the NHL in the 1970s.

As a player, Al Arbour was one of the few NHLers to wear eye glasses. He also has the distinction of winning back-to-back Stanley Cups with different teams. He manned the blueline for the Blackhawks when they won it all in 1961, then moved on to Toronto and won a Cup with the Leafs in 1962.

Arbour, Al

b. Sudbury, Ontario, 1 November 1932.

Al Arbour epitomized the term 'defensive defenseman' during his twelve NHL playing seasons, scoring only twelve goals in his career. He turned pro with the Detroit Red Wings in 1953 before moving on to the Chicago Blackhawks and the Toronto Maple Leafs. Arbour was chosen by St. Louis in the 1967 expansion draft and played his final four seasons with the Blues. After two brief stints as the coach of the Blues, Arbour stepped down to work as a scout for the Atlanta Flames. He became the third coach of the New York Islanders at the start of the 1973-74 season. With the help of outstanding draft picks, it took him only two seasons to turn the Islanders into a playoff contender. He was named the NHL coach of the year in 1979 and his team went on to win four consecutive Stanley Cups from 1980 to 1983. Arbour retired after the 1985-86 season and took a front office position with the Islanders, but returned to coaching, replacing Terry Simpson early in the 1988-89 campaign.

The Meadowlands Arena, home of the New Jersey Devils, is actually part of a three complex facility that also features a football stadium and a race track. The hockey stadium, known officially as the Brendan Byrne Meadowlands Arena, was named after a former New Jersey governor and opened in 1981. The facility seats 19,040 patrons for hockey.

Arenas

club	arena	seating capacity
Boston	Boston Garden	14,448
Buffalo	Memorial Auditorium	16,433
Calgary	Olympic Saddledome	20,002
Chicago	Chicago Stadium	17,317
Detroit	Joe Louis Sports Arena	19,275
Edmonton	Northlands Coliseum	17,313
Hartford	Hartford Civic Center Coliseum	15,580
Los Angeles	The Great Western Forum	16,005
Minnesota	Metropolitan Sports Center	15,093
Montreal	Montreal Forum	16,197
New Jersey	Byrne Meadowlands Arena	19,040
NY Islanders	Nassau Veterans' Memorial Coliseum	16,297
NY Rangers	Madison Square Garden	16,651
Philadelphia	The Spectrum	17,423
Pittsburgh	Civic Arena	16,025
Quebec	Colisee de Quebec	15,399
St. Louis	St. Louis Arena	17,188
Toronto	Maple Leaf Gardens	16,182
Vancouver	Pacific Coliseum	16,160
Washington	Capital Centre	18,130
Winnipeg	Winnipeg Arena	15,405

Armstrong, George

b. Skead, Ontario, 6 July 1930.
Hall of Fame: 1975

Rightwinger George Armstrong grew up near Sudbury, Ontario, the son of a Scotsman and his Indian wife. His heritage and his leadership ability earned the nickname 'The Chief'. He was a top junior player for Stratford and the Toronto Marlboros and played for the Marlboro senior team which won the Allan Cup in 1950. In 1,187 regular-season NHL games Armstrong recorded 296 goals and 417 assists for a total of 713 points. He was captain of the Maple Leaf teams that won four Stanley Cups in the 1960s.

Ashley, John

b. Galt, Ontario, 5 March 1930.
Hall of Fame: Referee, 1981

When he retired following the 1971-72 season, John Ashley was regarded as the top official in the NHL. He signed his first NHL contract in 1959-60 and went on to handle 17 games as a linesman and 605 games as a referee in regular-season play as well as working 59 Stanley Cup playoff matches. In 1971, he became the first man to referee the seventh game in each of three playoff series that required the maximum number of games. Following retirement as a referee, he was employed by the NHL, scouting young officials.

Atlanta Flames

The Atlanta Flames' franchise was born in 1972-73. Bill Putnam was named club president, Cliff Fletcher was chosen general manager and Bernie 'Boom Boom' Geoffrion was named coach. The team played eight seasons in Atlanta before shifting to Calgary for the 1980-81 campaign. The Flames made the playoffs in just their second season, losing to Stanley Cup-bound Philadelphia. In February 1975, Geoffrion stepped down as coach and was replaced by Fred Creighton. With stars like Willi Plett, Eric Vail and Guy Chouinard, the Flames regularly made it to post-season play, but did not progress far.

Avco World Trophy

Championship trophy of the World Hockey Association. The WHA played from 1972-73 to 1978-79 with New England winning in 1973, Houston in 1974 and 1975, Winnipeg in 1976, 1978 and 1979 and Quebec in 1977.

The NHL awards two most valuable player trophies each year. The regular-season MVP receives the Hart Trophy, at left. The top performer in the playoffs receives the Conn Smythe Trophy, at right.

Awards and Trophies

The following is a list of awards and trophies available to teams and players in the NHL

Team Awards

Clarence S. Campbell Bowl	Winner of the Campbell Conference finals
Presidents' Trophy	Team with the most regular-season points
Prince of Wales Trophy	Winner of the Price of Wales Conference finals
Stanley Cup	Winner of the Stanley Cup finals

Individual Awards

Jack Adams Award	Coach of the year
Budweiser/NHL Man of the Year	Player most active in community service
Lady Byng Memorial Trophy	Most gentlemanly player
Calder Memorial Trophy	Rookie of the year
King Clancy Memorial Trophy	Leadership and humanitarian contributions
Dodge Performance of the Year Award	Outstanding single NHL performance
Dodge Performer of the Year Award	Outstanding regular-season performer
Dodge Ram Tough Award	Player with most power-play, shorthanded, game-winning and game-tying goals
Hart Memorial Trophy	Most valuable player (selected by writers)
William M Jennings Trophy	Goaltender(s) allowing fewest goals
Bill Masterton Memorial Trophy	Perseverance, dedication and sportsmanship
James Norris Memorial Trophy	Best defenseman
Lester Patrick Trophy	Service to hockey in the United States
Lester B. Pearson Award	Most valuable player (selected by players)
Art Ross Trophy	Regular-season scoring leader
Frank J. Selke Trophy	Best defensive forward
Conn Smythe Trophy	Most valuable player in playoffs
Trico Goaltender Award	Best save percentage
Vezina Trophy	Best goaltender

Bailey, Irwin (Ace)

b. Bracebridge, Ontario, 3 July 1903.
Hall of Fame: 1975

Ace Bailey's NHL career ended suddenly in December of 1933 when a collision with Eddie Shore left him with a badly fractured skull. But in just 7½ seasons with the Maple Leafs, Bailey proved to be a top scoring winger, a fine checker and a complete team player. Bailey was an original Toronto Maple Leaf, having joined the Leafs' predecessor, the Toronto St. Patrick's. Bailey was the NHL's top scorer in 1928-29 and played on a Stanley Cup winner in 1932-33. When the famous Kid Line (Conacher-Jackson-Primeau) emerged as the Leafs' top scoring threat, Bailey was paired with Harold (Baldy) Cotton to become one of the finest penalty-killing units in the NHL. After recovering from his injury, Ace returned to hockey as a coach and as one of the minor officials at Maple Leaf Gardens.

Ballard, Harold

b. Toronto, Ontario, 30 July 1903; d. 11 April 1990.
Hall of Fame: Builder, 1977

Toronto Maple Leafs' owner Harold Ballard had a natural connection with hockey as his father was a leading skate manufacturer. Ballard managed the 1932 Allan Cup-winning Toronto Nationals and later became the financial backer of the senior and junior Toronto Marlboros. His Marlboro juniors won the Memorial Cup seven times and the seniors also won the Allan Cup in 1950. In 1961, he became one of three principal owners and chief executive of Maple Leaf Gardens, eventually acquiring complete control. He was a prime supporter of the first series with the Soviets and provided Maple Leaf Gardens without charge as a training camp for Team Canada in 1972.

Barilko, Bill

b. Timmins, Ontario, 25 March 1927; d. 26 August 1951.

Bill Barilko died at the height of his playing career in a plane crash a few months after scoring the winning goal in sudden-death overtime to clinch the Stanley Cup for the Toronto Maple Leafs in April 1951. Although Barilko never was an all-star, he had gained respect around the NHL for his fearsome 'snake-hip' bodychecks and his ability to block shots. Barilko became a Maple Leaf during the 1946-47 season, elevated from the Hollywood Wolves of the Pacific Coast League. He played on four Stanley Cup championship teams in five years prior to his untimely death at the age of 24.

Bathgate, Andy

b. Winnipeg, Manitoba, 28 August 1932.
Hall of Fame: 1975

Rightwinger Andy Bathgate was both a superb scorer and outstanding playmaker who recorded 1,008 points in 1,123 regular-season and playoff games. Despite a serious knee injury sustained in junior hockey, Bathgate broke in with the New York Rangers in 1952 and proved a durable NHLer, missing only five games in nine seasons. In 1958-59 he scored 40 goals, had 88 points and was named the league's MVP and, in 1961-62, tied Bobby Hull as the NHL's scoring leader. Bathgate was traded to Toronto in 1963-64, playing on his only Stanley Cup winner that season. He was later acquired by Detroit and then by Pittsburgh in the 1967 expansion draft. After one season with the Penguins and two in the minors, he completed his NHL career, returning to Pittsburgh in 1970-71. Despite playing in an era of superb rightwingers, Bathgate earned four NHL all-star selections.

Bauer, Father David

b. Waterloo, Ontario, 2 November 1924; d. 9 November 1988.
Hall of Fame, Builder: 1989

A skilled leftwinger and brother of Boston's Bobby Bauer, David Bauer was part of the Oshawa Generals' Memorial Cup-winning team in 1944. He declined the opportunity to turn pro, instead becoming a Basilian priest. He joined the teaching staff of St. Michael's College in Toronto, coaching the school's OHA junior A team to the 1961 Memorial Cup. Later in the 1960s he coached Canada's national hockey team, an elite amateur club of players who represented their country in international hockey competition while attending university. In its nine years of operation, this club rarely defeated strong national teams from the Soviet Union and Czechoslovakia, but represented Canada with dignity and sportsmanship that was a tribute to Father Bauer's leadership.

When Bill Barilko's plane disappeared while on a fishing trip during the summer of 1951, Conn Smythe vowed that no one would wear Barilko's number again. His playing number, 5, remains one of only two numbers retired by the Toronto Maple Leafs.

Beliveau, Jean

b. Trois Rivieres, Quebec, 31 August 1931.
Hall of Fame: 1972

Jean Beliveau was living hockey legend: a superbly talented centerman who was a natural leader and captain, a winner and one of the sport's finest ambassadors. Known as 'Le Gros Bill' because of his 6-3, 205-pound frame, Beliveau scored 507 goals during his 18 full seasons in the NHL. He was selected to NHL all-star teams on 10 occasions. He joined the Canadiens in 1953-54 and was the most highly-publicized rookie in the game. His exploits as a senior amateur player with the Quebec Aces had made him the best-known player outside of the NHL. In 1955-56 he was the NHL's scoring champion with 47 goals and 41 assists and was named MVP. Three seasons later, he scored 45 goals and, in 1963-64, won his second Hart Trophy. The following year he won the Conn Smythe Trophy as MVP in the Stanley Cup playoffs. In his final season, 1970-71, Beliveau collected 16 playoff assists and ended his career with his tenth Stanley Cup win.

Benedict, Clint

b. Ottawa, Ontario, 26 September 1892; d. 12 November 1976. Hall of Fame: 1965

In a 17-year career that began in 1913, goaltender Clint Benedict played on three Stanley Cup winners with the Ottawa Senators and one with the Montreal Maroons. In 56 playoff games, Benedict had 16 shutouts and an average of 2.16 goals-against per game. Benedict was one of the first goaltenders in pro hockey to wear a face mask. A shot by superstar Howie Morenz broke his nose and prompted Benedict to try a stiff leather mask. He later discarded it, claiming that it obscured his vision on low shots. Benedict also influenced a change in the rule that prohibited goaltenders stopping play by falling on the puck. Benedict stated that, "if you did it a bit sneaky and made it look accidental, you could fall on the puck without being penalized." Other netminders copied him and eventually it became part of the game.

Bentley, Doug

b. Delisle, Saskatchewan, 3 September 1916; d. 24 November 1972. Hall of Fame: 1964

Despite a playing weight of only 145 pounds, leftwinger Doug Bentley had all the attributes of a great hockey player. He was quick, a fine checker and a great scorer. After a junior and senior hockey career in Saskatchewan and Alberta, Bentley joined the Chicago Blackhawks in 1939. He played 12 seasons with the Hawks and, for several years, played with his brother Max and Bill Mosienko on the Pony Line, one of the NHL's finest forward combinations. Bentley won the NHL scoring title in 1942-43 and was named to the first all-star team on three occasions in the 1940s. A Chicago newspaper selected him as the city's best player of the half-century in 1950. After retiring from the NHL, Doug remained in the game as a player, coach and scout.

Bentley, Max

b. Delisle, Saskatchewan, 1 March 1920; d. 19 January 1984. Hall of Fame: 1966

Max Bentley tried out for three NHL teams before Chicago finally signed him in 1940. With the Blackhawks and, later, the Maple Leafs, Bentley established his credentials as one of the NHL's greatest playmakers. He centered Chicago's famous Pony Line with his brother Doug and Bill Mosienko. His 1947 trade from Chicago to Toronto sent shock waves throughout the NHL as Toronto gave up five high-quality players for Bentley and an amateur. Max played on three Stanley Cup championship teams with the Leafs. He was a first team all-star and won the Art Ross and Hart Trophies in 1945-46. He also captured the Art Ross Trophy as the NHL's leading scorer the previous season. Bentley scored 245 goals and had 299 assists for a total of 544 points in 646 regular-season games.

Bergeron, Michel

b. Montreal, Quebec, 12 June 1946.

A colorful personality with a volatile temperament, Michel Bergeron began his coaching career in midget in his Rosemont neighborhood of Montreal. He went behind the bench of the Trois-Rivieres Draveurs (QMJHL) in 1974-75 and led them to three league championships and two Memorial Cup finals. Signed as an assistant coach by the Quebec Nordiques in the summer of 1980, he replaced Maurice Filion as head coach two weeks into the 1980-81 season. In seven years his teams never missed the playoffs and went to the Wales Conference finals twice. He moved to the New York Rangers in 1987 but despite a winning percentage, failed to make the playoffs in 1987-88. His club made the playoffs the following seasons but Bergeron was fired on the final night of the regular season. He was immediately rehired as head coach of the Nordiques. His NHL lifetime record, including playoffs, through 1988-89 is 357 wins, 326 losses and 97 ties.

Bickell, J.P.

b. Toronto, Ontario, 26 September 1884; d. 22 August 1951. Hall of Fame: Builder, 1978

Financier J.P. Bickell was a silent partner in the Toronto St. Pats when control of that club was bought by Conn Smythe. Smythe convinced Bickell to become involved in the new club, known as the Maple Leafs, and to lend his support to the construction of a new arena. With Bickell's help, Maple Leaf Gardens stock was sold and the building erected in five months in the midst of the Depression. He became the first president, and chairman of the board of Maple Leaf Gardens, serving until his death.

Blake, Hector (Toe)

b. Victoria Mines, Ontario, 21 August 1912.
Hall of Fame: 1966

Toe Blake was part of an unprecedented 11 Stanley Cup championship teams. As a player he was part of one Cup winner with the Montreal Maroons and two more with the Canadiens. As coach of the Canadiens from 1955 to 1968, he led the club to eight triumphs in 13 years behind the bench. Blake joined the Maroons in 1934, but appeared in only nine games as this strong club won the Stanley Cup. A 1935 trade sent him across town to the Canadiens where he starred for 13 seasons. He was the NHL's MVP and top scorer in 1938-39, earned five all-star selections and was awarded the Lady Byng Trophy for gentlemanly play in 1945-46. He was part of the famous Punch Line with Elmer Lach and Maurice ('The Rocket') Richard. He scored 235 goals in 572 league games before a broken leg sustained in January of 1948 forced his retirement.

Blueline

A line of blue color, 12 inches wide, located 60 feet from the goal line and running across the width of the ice. There are two bluelines which divide the ice surface into either offensive or defensive zones, depending upon which team has possession of the puck. Linesmen closely monitor the bluelines for offside plays.

Bossy, Mike

b. Montreal, Quebec, 22 January 1957.

A fine junior player in Laval, Quebec, Mike Bossy was an instant NHL star, setting a rookie standard with 53 goals. He followed that up with a 69-goal sophomore season, the highest total of his career. Bossy remained one of the premier NHL sharpshooters through the early and mid-1980s, helping the Islanders to four Stanley Cup wins beginning in 1980. He began to suffer from back problems in 1986 and was forced to retire

Michel Bergeron or "le Petit Tigre" as he is known, was largely responsible for Guy Lafleur coming out of retirement and joining the New York Rangers in 1988. When Bergeron moved back to Quebec in 1989, Lafleur followed him and signed on to play for the Nordiques.

at the end of the 1986-87 season. His career totals included nine consecutive 50-goal seasons and 573 goals and 553 assists for 1,126 points in 752 games. Upon his retirement, he wrote an autobiography and now works as a broadcaster on French-language TV out of Quebec.

Boston Bruins

The Boston Bruins became the NHL's first American NHL franchise in 1924. Art Ross, a notable former player, was named coach of the team. The Bruins did not gain notoriety for their

Twelve different NHL teams had a chance to select Mike Bossy in the 1977 amateur draft, but were unwilling to take a chance on the Laval Nationals' product. The New York Islanders made Bossy their first round selection and he responded by firing at least 50 goals in each of his first nine campaigns, an NHL record.

Opposite page, top: The 1938-39 Boston Bruins, despite dominating the NHL in every category, needed three overtime winners from Mel "Sudden Death" Hill in the opening playoff round against the New York Rangers to win the seven-game series. Boston then defeated Toronto in five games to win the Stanley Cup. *Bottom:* The Bruins were also the NHL's top team in 1989-90, getting solid work on defense from Jim Wiemer (30) and Glen Wesley as well as standout goaltending from Andy Moog.

play on the ice until 1929, when they won their first Stanley Cup, led by Eddie Shore. They also won Cups in 1939 and 1941. Stars from these teams included Dit Clapper, Tiny Thompson, Cooney Weiland, Harry Oliver, Milt Schmidt, and Frank Brimsek. The Bruins' modern era began in 1966-67 with the arrival of rookie sensation Bobby Orr and new coach Harry Sinden. Manager Milt Schmidt completed a trade with Chicago the next year which brought Phil Esposito and Ken Hodge to the Bruins and put them in the playoffs for the first time in nine seasons. The Bruins won the Stanley Cup in 1970 and 1972. Sinden took over as g.m. in 1973 and Don Cherry became coach in 1974. Sinden was the architect of 'the Trade,' which sent Esposito and Carol Vadnais to the New York Rangers in exchange for Brad Park, Jean Ratelle, and Joe Zanussi in 1975. The club reached the Cup finals finals in 1977 and 1978, losing both times to the Montreal Canadiens. The Bruins iced hard-working, contending teams throughout the 1980s, reaching the Cup final once again in 1988 under coach Terry O'Reilly who was replaced a year later by former defenseman Mike Milbury.

CUMULATIVE RECORD

	GP	Won	Lost	Tied	Pct
Regular Season	4272	2040	1593	639	.452
Playoffs	415	202	207	6	.494
Series 87, W 41, L 46					
TOTALS	4687	2242	1800	645	.547

Bouchard, Emile (Butch)

b. Montreal, Quebec, 11 September 1920.
Hall of Fame: 1966

Butch Bouchard burst onto the hockey scene in Montreal in 1941-42, launching a 14-season career as a defenseman for the Canadiens. A big man, a playmaker and a leader, Bouchard was voted to the first all-star team three times and to the second twice. He scored 49 goals and had 144 assists and was captain of the Canadiens from 1948-49 to 1955-56. He played on four Cup winners. His son Pierre also played defense for the Canadiens and was a fan favorite in Montreal.

Boucher, Frank

b. Ottawa, Ontario 7 October 1901;
d. 12 December 1977.
Hall of Fame: 1958

Frank Boucher was one hockey's greatest playmakers and greatest gentlemen. He won the Lady Byng Trophy for gentlemanly play seven times in eight seasons and was finally given permanent possession of the original trophy. He began his pro career in Ottawa in 1921, playing on a star-studded team that included his brother George. He moved to the west coast the following year, playing four years for the Vancouver Maroons. When the Pacific Coast League broke up, he went to New York and wound up centering Bill and Bun Cook on one of the great lines of the era. Frank stayed with the Rangers' organization from 1926 until 1944. He played on two Stanley Cup winners in New York and coached the Rangers to a third championship in 1939-40. He was named to the NHL all-star team on four occasions.

Boucher, George (Buck)

b. Ottawa, Ontario, 18 August 1896;
d. 17 October 1960. Hall of Fame: 1960

George (Buck) Boucher played 20 years of pro hockey and was one of the best defensemen in the game. He joined the powerful Ottawa Senators in 1915 and was part of four Cup winners before being sold to the Montreal Maroons midway through the 1928-29 season. After two seasons and a half with the Maroons, he joined the Blackhawks in Chicago for his final NHL campaign. Boucher continued to play until 1934, and continued in the sport as a coach. He helped build the Ottawa RCAF team that won the Olympic championship in 1948 and coached an Ottawa club to Canada's senior hockey championship in 1949. His four brothers were also fine players and all but one played major-league hockey.

Bourque, Ray

b. Montreal, Quebec, 28 December 1960.

Ray Bourque follows in a long line of superb Bruins defensemen including Eddie Shore and Bobby Orr and ranks with the best to ever play the position. Bourque turned pro with Boston in 1979-80 and was an immediate hit, scoring 17 goals and 48 assists in 80 games. His 65 points were exceptional for a rookie and, not surprisingly, he won the Calder Trophy as the league's top freshman. Bourque soon emerged as the Bruins' leader and was a regular member of the NHL all-star team. He played for Team Canada in three Canada Cup tournaments (1981, 1984 and 1987) and was named to the 1987's all-tournament team. He won the Norris Trophy as the league's best defenseman in 1987 and 1988.

Bower, Johnny

b. Prince Albert, Saskatchewan, 8 November 1924. Hall of Fame: 1976

Goaltender Johnny Bower played almost 14

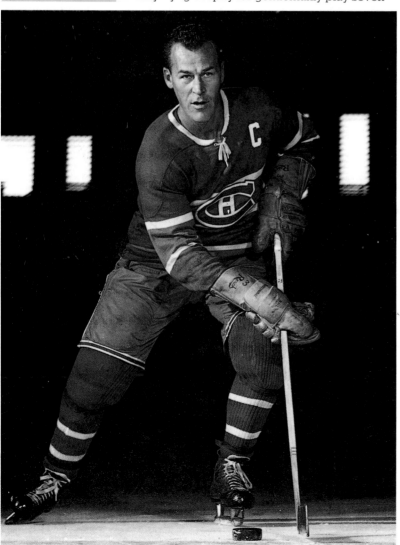

years in the minor leagues before sticking with a club in the NHL. Drafted in 1945 by Cleveland, he was the AHL's MVP and top goaltender on three occasions and played for the New York Rangers in 1953-54, but didn't land a permanent spot on an NHL roster until he was drafted by the Toronto Maple Leafs in 1958-59. He played 11 seasons with the Leafs and worked hard in every game and practice. With Bower, the Leafs won four Stanley Cups. He shared the Vezina Trophy in 1964-65 with Terry Sawchuk. His career regular-season goals-against average was 2.52 with 37 shutouts.

Bowman, Scotty

b. Montreal, Quebec, 18 September 1933.
Coach Scotty Bowman guided the Montreal Canadiens to five Stanley Cup wins including four straight from 1976-1979. He was known as a master strategist and motivator although he could be extremely harsh with his players. He left the Habs to become general manager and coach of the Buffalo Sabres in 1979-80 and made deals that enabled the Sabres to stockpile top draft choices, some of which ripened into stars.

However despite talented personnel, the club never lived up to expectations in the playoffs and Bowman was replaced in the 1986-87 season. He has remained active in hockey as a television commentator in both Canada and the United States.

Brimsek, Frank

b. Eveleth, Minnesota, 26 September 1915.
Hall of Fame: 1966
Frank Brimsek broke in as an NHL goaltender with Boston in 1938-39 and from the start mesmerized opposition shooters. In his first season he was selected as the NHL's top rookie and won the Vezina Trophy as the league's leading goaltender. He earned the nickname 'Mr. Zero', twice recording three consecutive shutouts. He became one of the first American-born players to star in the NHL. Except for his final season with Chicago, Brimsek was a Bruin throughout his NHL career. He played on two Stanley Cup winners, won two all-star team selections and a second Vezina Trophy. He played 10 years in the NHL, missing two seasons because of military service during World War II.

Surehanded Frank Brimsek was the first American-born professional player inducted into the Hockey Hall of Fame.

Ray Bourque, above, was the fourth defenseman drafted in 1979 behind Rob Ramage, Craig Hartsburg and Keith Brown. Bourque has dominated the blueline for a decade, and has been named to the first or second all-star squad in every year he has played in the NHL.

Broadbent, Harry (Punch)

b. Ottawa, Ontario, 13 July 1892; d. 6 March 1971.
Hall of Fame: 1962

Rightwinger Harry (Punch) Broadbent set an NHL record that still stands when he scored one or more goals in 16 consecutive games in 1921-22. He was adept with his elbows as well, once leading the NHL in both scoring and penalty minutes. Broadbent played his amateur hockey in Ottawa before joining that city's club in the National Hockey Association in 1912-13. He recorded 21 goals that season and two years later had 24, but left hockey to serve in the Canadian Forces in World War I. He returned to Ottawa in 1919, and played five seasons before joining the Montreal Maroons. He returned to Ottawa in 1927-28 and went to the New York Americans in 1928-29. He lost a great deal of money in the stock market crash of 1929, quit hockey and joined the Royal Canadian Air Force. He played on four Cup winners.

Broda, Walter (Turk)

b. Brandon, Manitoba, 15 May 1914;
d. 17 October 1972.
Hall of Fame: 1967

One of the game's greatest "money goalies", Turk Broda saved his best hockey for the playoffs. His play for the Detroit Olympics in winning the 1935 International League championship resulted in his contract being sold to the Toronto Maple Leafs for what was at that time a record price of $8,000. He played for the Leafs for 16 years, losing two seasons to military service in World War II. He won the Vezina Trophy in 1940-41 and 1947-48 and shared it with Al Rollins in 1950-51 when the two combined in one of the NHL's first successful two-goalie systems. Broda backstopped the Leafs to five Stanley Cup championships, allowing just 2.08 goals-against per game while recording 13 shutouts in 101 playoff contests.

Brown, George

b. 1880; d. 1937.
Hall of Fame: Builder, 1961

George V. Brown was a pioneer of hockey in Boston. He organized a top amateur club, the

Boston Athletic Association hockey team, and acted as manager of the Boston Arena. When the Bruins moved into the new Boston Garden in 1928, he helped form the Canadian-American League and entered a team. This was the forerunner of today's AHL. He was also a founder of the Boston Marathon and, at the time of his death, was general manager of Boston Garden. The Brown family remained on the Boston Garden management committee for 38 years.

Brown, Walter

b. 10 February 1905; d. 7 September 1964.
Hall of Fame: Builder, 1962
At the time of his death, Walter Brown was president of Boston Garden, chairman of the Basketball Hall of Fame, member of the Hockey Hall of Fame Governing Committee and past-president of the IIHF. He was also co-owner and president of the Boston Bruins hockey club and the Boston Celtics basketball team. A longtime supporter of amateur and college hockey, Brown succeeded his father George as general manager of Boston Garden in 1937. He coached the Boston Olympics between 1930 and 1940 when this team won five United States national amateur championships and one world title.

Bucyk, John

b. Edmonton, Alberta, 12 May 1935.
Hall of Fame: 1981
John Bucyk was a both a durable and productive NHLer, retiring after the 1977-78 season – his 23rd in the league – with 556 goals and 813 assists for 1,369 points. At the time of his retirement, he was the NHL's fourth-leading all-time scorer. A big leftwinger, Bucyk broke into the NHL with the Red Wings, playing two seasons in Detroit before being traded to Boston for all-star goaltender Terry Sawchuk. He played 21 seasons with the Bruins, winning Stanley Cups in 1970 and 1972. He also won the Lady Byng Trophy in 1971, a season in which he scored 51 goals.

Buffalo Sabres

The Buffalo Sabres joined the NHL in 1970 with ex-Leaf boss Punch Imlach serving as coach and general manager. Imlach's excellent drafting quickly made the Sabres competitive. Gil Perreault, Rick Martin, Jim Schoenfeld, Craig Ramsay, and Danny Gare were all key picks for Buffalo. Trades brought Don Luce and Rene Robert to the Sabres. Perreault, Martin, and Robert formed the famous and deadly accurate scoring line that became known as the 'French Connection.' The Sabres made the playoffs just three years after their start, and reached the Stanley Cup finals in 1975, bowing to the Philadelphia Flyers. Wholesale front office changes were made in 1978-79, with Billy Inglis named interim coach before Scotty Bowman, coach of four consecutive Cup-winners in Montreal, joined the team as coach and g.m. the following season. Bowman gave way to Gerry Meehan as g.m. midway through 1986-87 and Rick Dudley was appointed coach for 1989-90, the franchise's 20th season in the NHL.

CUMULATIVE RECORD	GP	Won	Lost	Tied	Pct
Regular Season	1592	766	571	255	.561
Playoffs	110	49	61	0	.445
Series 24 W9 L15					
TOTALS	1702	815	632	255	.554

The Buffalo Sabres celebrate a goal during the 1989–90 season. Led by Ray Sheppard (23) and Pierre Turgeon (77), the Sabres finished third over-all in the NHL with 98 points. Their 45 victories over the course of the campaign were second only to the Boston Bruins.

Burns, Pat

b. St. Henri, Quebec, 4 April 1952.
Pat Burns served for 17 years with the Gatineau, Quebec and Ottawa police departments before becoming coach of the Hull Olympiques of the QMJHL in 1983-84. In 1985-86 he led that team to the finals of the Memorial Cup and, later in 1986, served as assistant coach of Team Canada at the World Junior Championship in Czechoslovakia. Burns turned pro as coach of the Sherbrooke Canadiens, the AHL farm club of Montreal Canadiens. In June of 1988 he became head

coach in Montreal and, in 1988-89, led the Canadiens to their best regular-season finish since 1978-79. The Canadiens posted 53 wins and nine ties in winning the Adams Division, finishing second in the league overall. They won the Prince of Wales Trophy before losing a six-game series to Calgary in the Stanley Cup finals. Burns was awarded the Jack Adams Trophy as coach of the year, only the third rookie coach to be given this honor.

Montreal Canadiens' coach Pat Burns with assistant Jacques Laperriere. Burns led the Habs to the Stanley Cup finals in his first year behind the bench. Laperriere has served as an assistant to four different head coaches in his nine year tenure on the Canadiens' coaching staff.

Butterfield, Jack

b. Regina, Saskatchewan, 1 August 1919.
Hall of Fame: Builder, 1980

Jack Butterfield helped keep minor pro hockey alive during the years of NHL expansion and competition for players from the WHA. As president of the American Hockey League, a league which provided hundred of players to the NHL, Butterfield spearheaded indemnification negotiations, twice rewrote the AHL constitution and bylaws, and several times revised player contract forms to stay abreast of a constantly changing hockey world. Jack came well prepared to assume the AHL presidency in 1966. After his playing career was cut short by an injury, he stayed in the game working at various times as a team public relations man, trainer, business manager, rink manager, concessions manager, coach and, finally, general manager.

Calder, Frank

b. 17 November 1877; d. 4 February 1943.
Hall of Fame: Builder, 1947

Frank Calder was the first president of the NHL when the new league was formed in 1917. He had been secretary of the old NHA and had the respect of club owners. He served as league president until 1943, guiding the NHL through its first American expansion in 1924 and 1926. To commemorate his service to hockey, the Calder Memorial Trophy is awarded annually to the top rookie in the NHL.

Calgary Flames

One of the NHL's most successful franchises, the Flames began life in Atlanta, Georgia, in 1972-73. Shifted to Calgary in 1980-81, the team improved steadily behind star players Lanny McDonald (66 goals in 1982-83) and Kent Nilsson (131 points in 1980-81). Competing in the Smythe Division with the powerful Edmonton Oilers, the Flames first went to the Stanley Cup finals in 1986, losing to Montreal in five games. The club cracked the 100-point barrier in 1987-88 with 105, winning the first of two consecutive Presidents' Trophies awarded to the NHL club finishing first overall. The Flames reached the Stanley Cup finals again in 1989, this time defeating the Canadiens in six games. The Flames were the first NHL club to sign players released by the Soviet Ice Hockey Federation when Sergei Priakin joined the club late in the 1988-89 season. The current Flames roster is one of the most powerful in the NHL and includes goaltender Mike Vernon, defenseman Al MacInnis, and forwards Doug Gilmour, Joe Mullen and Joe Nieuwendyk.

CUMULATIVE RECORD	GP	Won	Lost	Tied	Pct
Regular Season	1436	673	539	224	.547
Playoffs	125	58	67	0	.464
Series 27 W12 L15					
TOTALS	1561	731	606	224	.540

California Golden Seals

This was the name given the Oakland Seals when Charlie Finley bought the franchise before the 1970-71 season. He changed the team's uniform colors and dressed them in white skates but they remained, for the most part, cellar dwellers. Before the 1972-73 season they suffered a severe setback when Paul Shmyr, Gerry Pinder, Tom Webster, Norm Ferguson, Bobby

Sheehan and Wayne Carleton jumped to the WHA. In February 1974, the NHL bought the Seals from Finley and Munson Campbell be- came president. Mel Swig, a San Francisco hotelier and former owner of the San Francisco Seals, purchased the team from the league in 1975. The losing ways continued, however, and fan support remained weak. In 1976-77 the franchise was moved to Cleveland.

California Seals

The California Seals were a charter member of the newly created West Division in the NHL's great expansion of 1967-68. They had rejected playing in the Cow Palace, home of the former San Francisco Seals of the Western League, because of the building's poor sight lines. Instead, they played in the Oakland-Alameda County Coliseum, known as the 'Jewel Box.' Fans from San Francisco did not come in great numbers so, in November of 1967, the California Seals became the Oakland Seals in an attempt to increase local market appeal.

Campbell, Clarence

b. Fleming, Saskatchewan, 9 July 1905; d. 24 June 1984. Hall of Fame: Builder, 1966

Clarence Campbell assumed the presidency of the NHL in 1946. A graduate of the University of Alberta and Oxford, Campbell played on a touring hockey team of Canadians studying in England that included future Canadian Prime Minister Lester Pearson. Back in Canada, Campbell worked as a sports administrator and refereed lacrosse and NHL hockey prior to World War II. Two of his outstanding achievements as president of the NHL were the establishment in 1946 of the NHL Pension Society and the successful guidance of the league's expansion from six to 12 teams in 1967-68. In 1977 he retired after 31 years on the job.

Canada Cup

The Canada Cup is the premier international hockey tournament played in Canada. It was inaugurated in 1976, and is open to the world's best professional and amateur players who play as national teams from Canada, the Soviet Union, Czechoslovakia, Sweden, Finland, and the United States. (West Germany substituted for Finland in 1984). Four tournaments have been held, with Canada winning in 1976, 1984 and 1987 and the Soviet Union winning in 1981. The Canada Cup trophy is a stylized maple leaf sculpted out of nickel. The tournament grew out of the success of the first Canada-Russia series in 1972 in which top NHL players competed for the first time against the Soviet Nationals.

Canadian Amateur Hockey Association (CAHA)

The CAHA is the governing body of amateur hockey in Canada and was formed in Ottawa, Ontario, on December 4, 1914. The group's objectives include the formation of uniform rules for amateur hockey across Canada, the promotion and organization of tournaments and the formation of amateur hockey associations on the provincial level.

Captain and Alternate Captain

Each hockey club selects a captain and up to three alternates from its roster of active players. These skaters wear a 'C' or 'A' of approximately three inches in height on the front of their jerseys. Only captains or alternate captains may speak with the on-ice officials during the course of a game.

Carbonneau, Guy

b. Sept-Iles, Quebec, 18 March 1960.

Guy Carbonneau is part of the Montreal Canadiens' long tradition of superior defensive forwards such as Claude Provost, Don Marshall, and Bob Gainey. Carbonneau won the Frank Selke Trophy awarded to the NHL's top defensive forward in 1988 and again in 1989 and when team captain Gainey retired after the 1988-89 season, was named co-captain along with Chris Chelios. He played some of his best hockey en route to the 1986 Stanley Cup.

Caron, Ron

b. Hull, Quebec, 19 December 1929.

After coaching in amateur hockey, Ron Caron was hired by the Montreal Canadiens' organization in 1957 as a part-time scout. In 1966 he was promoted to head scout of the Montreal Junior Canadiens and contributed to the building of two Memorial Cup championship teams. In 1968 he became chief scout of the Canadiens and also served as assistant to general manager Sam Pollock. The following year he doubled as general manager of the Montreal Voyageurs of the AHL, maintaining that position until 1978 when he was appointed director of scouting and player personnel for the Canadiens. Following the 1982-83 season he joined the St. Louis Blues as general manager. Inheriting a team that did not participate in the 1983 draft, Caron rebuilt through frequent trading to the point where the Blues won Norris Division titles in 1984-85 and 1986-87, and took Calgary to seven games before losing in the Campbell Conference final in 1986.

Gary Suter of the Calgary Flames battles Mike Gartner for a loose puck. Suter, the first member of the Calgary Flames to win the Calder Trophy as rookie of the year, has developed into one of the NHL's steadiest defenseman.

Opposite: Guy Carbonneau of the Montreal Canadiens is one of the NHL's finest two-way players, an unselfish contributor who excels in the defensive aspect of the game. When he was asked by coach Pat Burns during the 1988–89 season to contribute offensively as well, Carbonneau responded by scoring a career-high 26 goals and capturing his second consecutive Selke Trophy.

Carpenter, Doug

b. Cornwall, Ontario, 1 July 1942.
Coach Doug Carpenter contributed greatly to the Toronto Maple Leafs' dramatic improvement in 1989-90. Toronto was his second NHL head coaching job, having coached the New Jersey Devils from 1984-85 to 1986-87. He graduated from McGill University and played nine seasons in the Eastern Hockey League before he started coaching. He led the the Cornwall Royals to the Memorial Cup in 1980 and then worked in the Leafs' minor pro chain until joining the Devils in 1984. He also coached Team Canada to a silver medal in the 1985 World Championships.

Cattarinich, Joseph

b. Levis, Quebec, 13 November 1881;
d. 7 December 1938. Hall of Fame: Builder, 1977

Joseph Cattarinich played an important role in the development of the NHL. On November 3, 1921, along with Leo Dandurand and Louis Letourneau, Cattarinich purchased the Montreal Canadiens for $11,000 and built the club into the star-studded 'Flying Frenchmen' featuring Newsy Lalonde, Howie Morenz, Joe Malone, Aurel Joliat, Georges Vezina and others. Under this management the club won the NHL title and the Stanley Cup on three occasions. Letourneau retired in 1931 but Cattarinich and Dandurand kept the Canadiens until 1935 when the realities of the Depression forced them to sell the team for $165,000.

Centennial Cup

Awarded annually to the top junior A hockey team in North America by the Canadian Amateur Hockey Association. The trophy was donated in 1970 by the province of Manitoba to commemorate its centennial as a Canadian province. There are currently 94 teams eligible to compete for the Centennial Cup, with two located in the United States. The cup is classified as Tier II, and is the second-highest level of competition for junior hockey in Canada.

Central Scouting Bureau

Originally called the Central Scouting Service, the bureau was established by the NHL in 1975 in order to provide a source of information to member clubs on North American Entry Draft prospects. Ten scouts operate full-time and report their findings to a head office located in Toronto. Three times a year the Bureau prepares a ranking of the top 252 North American players eligible for the draft. This information is made available to all 21 NHL teams.

Chadwick, Bill

b. New York, New York, 10 October 1915.
Hall of Fame: Referee, 1964

Bill Chadwick became an NHL linesman in 1940, then moved up to referee hundreds of regular-season and Stanley Cup contests until he retired in 1955. Chadwick was playing for the New York Rovers of the Eastern Amateur League when his career as an official began. Forced to sit out a game because of minor injuries, he was asked to substitute for a referee who had failed to appear. He enjoyed officiating and became the first referee to use hand signals to indicate infractions.

Challenge Cup

The Challenge Cup was a three-game series played at Madison Square Garden on 8, 10 and 11 February 1979, between the national team of the Soviet Union and Team NHL, a collection of the league's all-stars. These three games replaced the regular mid-season NHL all-star game. The Soviets won two of the three games including a 6-0 shutout in the deciding contest to take the series.

Checking

Checking is the name given to the various ways in which one player can legally restrain or impede the progress of another. A legal check occurs when one player bumps or becomes entangled with another with contact occurring from in front or from the side. The player initiating the check must keep his stick down and not use his arms to hold his opponent. Backchecking describes the act of checking an opponent while skating back toward the checker's own defensive zone. Effective backchecking keeps the opposing team from mounting a co-ordinated attack. Forechecking describes the act of pursuing an opponent when he has gained possession of the puck in his own defensive zone. It serves to break up plays before they can be mounted and often results in gaining possession of the puck in the opponent's defensive zone. An old hockey saying goes: "Forecheck, backcheck, pay check."

Cheevers, Gerry

b. St. Catharines, Ontario, 7 December 1940.
Hall of Fame: 1985

Gerry Cheevers earned his reputation as a big-game goaltender and was a vital part in the strong Boston teams of the 1970s. The Bruins won the Cup in 1970 and 1972 and reached the finals in 1977 and 1978. Cheevers was popular with fans in Boston and throughout the NHL, playing an exciting style that saw him challenge opposing shooters, leave his crease to handle the puck and make passes that aided the Bruins' transition from defense to offense. While other goaltenders in the 1970s had slightly better statistics, many NHL coaches would have chosen Cheevers as the goaltender they'd want in the nets with a championship on the line. A product of the Toronto Maple Leafs' farm system, in 13 NHL seasons, his goals-against average was 2.89 in the regular season and 2.64 in the playoffs. He also played 3½ seasons with Cleveland in the WHA returning to Boston in 1976. He retired after the 1979-80 season and was appointed coach of the Bruins in July of that year.

Chelios, Chris

b. Chicago, Illinois, 25 January 1962.

A native of Chicago, Chelios starred on defense for the 1984 U.S. Olympic team and then went directly to the Montreal Canadiens where his excellent skating, hard checking and superb point shot enabled him to make an instant impact in the NHL. In 1989 he won the Norris Trophy as the NHL's best defenseman and, in 1989-90, was named co-captain of the Canadiens along with Guy Carbonneau.

Chicago Blackhawks

The Chicago Blackhawks entered the NHL in 1926 under the guidance of Major Frederic McLaughlin. Coached by Pete Muldoon, the Hawks finished third in the five-team American Division in their first season. After being eliminated from the playoffs, McLaughlin fired Muldoon who, in turn, 'cursed' the Hawks to never finish in first place. The Blackhawks finally gained on-ice respectability in 1934 with their first Stanley Cup triumph under coach-general manager Tommy Gorman. They again won the Cup in 1938 with baseball umpire Bill Stewart coaching the team. The Blackhawks made the playoffs only once in twelve tries between 1947 and 1958. During that stretch there were fears

that the franchise would fold, but new owners Arthur Wirtz and Jim Norris hired general manager Tommy Ivan and put emphasis on development of the team's farm system. This investment was rewarded in 1961 as the Hawks won the Stanley Cup with such players as Bobby Hull and Stan Mikita. The Blackhawks reached the Cup finals in 1962 and 1965 and became the first of the 'old' teams to shift from the East to the West Division after expansion in 1967. The team shook off the 'Curse of Muldoon', finishing first in 1967-68 and then went on to four consecutive first-place finishes beginning in 1969-70, the season in which rookie goaltender Tony Esposito recorded 15 shutouts. Bobby Hull left the team to join the Winnipeg Jets of the WHA in 1972 and Bobby Orr joined it in an unsuccessful attempt to come back from knee surgery in 1976. Bob Pulford became g.m. in 1977 and Mike Keenan coach in 1988. The Blackhawks led the Norris Division for much of the 1989-90 schedule.

CUMULATIVE RECORD	GP	Won	Lost	Tied	Pct
Regular Season	4206	1696	1853	657	.481
Playoffs	340	154	181	5	.460
Series 76 W34 L42					
TOTALS	4546	1850	2034	662	.480

Clancy, Francis (King)

b. Ottawa, Ontario, 25 February 1903;
d. 10 November 1986. Hall of Fame: 1958

It is unlikely that any player enjoyed playing hockey more than King Clancy. A whirling skater with an irrepressible Irish twinkle, the 155-pound rushing defenseman broke in with the powerhouse Ottawa Senators in 1921, becoming a regular two seasons later. He played for two Cup winners in Ottawa, before becoming the central figure in a deal that saw Clancy traded to the Maple Leafs for $35,000 and two players in 1930. Toronto manager Conn Smythe saw Clancy as the piece of the puzzle the Leafs needed to win the Stanley Cup, a feat the team accomplished in 1931-32. Clancy was named to the NHL all-star team in four consecutive seasons and remained one of the NHL's best defensemen until his retirement early in the 1936-37 season. Clancy stayed in the game first as a coach and then as a referee. He returned to the Leafs as coach from 1950 to 1953 before moving into the club's front office. He remained a cheerful figure around Maple Leaf Gardens until his passing in 1986.

After King Clancy retired as a player, he coached the Montreal Maroons for a season before becoming a referee. He was named NHL referee-in-chief prior to the start of the 1949-50 season, but decided to hang up the whistle and return to the coaching ranks with the Montreal Canadiens' farm team in Cincinnati. From there, he rejoined the Leafs' organization, serving as coach, manager and vice-president until his death in 1986.

Clapper, Aubrey (Dit)

b. Newmarket, Ontario, 9 January 1907;
d. 21 January 1978. Hall of Fame: 1947

Dit Clapper was the first man to play 20 seasons in the NHL. He was a precocious talent, playing

junior at age 13. He joined the Bruins six years later and played his entire professional career with Boston. He was one of the NHL's biggest players and played nine seasons at right wing before switching to defense. He scored 228 goals and 246 assists in his career, including 41 goals in just 44 games in 1929-30. He was part of three Stanley Cup winners and was named to each of the first and second all-star teams on three occasions. Upon his retirement in 1947, he became coach of the Bruins, a post he held for two seasons.

Chris Chelios, the Habs' secretary of defense and a steady leader. Though injury-hit for much of the 1989–90 season, Chelios is still one of the NHL's top rearguards.

Opposite: Gerry Cheevers of the Boston Bruins wearing his "stitches" goalie mask. Cheevers began having stitches painted on his mask after he was hit during a practice session. Cheevers had the trainer paint a scar on the mask to simulate the damage he avoided by wearing the mask, and kept up the practice throughout the remainder of his career.

Clark, Wendel

b. Kelvington, Saskatchewan, 25, October 1966.

Drafted first overall by the Toronto Maple Leafs in 1985, Wendel Clark, who played both defense and forward in junior, was assigned to left wing by the Leafs and immediately established himself as a top-flight scorer. In 66 games as a rookie he scored 34 goals. In 1986-87 he played a full 80 games and seemed destined to reach the upper plateau in the league. But back problems slowed his development. He played only 28 and 15 games in the next two seasons and was in and out of the lineup 1989-90. He remained an effective and forceful player when able to compete.

Bobby Clarke moved from the ice to the front office with the Philadelphia Flyers, serving as general manager from 1984 until April of 1990.

Clarke, Bobby

b. Flin Flon, Manitoba, 13 August 1949.
Hall of Fame: 1987

Tenacious center Bobby Clarke was one of the hardest-working players in the NHL throughout

his 15-year career with the Philadelphia Flyers. Despite suffering from diabetes, Clarke had the desire and stamina necessary to play on the Flyers' first line, kill penalties and work the powerplay. Drafted 17th overall in 1969, Clarke claimed a place in the Philadelphia lineup. His productivity improved each year until he became the first expansion-team player to record a 100-point season in 1972-73, a season which saw him named team captain and win the first of three Hart Trophies as league MVP at age 23. One of the best faceoff men in the NHL, Clarke's Flyers won the Stanley Cup in 1974 and 1975. Clarke became general manager of the Flyers in 1984-85.

Cleghorn, Sprague

b. Montreal, Quebec, 1890; d. 11 July 1956.
Hall of Fame: 1958

Veteran observers of hockey have always insisted that defenseman Sprague Cleghorn was one of the most talented and roughest players to ever play the game. His career in the NHA and NHL spanned 1911 to 1928 and saw him suit up for Renfrew, the Montreal Wanderers, Ottawa, Toronto, the Montreal Canadiens and Boston. In Renfrew, Ontario, he was paired on defense with Cyclone Taylor, the premier rushing defenseman of the era. Cleghorn adopted Taylor's style with great success, once scoring five goals in a game and finishing his career with 163. His penchant for rough play placed him at the center of many on-ice brawls, the worst of which earned him a $200 fine and a suspension from the final game of the 1923 NHL playoffs. He played on Stanley Cup winners with the Ottawa Senators in 1920 and the Canadiens in 1924.

Cleveland Barons

There were two sets of Cleveland Barons [n] minor-pro and NHL. The minor pro franchise was one of the most successful independent teams in the 1940s and early 1950s and received serious consideration for an NHL franchise. The NHL Cleveland Barons resulted from the shifting of the Oakland Seals to Ohio in 1976. Fan support was inadequate and, after just two years, the club merged with the Minnesota North Stars. Cleveland's players moved to Minnesota, ending the NHL era in Ohio.

Coffey, Paul

b. Weston, Ontario, 1 June 1961.

Paul Coffey became the NHL's top rushing defenseman of the 1980s, earning four Stanley Cups, two Norris Trophies and five all-star selections with the Edmonton Oilers over seven seasons beginning in 1980-81. He was traded to

Pittsburgh in November of 1987 and after missing much of the 1987-88 campaign due to injury, recorded 30 goals, 113 points and a first team all-star selection in 1988-89.

Colorado Rockies

When the Kansas City Scouts achieved only 36 points in front of small crowds in their second season (1975-76), the franchise was moved to Denver for 1976-77 and was renamed the Colorado Rockies. In 1977-78, rookie defenseman Barry Beck registered 60 points and finished second in the Calder Trophy voting as the Rockies wound up second in the Smythe Division and made their only appearance in postseason play. The Rockies had one general manager, Ray Miron, and a plethora of coaches, including Johnny Wilson, Pat Kelly, Aldo Guidolin, Don Cherry, Billy MacMillan, Bert Marshall and Marshall Johnston. A further indicator of the franchise's instability was its willingness to trade its stars: Beck went to the Rangers in 1979 and Lanny McDonald to Calgary in 1981. The franchise was shifted to New Jersey where it played as the Devils beginning with the 1982-83 season.

Conacher, Charlie

b. Toronto, Ontario, 10 December 1909; d. 30 December 1967.
Hall of Fame: 1961

Rightwinger Charlie Conacher was a slick puckhandler with a hard shot who jumped directly to the Toronto Maple Leafs from junior hockey in 1929-30. He played nine seasons with the Leafs, one with Detroit and two with the New York Americans. Conacher led or was tied for the lead in goal scoring for four consecutive seasons beginning in 1932. He earned five all-star selections and was a member of the Maple Leafs' first Cup winner in 1932.

Connell, Alex

b. Ottawa, Ontario, 8 February 1900; d. 10 May 1958.
Hall of Fame: 1958

In 1927-28 goaltender Alex Connell set an NHL record with six consecutive shutouts and 446 minutes without allowing a goal. A fine athlete, Connell began tending goal while serving in the Canadian army in World War I. He played senior amateur hockey in Ottawa, turning pro with the Ottawa Senators in 1924 when Clint Benedict went to the Montreal Maroons. Connell's Senators won the Stanley Cup in 1926-27, the year before he posted his remarkable shutout streak. He allowed just 57 goals in 44 games that season. He initially retired in 1933 but returned to the NHL with the Montreal Maroons

in 1934. With Connell in goal, the Maroons won the Stanley Cup in 1935.

Cook, Bill

b. Brantford, Ontario, 8 October 1896; d. 6 April 1986.
Hall of Fame: 1952

Bill Cook scored 228 goals and had 140 assists in 11 seasons with the New York Rangers. Cook was an original member of the first Ranger club in 1926-27, going to New York after five successful seasons with Saskatoon in the Western League. In Manhattan, he played rightwing on a line with his brother Bun Cook and Frank Boucher, winning the NHL scoring race with 33

Alex Connell was an outstanding sportsman who had never played hockey prior to World War I. While stationed in Kingston during the War, he played in goal because he couldn't skate. He went to establish himself as an all-star goalie with Ottawa, the Montreal Maroons and Detroit.

Paul Coffey set an NHL record for defenseman in 1985–86 when he scored 48 goals, passing Bobby Orr's mark of 46 set eleven years earlier in 1974–75.

goals in 44 games that first season. He led or tied for the lead on two other occasions, was a four-time all-star and played on Stanley Cup winners in 1928 and 1933.

Cournoyer, Yvan

b. Drummondville, Quebec, 22 November 1943.
Hall of Fame: 1982

Rightwinger Yvan Cournoyer combined speed, skating ability and puck skills to score 428 regular-season goals in 15 seasons for the Montreal Canadiens. A small player at just 5-7, 178 pounds, Cournoyer proved durable enough to play 1,115 regular-season and playoff games en route to 10 Stanley Cup wins for Montreal. He was a four-time all-star and scored 25 or more goals in 12 consecutive seasons. He won the Conn Smythe Trophy as playoff MVP in 1973 and, at the time of his retirement, shared the record for most points in a Stanley Cup final series with 12. Throughout his career, Cournoyer averaged only 17 penalty minutes per season.

Cowley, Bill

b. Bristol, Quebec, 12 June 1912.
Hall of Fame: 1958

Playmaking center Bill Cowley averaged almost a point per game in 13 NHL seasons, with 195 goals and 353 assists for 548 points in 549 games. A product of the Ottawa minor hockey system, he joined the NHL's St. Louis Eagles club, which was the old Ottawa Senators franchise relocated in the U.S. for the 1934-35 season. After a year with the Eagles, he joined the Boston Bruins and remained with them until retiring after 1946-47. He played on two Cup winners, was selected to five all-star teams and was twice voted winner of the Hart Trophy as league MVP. A pinpoint passer, in 1943-44 Cowley had 72 points in 36 games, only to lose the scoring title when shoulder and knee injuries forced him out of the lineup for 12 games.

Crisp, Terry

b. Parry Sound, Ontario, 28 May 1943.

A former player with the Philadelphia Flyers and New York Islanders, Crisp was an effective checking forward. He later turned to coaching with Sault Ste. Marie in the OHL and Moncton of the AHL before moving up to the NHL with the Calgary Flames in 1987. He proved to be a master motivator, both emotional and dedicated, leading the Flames to the Stanley Cup in 1989. That Calgary club finished first overall in the regular season and then defeated Vancouver, Los Angeles, Chicago and Montreal to win its first Stanley Cup.

Cunniff, John

b. South Boston, Massachusetts, 9 July 1944.

Leftwinger John Cunniff was an all-American at Boston College and a member of the 1968 U.S. Olympic team. He played in the AHL, CHL and WHA before becoming general manager and coach for Cape Cod in the now defunct North American Hockey League. He was named coach of the AHL Binghamton Whalers in 1982-83 but was promoted to the NHL Whalers' staff before the season was over. He remained with the Whalers working as a scout for three seasons before joining the Boston Bruins as assistant coach in November of 1986. He was hired by New Jersey as assistant coach in May of 1989 and was promoted to head coach in November of the same year.

Czechoslovakia

Relatively small in size compared to its hockey playing neighbors such as the Soviet Union, West Germany, Sweden, and Finland, Czechoslovakia nevertheless has emerged as a hockey power. The country has enjoyed a long and rich

Terry Crisp began his playing career in Boston, and after stops in St. Louis and New York, was traded to Philadelphia. While with the Flyers he earned two Stanley Cup rings, playing a key role as a defensive specialist in Philadelphia's championship seasons of 1974 and 1975.

hockey history dating back to pre-World War II days. The game was most popular in the provinces of Bohemia, Moravia, and Slovakia. The Czechs were particularly inspired by Stan Mikita (formerly Stanaslov Gvoth) who emigrated from Czechoslovakia to St. Catharines, Ontario, where he developed into a superior hockey player, later to star for the Chicago Blackhawks and gain entry to the Hockey Hall of Fame. The Czechs won the IIHF World Championships in 1947, 1949, 1972, 1976, 1977 and 1985. NHL teams began to covet Czech players. The Rangers, for example, sought Vaclav Nedomansky, a gifted forward who eventually made it to the WHA and, briefly, the NHL. The Czechs who made the biggest impact in North America were the Stastny brothers, Peter, Anton, and Marian who played for the Quebec Nordiques just after the franchise joined the NHL. Peter emerged as one of the NHL's top scorers and was captain of the Quebec club until he was traded to New Jersey in March 1990. Other Czech stars in the NHL include defenseman Petr Svoboda, and forwards Petr Klima, David Volek and Vladimir Ruzicka.

Dandurand, Leo

b. Bourbonnais, Illinois, 9 July 1889; d. 26 June 1964. Hall of Fame: Builder, 1963

Leo Dandurand was an extraordinary sports executive able to make a success of almost every venture he undertook. Along with Joseph Cattarinich and Louis Letourneau, he became known as one of the "Three Musketeers of Sport". This trio bought the Montreal Canadiens on November 3, 1921, for $11,000 and built the club into the "Flying Frenchmen" featuring many or the top players of the day. Sixteen years later, the club was sold for $165,000. Dandurand was also a director of Montreal Royals baseball club, and was involved in pro football and horse racing in Montreal. In earlier years, he had been a referee in the National Hockey Association.

Darragh, Jack

b. Ottawa, Ontario, 4 December 1890; d. 25 June 1924. Hall of Fame: 1962

Jack Darragh played his entire hockey career in his hometown of Ottawa. He was part of four Stanley Cup championship teams, including 1911, his first pro season, 1920, 1921 and, after

coming out of a one-season retirement, 1923. Renowned as a stickhandler and scorer who avoided unnecessary penalties, Darragh was a lefthanded shot who usually played rightwing. He scored 24 goals in 22 games in 1919-20, and was known as a clutch player capable of scoring big goals in crucial games. He scored 12 goals in as many games in the 1920 and 1921 playoffs.

Dawson City Klondikers

It is unrecorded whether this was a regular squad, or one organized for its one moment in the spotlight. In 1904, Joe Boyle, an entrepreneur from Dawson City in the Yukon organized a local team to challenge the Ottawa Silver Seven for the Stanley Cup. Team members travelled on bicycle, dog sled, boat and train to arrive at Edgar Dey's rink in Ottawa for a two-game series that began January 13th. The Ottawa team defeated the Klondikers 9-2 in the fist game and 23-2 in the second game three days later with Ottawa's Frank McGee scoring 14 goals.

Day, Clarence (Hap)

b. Owen Sound, Ontario, 1 June 1901; d. 17 February 1990. Hall of Fame: 1961

Defenseman Hap Day was studying pharmacy at the University of Toronto when Charlie Querrie convinced him to play professionally with Toronto in the 1924-25 season. After two seasons on left wing, he became a defenseman and was paired with King Clancy. He was captain of the 1931-32 Cup-winning Maple Leafs and had three goals and three assists in seven playoff games. He

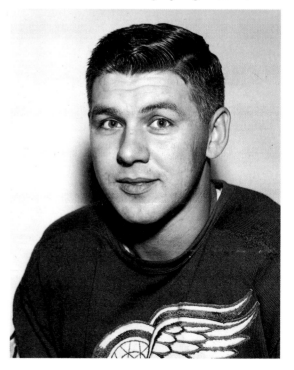

remained with the Leafs through 1937, joining the New York Americans for his final campaign as a player. He served as a referee for two seasons and then returned to Toronto to coach for 10 years beginning in 1940-41. Day's Leaf clubs won five Stanley Cups in the 1940s. He became team manager in 1950, finally retiring from hockey in 1957.

Delayed Offside

A delayed offside or slow whistle occurs when a player on the attacking team precedes the puck over the opposition blueline but does not gain possession. The linesman signals an offside infraction, but does not blow the whistle if the defending teams gains possession. If the puck is carried out over the blueline before it is touched by an attacker, no offside is called and play continues.

Delayed Penalty

When two players of the same team are serving a penalty, and a third player of the same team is penalized, the third player's penalty time does not begin until the penalty time of the first two players is completed. The third player is required to go to the penalty box directly, but can be replaced on the ice by a substitute until the time of his penalty begins.

Delayed Whistle

When the referee signals a penalty against a player for the team which does not have possession of the puck, he delays blowing the whistle until the puck is either touched by the penalized team, frozen or out of play. If the non-penalized team scores a goal, the penalty being indicated by the referee is waived if it is a minor infraction. If the non-penalized team scores on its own goal without a member of the penalized team touching the puck, the goal stands and the penalty is called. Because play stops when a member of the penalized team touches the puck, the goaltender for the non-penalized team is free to skate to his bench to be replaced by an extra attacker.

Delvecchio, Alex

b. Fort William, Ontario, 4 December 1931.
Hall of Fame: 1977
Center Alex Delvecchio played more than 22 seasons with the Detroit Red Wings before retiring in November 1973 at which time he ranked second to longtime linemate Gordie Howe in NHL records for games played, seasons, assists and points. He finished with 456 goals and 825 assists for 1,281 regular-season points and was a three-time winner of the Lady

Byng Trophy for gentlemanly conduct. He earned two all-star selections and was durable, missing only 43 games throughout his lengthy career. He was part of three Cup-winners in Detroit.

Demers, Jacques

b. Montreal, Quebec, 25 August 1944.
Jacques Demers coached in the Quebec Junior League, the WHA and the NHL before being hired by the St. Louis Blues in 1983. At the time the Blues were struggling, but Demers turned the team around, extracting every bit of potential from his skaters en route to the Campbell Conference final in 1986. Despite being heavy underdogs, the Blues extended Calgary to seven games. Demers proved popular with players, fans and media, and was one of the most quotable and emotional coaches in the league. He joined the Detroit Red Wings for 1986-87, guiding the club into the playoffs in 1987, 1988 and 1989.

Jacques Demers guided the Detroit Red Wings from the basement of the Norris Division to the Campbell Conference Championship round in 1987 and again in 1988, winning coach of the year honors in both campaigns.

The Red Wings acquired high-scoring Jimmy Carson from Edmonton as part of a multi-player deal in November of 1989 that saw Petr Klima, Joe Murphy, Adam Graves and Jeff Sharples join the Oilers while Carson, Kevin McClelland and Edmonton's fifth-round pick in the 1991 draft went to Detroit.

Denneny, Cy

b. Farran's Point, Ontario, 23 December 1891; d. 9 September 1970. Hall of Fame: 1959

Leftwinger Cy Denneny's accurate shot resulted in 246 goals and five Stanley Cup championships in 14 professional seasons. He joined the NHA's Toronto Shamrocks in 1914 and played there for two seasons before going to Ottawa. He was a member of the Senators through four Cup wins and 11 seasons before becoming playing coach of the Boston Bruins in 1928-29. Boston won the Cup that season and Denneny retired as a player. He was a referee for one season and then coached until 1933.

Detroit Cougars

First NHL franchise in Detroit, Michigan. Began operations in 1926-27 under manager Art Duncan playing in the American Division of the NHL. The club's name was changed to Falcons in 1930-31.

Detroit Falcons

Detroit's NHL team from 1930-31 to 1932-33 was known as the Falcons. After going into receivership in 1933, the team was reorganized and renamed as the Red Wings. The Falcons played in the American Division of the NHL, making the

playoffs twice. Leading members of the club included Ebbie Goodfellow, Herb Lewis, Larry Aurie and coach Jack Adams.

Detroit Red Wings

Professional hockey came to the Detroit area in 1926. The following year Jack Adams joined the Detroit Cougars and they began play in the new Olympia Stadium. Money was tight and Chicago industrialist James Norris bought the team [n] now called the Falcons [n] and the arena in 1933. Norris changed the team's name to Red Wings and the club won its first league championship in 1933-34 under Jack Adams. In 1935-36 they finished first in the regular season and won the first of seven Stanley Cups. Over the years, some of the most illustrious names in hockey have been identified with the Red Wings, Gordie Howe foremost among them. More than 80 Red Wings have enjoyed all-star status and Detroit players have captured more than 40 individual league awards. The most amazing string of titles in NHL history stretched from 1948-49 to 1954-55, when the Wings won a record seven consecutive league championships. In that span they captured four Stanley Cups. The team declined through the 1970s and into the early 1980s. The Norris family sold the club to Mike Ilitch who hired g.m. Jimmy Devellano to rebuild the club in 1982. Devellano scouted and signed Steve Yzerman and hired Jacques Demers as coach. The team rebounded, playing near the top of the Norris Division with capacity crowds filling the new Joe Louis Arena. The 1989-90 season was much less successful and the Red Wings finished out of the playoffs, winning only 28 games all term.

CUMULATIVE RECORD	GP	Won	Lost	Tied	Pct
Regular Season	4206	1725	1804	675	.490
Playoffs	319	155	163	1	.487
Series 67 W35 L32					
TOTALS	4525	1880	1967	676	.490

Devellano, Jimmy

b. Toronto, Ontario, 18 January 1943.
Jimmy Devellano got his start in Toronto minor hockey before being hired by Bill Torrey, g.m. of the New York Islanders, when Torrey was putting together his team in the 1970s. With Devellano helping in player procurement, the Islanders acquired such youngsters as John Tonelli, Mike Bossy, Bryan Trottier, and Clark Gillies and won four straight Stanley Cups starting in 1980. Credited with helping create this dynasty, Devellano was hired as g.m. of the Red Wings in 1982. He picked Steve Yzerman

Marcel Dionne retired prior to the 1989–90 season in much the same manner as he played throughout his career; quietly and without great fanfare. Despite ranking second on the NHL's all-time goal scoring list and third on the all-time points parade, Dionne never received the accolades deserving of a player of his calibre.

fourth overall in the 1983 Entry Draft and saw his young star rapidly develop into a franchise player. The Wings improved, finishing first in the Norris Division in 1988 and 1989.

Dionne, Marcel

b. Drummondville, Quebec, 3 August 1951.
Marcel Dionne launched his career with the Detroit Red Wings as a developing superstar. In 1971-72, his 77 points as a rookie set a mark for first-year NHLers, and the next season he upped the total to 90, with 40 goals and 50 assists. He broke 100 points in 1974-75 with 47 goals and 74 assists and signed as a free agent with the Los Angeles Kings in 1975. He had his best years in California, starring with Charlie Simmer and Dave Taylor on the Triple Crown Line. Dionne remained an L.A. hero until 1987 when he was traded to the Rangers for Bobby Carpenter and Tom Laidlaw. He retired in 1989 as the NHL's third- leading all-time scorer with 731 goals and 1,040 assists for 1,771 points.

Division of the Ice Surface

The ice surface is divided in the following manner: a red goal line (two inches in width) is drawn across the ice ten feet from and parallel to each end of the rink. Two bluelines (one foot in width) are drawn sixty feet from and parallel to the goal lines. The area from the bluelines to the goal lines is referred to as the defensive zone. The area between the bluelines is referred to as the neutral zone. This neutral zone is further divided by a center or redline (one foot in width) across and parallel to the goal lines, dividing the ice surface in half. The redline, introduced by the NHL in 1943, is used in the calling of icing and off-side infractions. This introduction of the redline coincided with the initiation of forward passing, ushering in the 'modern era' of hockey. The blueline was first introduced in the Pacific Coast Hockey Association in 1911.

Drillon, Gordie

b. Moncton, New Brunswick, 23 October 1914; d. 22 September 1986. Hall of Fame: 1975

Gordie Drillon broke in with the Toronto Maple Leafs in 1936-37 when management decided to rest Charlie Conacher. The rightwinger proved to be a talented goal scorer, finishing the season on a line with Hall of Famers Syl Apps and Busher Jackson. Bob Davidson replaced Jackson as Drillon's linemate the following season and Gordie went on to lead the NHL in goals and points, winning the Lady Byng Trophy and a first all-star selection. He played a total of six seasons with the Leafs and one with the Canadiens, scoring a total of 155 goals for a single-season average of more than 22. Traded to Montreal for

Before he went on to stardom with the Montreal Canadiens, Ken Dryden was an all-American for three consecutive years while tending goal for Cornell University. He set school records for goals-against average and shutouts during a varsity career that began in 1966 and ended in 1969, when Dryden joined the Canadian National team.

1942-43, he scored a career-high 28 goals in his final NHL season. Drillon was a three-time NHL all-star.

Drinkwater, Graham

b. Montreal, Quebec, 22 February 1875; d. 26 September 1946. Hall of Fame: 1950

Defenseman/forward Graham Drinkwater was one of hockey's first star performers. As a student at McGill University in Montreal, he was part of championship football and hockey teams playing at the junior and intermediate levels. He left McGill to join the Montreal Victorias in 1895 and found himself part of a Stanley Cup challenge winner. Drinkwater's club relinquished the Cup to the Winnipeg Victorias in February of 1896, but reclaimed it in December of that year. They successfully defended the trophy through 1899 when the Shamrocks, another Montreal club, claimed possession of the Cup as champions of the Canadian Amateur Hockey League. Drinkwater was captain of the Victorias when the club won its final Stanley Cup challenge in February of 1899.

Dryden, Ken

b. Hamilton, Ontario, 8 August 1947. Hall of Fame: 1983

Ken Dryden made an impressive debut in goal for the Montreal Canadiens in 1971. With six games remaining in the regular season, Dryden was called up to the NHL, winning the Conn Smythe Trophy as playoff MVP as the Canadiens skated to an upset Stanley Cup win. Still technically a rookie, he won the Calder Trophy the following season and in seven-plus seasons with the Canadiens had 46 shutouts and a 2.24 goals-against average. With Dryden in net the Canadiens won six Stanley Cups including four in a row in the late 1970s. Dryden was a five-time all-star and five-time winner or co-winner of the Vezina Trophy for fewest goals-against. He retired after the 1978-79 season.

Dudley, George

b. Midland, Ontario, 19 April 1894; d. 8 May 1960. Hall of Fame: Builder, 1958

George Dudley was active in hockey for more than 50 years. He played the game in his youth, but moved to the executive level after obtaining his law degree in 1917. From 1940 to 1942 he was president of the CAHA, became secretary in 1945 and later served as secretary-manager. He was instrumental in arranging some of the first visits to Canada by hockey teams from Russia. At the time of his death in 1960, he was treasurer of the OHA, president of the IIHF and head of hockey for the 1960 Olympics.

Dudley, Rick

b. Toronto, Ontario, 31 January 1949.
Rick Dudley played his first pro hockey in the Minnesota North Stars' organization, but was hampered by a leg injury in his first two seasons. Buffalo obtained his rights and he made his NHL debut in 1972-73 with the Sabres. He later joined Cincinnati of the WHA but returned to Buffalo in 1979. He finished his playing career in Winnipeg and turned to coaching in 1982-83. In seven minor-league seasons, he compiled a .655 winning percentage before being appointed head coach of the Sabres in 1989.

Dump and Chase

A style of play which has the attacking team shoot or dump the puck into its opponent's defensive zone and then try to either get to the puck first in the opposing end or forecheck aggressively in an attempt to force a bad defensive play.

Dunderdale, Thomas

b. Benella, Australia, 6 May 1887; d. 15 December 1960. Hall of Fame: 1974
Australian-born Thomas Dunderdale grew up in Ottawa and Winnipeg but began his pro career with Montreal Shamrocks of the NHA in 1910. He joined Quebec the following season before moving to Victoria, B.C., to play in the newly-formed Pacific Coast Hockey Association. He became the PCHA's all-time leading scorer, with 191 goals in 251 games over 12 seasons with Victoria and Portland. A center and rover, Dunderdale had more than 20 goals on five occasions and led the league with 24 goals in just 15 games in 1912-13 and 23 goals in 1913-14. He played with Edmonton and Saskatoon in 1923-24 and then turned to coaching and managing clubs in Los Angeles, Edmonton and Winnipeg.

Durnan, Bill

b. Toronto, Ontario, 22 January 1915; d. 31 October 1972. Hall of Fame: 1963
Ambidextrous goaltender Bill Durnan played with top junior and senior teams in northern Ontario in the 1930s. He was in goal for an Allan Cup championship with the Kirkland Lake Blue Devils in 1939-40 and later moved into the Montreal Canadiens' system, playing with the Montreal Royals senior club. He jumped to the NHL in 1943-44 and was a sensation in Montreal, winning the Vezina in his rookie year. He went on to play seven seasons for the Habs, winning six first all-star team berths and six Vezina Trophies. His Canadiens won the championship four times and the Stanley Cup twice. In 1948-49

he set a modern NHL record with 309 minutes of shutout goaltending. His lifetime goals-against average was just 2.36 per game.

Dutton, Mervyn (Red)

b. Russell, Manitoba, 23 July 1898; d. 15 March 1987. Hall of Fame: 1958
Despite a serious leg injury sustained during the battle of Vimy Ridge, rugged defenseman Red Dutton was able to play 15 years of professional hockey. After five seasons with Calgary in the WCHL, Dutton joined the Montreal Maroons of the NHL. He moved to the New York Americans in 1930 and played six seasons, finally taking over as playing-manager in 1936. He remained as team manager until the franchise disbanded in 1942. When Frank Calder, the NHL's first president, died in 1943, Dutton was made managing director and the president of the league. He was succeeded by Clarence Campbell in 1946.

Red Dutton overcame a serious leg injury suffered in World War I by skating up to seven hours a day for as many as seven different teams, often playing four games a night to work his way back into shape. He impressed more than one set of scouts, and when a Calgary team official pressed 500 dollars into his palm, his 15-year professional career began. He retired in 1936 after six seasons with the New York Americans.

Dye, Cecil (Babe)

b. Hamilton, Ontario, 13 May 1898; d. 2 January 1962. Hall of Fame: 1970

Babe Dye was a top performer in three sports: hockey, football and baseball. At just 5-8 and 150 lbs., Dye's success as a rightwinger depended on superb stickhandling and a phenomenally hard shot. He played with Ontario junior champion Toronto Aura Lee, joining the Toronto St. Patrick's of the NHL in 1919-20. In his first seven big league seasons, he scored 185 goals in 181 games including playoffs. He led the NHL in scoring four times including 1924-25 when he had 38 goals in 29 contests. His one Stanley Cup win came in 1921-22 when he scored nine goals in the five-game final against Vancouver. He went to Chicago when the NHL expanded in 1926-27, but after one season with the Blackhawks a broken leg sustained in training camp effectively ended his career. He attempted a comeback with the New York Americans in 1928-29, but scored only one goal in 41 games giving him a total of 200 regular season goals.

Cecil "Babe" Dye played a significant part in the formation of the Toronto Maple Leafs, although he was not aware of the role he played. Conn Smythe was offered Dye's services while Smythe was organizing the New York Rangers. Smythe declined and the New York scribes were unmerciful in their criticism of his decision. Smythe was fired from the Rangers and went on to form the Toronto Maple Leafs. Dye eventually played for Smythe when he joined the Leafs for a brief period during the 1930-31 season.

Alan Eagleson may have never had the chance to play a dominant role on the international hockey front were it not for an ironic twist of fate. In the 1963 Canadian federal election, Eagleson ran for the Progressive Conservatives in the federal riding of York West, but lost to Liberal Red Kelly, a star with the Toronto Maple Leafs. Eagleson then decided to concentrate on other pursuits, including sports management. In this case, politics' loss has been hockey's gain.

Eagleson, Alan

b. St. Catharines, Ontario, 24 April 1933. Hall of Fame: Builder, 1989

As a player agent, Alan Eagleson negotiated Bobby Orr's first professional contract in 1966, legitimizing the agent's role in hockey. A successful lawyer practising in Toronto, Eagleson's efforts on behalf of his hockey clients led to the formation of the National Hockey League Players' Association. Serving as its executive director, Eagleson's efforts resulted in vastly increased salaries and pension benefits for NHL players. He also worked tirelessly as Canada's chief negotiator in international hockey, bringing together government, business and hockey interests to stage the first Team Canada-Russia series in 1972 and Canada Cup international tournaments in 1976, 1981, 1984 and 1987.

Edmonton Oilers

Originally a team in the World Hockey Association, the franchise began play in 1972-73 as the Alberta Oilers. Renamed Edmonton prior to the next season, the club went through five unspectacular seasons before acquiring 17-year old Wayne Gretzky from the folding Indianapolis Racers early in 1978-79. In 1979 the Oilers were one of four former WHA teams accepted into the NHL and though they struggled early, by 1982 they were serious Cup contenders. Coach and general manager Glen Sather's picks in the 1979, 1980, 1981 entry drafts included Kevin Lowe, Mark Messier, Glenn Anderson, Paul Coffey, Jari Kurri, Andy Moog and Grant Fuhr and these players along with Gretzky were the keys to the Oilers reaching the Stanley Cup finals in 1983. Though they lost to the New York Islanders in the finals that year, the Oilers had become a highly-skilled, fast-skating outfit that scored

goals in bunches. They overwhelmed their opposition in the mid to late 1980s, winning the Stanley Cup in 1984, 1985, 1987 and 1988. The trading of superstar Wayne Gretzky in August of 1988 changed the makeup of the club, but in the 1989-90 season the Oilers reasserted themselves as one of the most talented clubs in the NHL and won their fifth Stanley Cup.

CUMULATIVE RECORD	GP	Won	Lost	Tied	Pct
Regular Season (NHL)	880	484	278	118	.617
Playoffs	148	105	43	0	.709
Series: 31 W25 L6					
TOTALS	1028	589	321	118	.630

Entry Draft

The Entry Draft is the formalized process by which young hockey talent is acquired by NHL clubs. Each team is entitled to a selection in each of the twelve rounds that make up the Entry Draft which takes place in June of each year. These selections can be traded from club to club allowing a given team to have more or less than 12 picks in a given year. Order of selection is determined by the regular-season record of each of the 21 NHL clubs at the end of the season preceding each year's draft. The five teams

Bill Ranford backstopped Edmonton to the 1990 Stanley Cup, winning the Conn Smythe Trophy as playoff MVP. The Oilers beat Boston in five games.

which do not qualify for playoff competition pick first, based upon the inverse order of their records. The remaining 16 teams then follow with their order of selection based on the same criteria. In simple terms, the team with the worst record picks first and the team with the best record picks last in an attempt to equalize the relative strengths of the league's teams. Players ages 18, 19 and 20 are eligible for selection in the Entry Draft with 18-year-olds only eligible in the first three rounds. Previous to 1979, it was known as the Amateur Draft.

Esposito, Anthony (Tony)

b. Sault Ste. Marie, Ontario, 23 April 1943.
Hall of Fame: 1988

Five-time all-star goaltender Tony Esposito was a product of American college hockey who played 13 games for Montreal in 1968-69. Drafted by the Chicago Blackhawks in the ensuing off-season, Esposito emerged as that club's number one goaltender in 1969-70 with a 2.17 goals-against average and a modern record 15 shutouts in 63 games played. He was awarded

Tony Esposito never missed the playoffs in his 14-year stay with the Chicago Blackhawks. Although he reached the Cup finals with the Hawks on two occasions, Esposito never won a Stanley Cup ring, one of the few honors to elude his grasp in his career.

the Vezina and Calder Trophies as well as earning a first team all-star selection. He retired in 1984 after 16 NHL seasons, ranking third in all-time wins with 423 and seventh in shutouts with 76. He later served as vice-president and general manager of the Pittsburgh Penguins.

Esposito, Phil

b. Sault Ste. Marie, Ontario, 20 February 1942. Hall of Fame: 1984

Unlike most NHLers, center Phil Esposito played very little youth hockey. Never a great skater, he made his mark in the NHL through his great strength and his scoring touch. He began his NHL career with Chicago in 1963-64 before being traded to Boston as part of a six-player deal in 1967. Along with Bobby Orr, he was a cornerstone of the Bruins' revitalization that saw the Boston club win the Stanley Cup in 1970 and 1972. As a Bruin, Esposito won five NHL scoring titles and finished second twice. He was an eight-time all-star, a two-time MVP and, in 1968-69, the first player to score more than 100 points in a season. His single-season goal-scoring mark of 76 goals set in 1970-71 has been surpassed only by Wayne Gretzky and Mario Lemieux.

Expansion

The National Hockey League first expanded in 1924-25, growing from four franchises to six with the addition of the Montreal Maroons and Boston. Pittsburgh joined the following season and the New York Rangers, Chicago and Detroit followed in 1926-27 as the league now played in two divisions (American and Canadian). Franchise closures in the 1930s and 1940s reduced the play to a single division in 1938-39 and a six-team configuration in 1942-43. The six-team NHL (often erroneously referred to as the 'original six') doubled in size and returned to a two-division format in 1967-78 when six clubs (Los Angeles, Minnesota, Oakland, Philadelphia, Pittsburgh and St. Louis) were added. Smaller expansions in 1970-71 (Buffalo and Vancouver), 1972-73 (Atlanta and the New York Islanders) and 1974-75 (Washington and Kansas City) resulted in the league being divided into four divisions playing in two conferences. The 1979-80 season saw a further expansion as four teams that had played in the rival WHA (Edmonton, Hartford, Quebec and Winnipeg) joined the NHL. As the 1980s ended, the NHL, currently a 21-team league, announced plans to add as many as seven new clubs by the end of the 1990s.

Expansion Draft

A formula by which new teams entering an existing league are stocked with players. Usually, each established club is allowed to protect a set number of players (normally from 15 to 18). The expansion clubs then draft from the unprotected pool of players. Depending on the rules of the expansion draft, established clubs losing players are allowed to protect one additional player for every player chosen from their unprotected lists.

Extra Attacker

When a team replaces its goaltender with an extra skater, this player is called the extra attacker. The extra attacker is commonly used in three situations: when a team trailing by one or two goals late in a game and must go all out to score; when a delayed penalty is called and the team which will eventually have the man advantage is still in possession of the puck; and when a faceoff occurs deep in the offensive zone with only two or three seconds left in the period. Some say the first coach to pull his goaltender in favor of an extra attacker was Ed Wildey of the Young Rangers, a juvenile team in Toronto. Art Ross of the Boston Bruins is generally conceded to be the first to pull his goaltender in a Stanley Cup playoff game when, on March 26, 1931, he lifted Tiny Thompson in the last minute but the Bruins failed to score on the Canadiens.

Face-off

The method of beginning play in hockey at the start of a period or after any stoppage is referred to as the face-off. Two players stand facing each other, roughly one foot apart, with their sticks on the ice. The visiting team's player taking the face-off must place his stick on the ice first. The referee or linesman drops the puck between the players and they attempt to either gain control of the puck or pass it to a teammate. A face-off can occur at any spot on the ice, except within 15 feet of the goal or the boards. Face-offs are usually held on one of the nine designated face-off dots drawn on the ice-surface. These dots are located on either side of the goal in each team's defensive zone, just outside both bluelines in the neutral zone on both sides of the ice, and at the middle of the center redline.

Farm Club

A minor professional team which grooms players to eventually play for its major-league affiliate is called a farm club. Modern NHL teams place their top professional prospects on clubs in the American Hockey League or International Hockey League.

Federko, Bernie

b. Foam Lake, Saskatchewan, 12 May 1956.

A steady center who topped 1,000 points at the end of the 1987-88 season, Bernie Federko played 13 seasons with the St. Louis Blues before being traded to Detroit in June of 1989. He had four 100-point seasons, including a career-best 41 goals and 66 assists for 107 points in 1983-84. Federko had 50 or more assists in 10 consecutive seasons beginning in 1978-79.

Ferguson, John

b. Vancouver, British Columbia, 5 September 1938.

John Ferguson was a tough minor-pro with Cleveland of the AHL when he was hired by the Montreal Canadiens to act as the team's policeman in 1963-64. Ferguson's strength and intimidating manner discouraged opposition players from fouling the Canadiens' small forwards and,

Brent Sutter, right, and Carey Wilson prepare to do battle in the face-off circle, the one-on-one confrontation that follows every stoppage in play during a hockey game.

with him in the lineup, the club won five Stanley Cups in eight seasons. He retired in 1971 and later was appointed assistant coach for Team Canada in its 1972 series with the Soviet Union. In 1976 he became general manager-coach of the New York Rangers and later joined the Winnipeg Jets as g.m. He stayed with the Jets until 1988 and is now president of Windsor Raceway in Windsor, Ontario.

Ferreira, Jack

b. Providence, Rhode Island, 9 June 1944.
Named general manager of the Minnesota North Stars in 1988, Jack Ferreira had been active in professional hockey since 1972 when he was appointed assistant g.m. of the WHA's New England Whalers. He later joined the Calgary Flames as U.S. and college scout and the New York Rangers as director of player development before accepting the top job in Minnesota.

Fetisov, Viacheslav

b. Moscow, Soviet Union, 20 May 1958.
When he joined the New Jersey Devils for the 1989-90 season, Slava Fetisov was ranked as one of the top defensemen in the world. He was a nine-time Soviet league all-star; a four-time winner of the Pravda Trophy as top-scoring defenseman; and recipient of the Gold Stick Award as Europe's best player in 1984. Fetisov played for and was eventually appointed captain of the Central Red Army hockey team. Army

Finland's ice hockey team made its first appearance on the international hockey scene at the 1952 Olympic Games in Oslo. Although they have yet to win an Olympic gold medal, the Finns did win the World Junior crown in 1986–87.

team won the league title in each of Fetisov's 12 full seasons. He made his World Championship debut at age 17 in 1977 and, twelve years later in 1989, led his team to a 10-0 record and a gold medal, while winning the best defenseman and MVP awards. He scored 153 goals and 373 points in 478 Soviet league games; in international competition he participated in 153 games, scoring 55 goals and 147 points.

Filion, Maurice

b. Montreal, Quebec, 12 February 1932.

Maurice Filion was named general manager of the Quebec Nordiques early in 1990 replacing Martin Madden. A member of the Quebec organization since the inception of the WHA, he has served at various times as coach, scout, vice-president of hockey operations and g.m. He played junior hockey in Trois-Rivieres, Quebec, and started his coaching career with the senior A Montreal Olympiques in 1961-62, taking this team to the Allan Cup final. He later coached several teams in junior A including Guy Lafleur's Memorial Cup champion Quebec Remparts in 1971.

Finland

Like the Soviet Union, Sweden and Canada, Finland is ideally suited for producing professional hockey players. The Finnish league consists of 12 teams playing a 44 game schedule. TPS Turku was both regular-season and playoff champion in 1988-89. The Finnish national junior team won the IIHF World Junior Championship in 1986-87. Eighty-four Finns have been selected in the NHL Entry Draft since 1969, with Edmonton's Jari Kurri the best known. Other Finnish NHLers include Reijo Ruotsalainen, Esa Tikkanen and Jyrki Lumme.

Fletcher, Cliff

b. Montreal, Quebec, 16 August 1935.

Cliff Fletcher got his NHL administrative start under Scotty Bowman when Bowman was developing the St. Louis Blues in the early days of expansion. When the Atlanta Flames were admitted to the NHL as an expansion team in 1972-73, Fletcher was hired as g.m., proving his administrative capabilities by developing the Flames into a playoff team faster than most observers believed possible. The Flames shifted to Calgary in 1980 with Fletcher remaining in charge. As the 1980s unfolded, Fletcher found himself having to build a team that could compete with the Wayne Gretzky-led Edmonton Oilers, their fierce cross-state rivals. The Flames reached the finals in 1986 and won the Cup in 1989.

Emile Francis was named executive of the year by both The Hockey News and The Sporting News in 1981. In 1982, the NHL honored him as well, presenting him with the Lester Patrick Trophy for his outstanding contributions to hockey in the United States.

Francis, Emile

b. North Battleford, Saskatchewan, 13 September 1926. Hall of Fame: Builder, 1982

Emile Francis was known as 'The Cat' during his 14 years of as a pro goaltender, but it was his efforts as a coach, manager and executive that earned him a place in the Hockey Hall of Fame. He began his coaching career in 1960 with the Rangers' sponsored junior team at Guelph, Ontario. He rose rapidly to the NHL and was soon general manager of the Rangers. He held this job for 10 seasons, going behind the bench to take over as coach on three occasions. He joined the St. Louis Blues in April, 1976, as executive vice-president, general manager and coach and in May of 1983, was named president and general manager of the Hartford Whalers.

Fredrickson, Frank

b. Winnipeg, Manitoba, 11 June 1895; d. 28 May 1979. Hall of Fame: 1958

Fredrickson established himself as an amateur standout before becoming a star in the Pacific Coast Hockey Association, Western Canada League and the NHL. He played his first senior hockey with the Winnipeg Falcons during the 1913-14 season, and led this club to both an Allan Cup and Olympic triumph in 1919 and 1920. He signed with the Victoria Aristocrats (later Cougars) in 1920, and remained with the WHL team until it was sold to eastern interests. He won a Stanley Cup with the Cougars in 1925. His career took him to Detroit of the NHL, to Boston, and finally to Pittsburgh. He was coach, manager and center for Pittsburgh when a leg injury ended his playing days. He retired after the 1930-31 season.

Grant Fuhr led all NHL goaltenders in 4 different categories including games, wins and shutouts during the 1987–88 regular season. In the playoffs he continued his outstanding play, winning 16 games and losing only two as the Oilers won their fourth Stanley Cup.

Fuhr, Grant

b. Spruce Grove, Alberta, 28 September 1962.

Few goaltenders during the decade of the 1980s received as much positive acclaim as Grant Fuhr. He was a second team all-star in his rookie season, 1981-82 and soon displaced Andy Moog as the Oilers' number one goaltender. In 1984 Stanley Cup finals, Fuhr shutout the New York Islanders in the opening game in Nassau Coliseum. That proved to be the turning point in the series and inspired Edmonton to its first Stanley Cup. With Fuhr in the crease Edmonton won the Cup again in 1985. Fuhr also played superbly in 1987 and 1988 when the Oilers again won two consecutive Stanley Cups. He was the goaltender for Team Canada in the 1987 Canada Cup and set an NHL record for games played with 75 en route to the Vezina Trophy in 1988, but was injured for much of the 1989-90 season.

Gadsby, Bill

b. Calgary, Alberta, 8 August 1927.
Hall of Fame: 1970

Tough situations were almost commonplace to defenseman Bill Gadsby, but both on and off the ice he faced them the same way – head on. In 1952, while captain of the Blackhawks, Gadsby was struck by polio, but beat this crippling disease to go on to become one of the few players to endure 20 NHL seasons. Signed by

Chicago from junior hockey in Edmonton, Gadsby joined the Hawks early in the 1946-47 season. He was traded to New York during the 1954-55 campaign, and then to Detroit in 1961-62, finishing his career with the Wings. He coached the Wings during the 1968-69 and 1969-70 seasons. A seven-time all-star, he never played on a Stanley Cup winner.

Gainey, Bob

b. Peterborough, Ontario, 13 December 1953.
At one point in the prime of his career, Soviet hockey experts revealed that they considered Bob Gainey to be the best all-round player in the world. At his peak, Gainey excelled in every aspect of the game. He was a powerful forward with long strides who could score key goals when necessary. In addition, he was one of the top forecheckers and backcheckers in the league, winning the Frank Selke Trophy as the NHL's best defensive forward the first four years it was awarded. Gainey was a mainstay of the Montreal Canadiens' teams that won four consecutive Stanley Cups from 1976 to 1979. He captained the team to yet another Stanley Cup in 1986 and took the Canadiens to the finals again in 1989 when they were eliminated by the Calgary Flames. Following the series, Gainey announced his retirement as a professional hockey player but continued working in the game as a player-coach in France.

Rod Gilbert still holds five individual records for the New York Rangers, including career marks in goals, assists and points. His 1,065 games played for the Broadway Blues ranks him second to Harry Howell.

Gardiner, Chuck

b. Edinburgh, Scotland, 31 December 1904; d. 13 June 1934. Hall of Fame: 1945

A superb goaltender, felled by a brain tumor at the height of his career, Chuck Gardiner originally played the position because he was a poor skater. His skills as a netminder enabled him to play competitive intermediate hockey in Manitoba at the age of 14, graduate up to senior play in 1925 and turn pro with the Winnipeg Maroons in 1926. He joined the NHL's Chicago Blackhawks in 1927-28, and in seven seasons posted a 2.13 goals-against per game average with 42 shut-outs. In 21 Stanley Cup matches, his goals-against average was a miniscule 1.66. He won the Vezina Trophy in 1931-32 and 1933-34 and earned four all-star berths, playing a daring style that saw him frequently leave his crease to beat opposing forwards to loose pucks.

Geoffrion, Bernie (Boom-Boom)

b. Montreal, Quebec, 14 February 1931. Hall of Fame: 1972

Rightwinger Bernie Geoffrion stepped from the Montreal Nationals junior team to the Canadiens in 1951, scoring eight goals in 18 games. He registered 393 NHL goals before retiring following the 1967-68 season – fifth on the all-time NHL scoring list at the time. An eight-time all-star, Geoffrion blazed his name into the record book on several occasions; he was named the rookie of the year during 1951-52, twice won the NHL scoring championship, and once the Hart Trophy as the most valuable player to his team. Geoffrion was the second player to score 50 goals in a season (1960-61), the year he achieved a career-best 95 points. He retired as a player after the 1963-64 season, but, after two seasons,

Bill Gadsby played 1,248 games in the NHL amassing 567 points and more than 600 stitches. His final NHL appearance was in the sixth game of the 1966 Stanley Cup finals, a game Gadsby played despite a broken toe on his right foot and a battered left elbow.

returned to the NHL as a Ranger. Physical infirmities ended his playing career in 1967-68, and he turned to coaching – first with the Quebec Aces, and then in the NHL with the Rangers, the Atlanta Flames and the Canadiens.

Gerard, Eddie

b. Ottawa, Ontario, 22 February 1890; d. 8 December 1937. Hall of Fame: 1945

A star participant in football, paddling, cricket, tennis, lacrosse and hockey, Gerard turned professional with the Ottawa Senators in the 1913-14 season and became their captain in the 1920-21 campaign. During his 10 years with the club he was on four Stanley Cup winners, although one championship came while on loan to the Toronto St. Pats. Gerard played his defense position well and cleanly, retiring in 1924 because of asthma. He coached the Montreal Maroons to a Cup victory in 1926, and remained with them until 1930, when he joined the New York Americans. He concluded his · career with the St. Louis Eagles in 1934-35.

Giacomin, Ed

b. Sudbury, Ontario, 6 June 1939. Hall of Fame: 1987

Goaltender Ed Giacomin spent seven years in the minors before joining the New York Rangers in 1965-66 when the franchise was rebuilding. He had nine shutouts and earned a first team all-star selection the following year and went on to become a New York fan favorite with his acrobatic style and puck handling skills. He played with the Rangers until 1978, earning five all-star selections, 289 wins and 54 shutouts. He was traded to Detroit in 1975-76, retiring in 1978 with a lifetime 2.82 goals-against average.

> Bernie "Boom-Boom" Geoffrion may not have invented the slapshot, but he was the first NHL player to develop the accuracy needed to control it. He is one of the few players to retire, coach in the minor leagues and then return to the NHL as an active player.

> The goal net and its surrounding crease are the personal domain of the goaltender, and many netminders are fiercely protective of this area. New rules to prevent players from invading the goalie's inner sanctum are being considered.

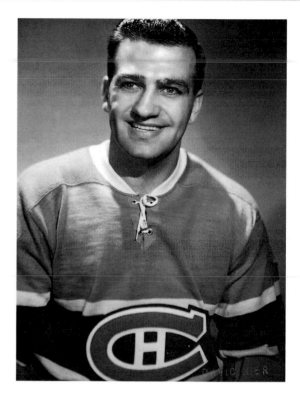

Gibson, Jack (Doc)

b. Berlin, Ontario, 10 September 1880; d. 7 October 1955. Hall of Fame: Builder, 1976

Jack Gibson organized hockey's first pro league – the International League of 1904-05 – with three teams in Michigan plus Pittsburgh and the Canadian Soo. Gibson, who set up a dental practice in Houghton, Michigan, had been a member of Ontario's Intermediate champions in 1897. He organized a team in Houghton called the Portage Lakers that, in 1903-04, won 24 of 26 games, defeating opponents from Pittsburgh, St. Paul and St. Louis as well as the Montreal Wanderers. The International (Pro) League was organized the next season and featured many of the top players of the day. Portage Lake, in 1905 and 1906, challenged Ottawa and Montreal to championship series, but both challenges were refused. As the popularity of professional hockey grew in Canada, lucrative contracts were offered to Portage Lake's top players, effectively ending the International (Pro) League.

Gilbert, Rod

b. Montreal, Quebec, 1 July 1941. Hall of Fame: 1982

Gilbert overcame almost insurmountable odds to become one of the top rightwingers in the NHL. During a junior game he skated over a piece of debris on the ice and suffered a broken back. He almost lost his left leg during two operations to correct the damage. Gilbert, an excellent skater and puckhandler, played almost 16 full seasons with the New York Rangers, setting or equalling 20 team records. When he retired in 1977, Rod trailed only one other rightwinger (Gordie Howe) in total points. He had 406 goals and 615 assists in 1,065 games, plus 34 goals and 33 assists in 79 playoff encounters. He was twice named an NHL all-star, and in 1976 was awarded the Masterton Trophy.

Goal Crease

In front of each goal is a goal crease area marked by red lines two inches in width. The goal crease is laid out as follows: one foot from the outside of each goal post, lines four feet in length shall be drawn at right angles to the goal line and the points of these lines furthest from the goal line shall be joined by another line. In addition, a semi-circle six feet in radius shall be drawn using the center of the goal line as the center point. The space extending vertically four feet to the top of the goal frame, behind the crease lines, is also considered part of the goal crease. If the puck enters the net while a player on the attacking team has both skates on the ice inside the goal crease, no goal is awarded.

Goal Light

When a goal has been scored, the goal judge activates a red goal light above his cage the instant the puck fully enters the goal area. At the end of a period or overtime session, a green or blue light comes on, signalling the expiration of time. When this time expired light is on, the red goal light is locked out so that a goal scored after the clock ticks down to zero will not register.

Goal Mouth

The area, of approximately ten feet, directly in front of the net and crease. Players vying for the puck by this area are often said to be in a "goal mouth scramble".

Goal Post

Exactly ten feet from the end of the rink, on the goal line, is a set of two red goal posts constructed of steel tubing that extend four feet above the ice. A crossbar connects the top of both goal posts, forming an opening four feet high by six feet wide. The goal net extends 44 inches behind the posts. In NHL arenas, goal post are kept in place by magnets fixed in the ice. Goalkeepers often say that the goal posts are their best friends because they occasionally stop shots that have the goalie beaten. A shot that hits the goal post or crossbar of the net does not count as a shot on goal.

Goodfellow, Ebbie

b. Ottawa, Ontario, 9 April 1906; d. 10 September 1955. Hall of Fame: 1963

Goodfellow's amateur career was played with the Ottawa Montagnards where, in 1927-28, he was an all-star center and leading scorer for the city championship club. He was spotted by Detroit, which assigned him to the Olympics of the International League where, in 1928-29, he achieved all-star status and led the league in scoring. He joined the NHL in 1929, and in his second season led the NHL's American Division in goals (25). Twice a first team, and once a second team, all-star, Goodfellow was named the NHL's MVP in 1939-40, and was a three-time Stanley Cup winner. He captained the Red Wings for five seasons, and was a member of the Hockey Hall of Fame's selection committee.

Gorman, Tommy

b. Ottawa, Ontario, 9 June 1886; d. 15 May 1961. Hall of Fame: Builder, 1963

Tommy Gorman was surrounded by sports activity all his life. He played lacrosse well and was a member of the Canadian Olympic team in 1908. He held the NHA together when he picked up the Ottawa franchise during World War I and, in 1917, participated in the founding of the NHL. He managed or coached seven Stanley Cup teams in Ottawa, Montreal and Chicago.

Goulet, Michel

b. Peribonka, Quebec, 21 April 1960.

Michel Goulet was one of the 'Baby Bulls', an underage junior signed by the Birmingham Bulls of the World Hockey Association. After his year with Birmingham, Goulet graduated to the Quebec Nordiques and established himself as one of the premier goal scorers of the NHL. He had seven consecutive 40-goal seasons beginning in 1981-82 and topped 50 on four occasions. He remained at the very top of his game through the end of the 1980s. He was traded to Chicago in March 1990.

Great Britain

Professional hockey has enjoyed success in Britain as far back as the 1930s when teams employed Canadian expatriates to fill their rosters. Great Britain won the gold medal in hockey at the 1936 Olympics using a team of Canadian servicemen of British parentage. Professional games proved very popular at such buildings as Harringay Arena and Wembley Stadium in London as well as Paisley, Scotland and other areas in the north. The ice game declined in popularity in the 1960s but began to

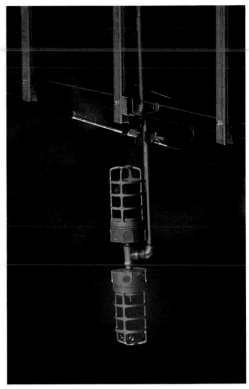

enjoy a renaissance thereafter. At one point, the Detroit Red Wings placed a farm team in London in the hope of developing a European professional league. By the 1980s hockey had become exceptionally popular again in Great Britain with a number of former NHL stars such as Garry Unger playing or coaching in Great Britain. Ten teams compete in the Heineken British League, playing a 36-game schedule. Keith Gretzky, younger brother to Wayne and a Buffalo Sabres' draft pick, played in this league in 1989-90.

Gretzky, Wayne

b. Brantford, Ontario, 26 January, 1961.

Wayne Gretzky has rewritten the NHL record book like no other player to come before him in the game. In less than 11 NHL seasons, he has broken almost every conceivable single-season and career scoring record in both regular-season and playoff competition. Gretzky broke into pro hockey with the Indianapolis Racers of the WHA. The financially troubled Racers dealt him to Edmonton and when the Oilers joined the NHL in 1979-80, Gretzky immediately silenced the critics who said that he wouldn't be able to stand the checking and bumping in the NHL. The Gretzky-led Oilers of the early 1980s were one of the league's most exciting teams. Gretzky scored 92 goals in 1981-82 and rattled off four seasons with more than 200 points. By 1983, the Oilers reached the Stanley Cup finals and a year later, were champions. The Oilers, led by

Gretzky, won four Stanley Cups. Gretzky won the Hart Trophy as NHL MVP nine out of ten times in the 1980s. He was the league's leading scorer seven times in the decade and set and improved upon the NHL single-season assist record five times. He surpassed Gordie Howe as the NHL's all-time leading point scorer early in the 1989-90 season. He was the central figure in the most dramatic trade in the history of sport, moving to Los Angeles in August of 1988. With the Kings, he has continued to function as the NHL's most effective ambassador, turning hockey into a hot ticket in Los Angeles. Some of "The Great One's" other records include: Most assists in a single game, most goals in a single period, longest consecutive point-scoring streak and most playoff points. In fact, he holds over 30 different scoring records for game, regular season, playoffs, and career.

Griffis, Si

b. 22 September 1883; d. 9 July 1950.
Hockey Hall of Fame: 1950

Griffis first came to prominence with the great Kenora team that won the Stanley Cup in 1906-07. Although he was one of the bigger men in hockey at 195 pounds, he became known as the fastest man in the game, starting at rover in the seven-man game of that era but later moving to cover point (defense). Griffis also captained the Vancouver Millionaires when they won the Cup in 1914-15. He remained with the team until his retirement in 1918.

Habs

'Habs' has been a nickname for the Montreal Canadiens for decades. It is derived from the Quebec French term 'habitant' which is a synonym for local farmer or person of the land.

Hainsworth, George

b. Toronto, Ontario, 26 June 1895; d. 9 October 1950. Hall of Fame: 1961

Goaltender George Hainsworth set two records in 1928-29, allowing only 43 goals in 44 games while recording 22 shutouts. He turned pro with Saskatoon in 1923-24 and remained with that team until shifting to the Montreal Canadiens in 1926-27. In Montreal, he won the Vezina Trophy

Glenn Hall's 502 consecutive games played by a goaltender is a record that will never be beaten. He played every minute of every game for the Red Wings from 1955 to 1957, and when traded to the Blackhawks, continued that streak until 7 November 1962. What is even more remarkable is that he played without a face mask.

in his first three seasons. He was traded to Toronto after 1932-33, remaining with the Maple Leafs until his retirement midway through 1936-37. He came back to appear in a few games for the Canadiens later that season.

Hall, Glenn

b. Humboldt, Saskatchewan, 3 October 1931. Hall of Fame: 1975

Glenn Hall was consistently one of the league's outstanding goaltenders and an 11-time all-star, finishing with a career goals-against average of 2.51. He was the NHL's top rookie in 1955-56 and went on to record 84 regular-season shutouts in 18 seasons with Detroit, Chicago and St. Louis. He holds NHL records for consecutive games by a goaltender (502), most playoff games (113) and most minutes played (6,899). He won the Vezina Trophy three times and led the St. Louis Blues to the Stanley Cup finals in each of the first three seasons after expansion in 1967.

Hall, Joe

b. Staffordshire, England, 3 May 1882; d. 5 April 1919. Hall of Fame: 1961

One of the true slam-bang defensemen in the game's history, Hall was a professional player for 14 years. He started playing hockey in 1897, and turned pro with Kenora in 1905-06. He moved east to play with the Montreal Shamrocks from 1907-1910, played with the Quebec Bulldogs from 1910-1916 (two Stanley Cups) and finished his career with the Montreal Canadiens. The Canadiens won the NHL title in 1918-19 and headed west to play Seattle for the Stanley Cup. The series was cancelled after five games because of a flu epidemic, and Hall was the most seriously stricken of the players; he died from the illness on 5 April.

Hamilton Tigers

The Hamilton Tigers franchise of the National Hockey League came into existence in 1920. When the Quebec Bulldogs could no longer support a team the franchise was moved to Hamilton. In 1925 the Tigers finished at the top of the NHL with a 19-10-1 record. Due to a player strike, they were dropped from the playoffs, and the franchise transferred to New York to become the Americans. Outstanding players on the team included Joe Malone, Goldie Prodgers, Mickey Roach and Jake Forbes.

Hanley, Bill

b. Ireland, 28 November 1915. Hall of Fame: Builder, 1986

Bill Hanley began his career in hockey as a

timekeeper. He was soon asked to assist George Panter, business manager of the OHA, and began to work in hockey full-time. He worked with Panter and Hall of Famers George Dudley and W.A. Hewitt, staying with the OHA as secretary-manager until his retirement in 1974. During his tenure, Hanley saw many changes in the game including the switch from the two to three on-ice officials and the elimination of the off-side pass.

Hartford Whalers

The Hartford franchise, which began operations as the New England Whalers, was a charter member of the WHA, beginning play in 1972. Jack Kelly, longtime coach of Boston University, was the first to manage and coach the Whalers. Former Montreal Canadiens' center Larry Pleau of Lynn, Massachusetts, was the first Whaler signed by Kelly, followed by NHL regulars Brad Selwood, Rick Ley, and Jim Dorey, all former Toronto Maple Leafs, and Tim Sheehy of Boston College. On July 27, 1972, the Whalers signed former Boston Bruins defenseman Ted Green as captain, following with other NHLers like Tom Webster, Al Smith, and Tom Williams. On October 12, 1972, the Whalers played their first home game at Boston Garden before a crowd of 14,442, defeating the Philadelphia Blazers 4-3. A well-balanced unit, the Whalers went on to finish first and win the WHA's first championship. However, the Whalers were unable to compete with the drawing power of the Boston Bruins at the venerable Boston Garden, necessitating a shift to the new Hartford Civic Center. Gordie, Mark, and Marty Howe joined the Whalers in 1977. The Whalers were one of the four WHA teams included in the amalgamation of the two leagues, officially becoming the 'Hartford' Whalers in 1980. The Whalers finished first in the Adams Division with 93 points in 1986-87 and have reached the playoffs every year since 1986.

CUMULATIVE RECORD	GP	Won	Lost	Tied	Pct
Regular Season (NHL)	880	339	428	113	.449
Playoffs	36	13	23	0	.361
Series: 7 W1 L6					
TOTALS	916	352	451	113	.446

Harvey, Doug

b. Montreal, Quebec, 19 December 1924; d. 26 December 1989. Hall of Fame: 1973

Harvey played 21 seasons of professional hockey, winning six Stanley Cups during 14 seasons with the Montreal Canadiens. He won the Norris Trophy as the NHL's top defenseman seven times. An excellent shot-blocker, Harvey had uncanny puck control and could set the pace of a game. Such was the caliber of his skating,

shooting and passing that he was named to NHL all-star teams 11 times. His passing ability is demonstrated by his 452 assists in regular-season play. He was traded from Montreal to the Rangers in 1961-62 to become a playing coach, and was later traded to Detroit. He was drafted by the expansion Blues, and finished his career in St. Louis.

Hat Trick

Three goals scored by a player in one game is a known as a hat trick. A pure or natural hat trick occurs when a player scores three consecutive goals or scores three goals in one period.

Hawerchuk, Dale

b. Toronto, Ontario, 4 April 1963.
A high-scoring center with the Winnipeg Jets, Dale Hawerchuk made his junior debut with the Cornwall Royals of the QMJHL in 1979-80. The next year he was named player of the year not only in his league but in all of major junior hockey. Hawerchuk won the Calder Trophy as rookie of the year with the Jets in 1981-82. He was named captain before the 1984-85 season, a year in which he scored 53 goals and 130 points; was runner-up for the Hart Trophy; and named to the second all-star team. He played with Team Canada in the 1987 Canada Cup and captained Team Canada to a silver medal in the 1989 World Championships.

Hay, Charles

b. Kingston, Ontario, 1902; d. 24 October 1973.
Hall of Fame: Builder, 1974
Charles Hay will be remembered as the nego-tiator who brought together the best players from Canada and the Soviet Union in 1972. He was a founder and, later, president of Hockey Canada, an organization set up to operate a national hockey team to represent Canada in international competition. The resulting September 1972 'Super Series' is considered by many to have been the greatest sports event in Canadian history. His son, Bill, played eight seasons with Chicago in the NHL.

Hay, George

b. Listowel, Ontario, 10 January 1898;
d. 13 July 1975.
Hall of Fame: 1958
Many experts called Hay the greatest stickhand-ler in hockey when he played in the NHL during the 1920s. He played junior with the Winnipeg Monarchs in 1915 and 1916, later turning profes-sional with the Regina Caps. During four years in the Saskatchewan capital, Hay scored 87 goals and had 57 assists. He moved on to Portland and joined the NHL when the team was sold to Chicago. Dealt to Detroit prior to the 1927-28 season, Hay led the Cougars (later the Red Wings) with 22 goals and 10 assists. The NHL's 10 coaches selected an all-star team that year, and Hay was part of the forward unit.

Ron Hextall is the first and only NHL goalie to actually shoot and score a goal, a feat he has accomplished twice. Hextall scored his first NHL goal against the Boston Bruins on 8 December 1987, then added a playoff goal as well when he scored against Washington on 11 April 1989.

Hayes, George

b. Montreal, Quebec, 21 June 1914;
d. 19 November 1987.
Hall of Fame: Linesman, 1988
George Hayes was the first NHL official to work more than 1,000 games. Despite disputes with league executives, Hayes was acknowledged as the finest linesman of his day. He signed his first NHL contract in 1946. From 1946-47 to 1964-65 he worked 1,544 regular-season, 149 playoff and 11 all-star games.

Henderson, Paul

b. Kincardine, Ontario, 28 January 1943.
Nothing will ever dim the memory of long-time Toronto Maple Leaf Paul Henderson's heroics in the classic 1972 series between Team Canada and the Soviet Nationals. Despite predictions that the NHLers who made up Team Canada would win every game, the Soviets held a 3-1-1

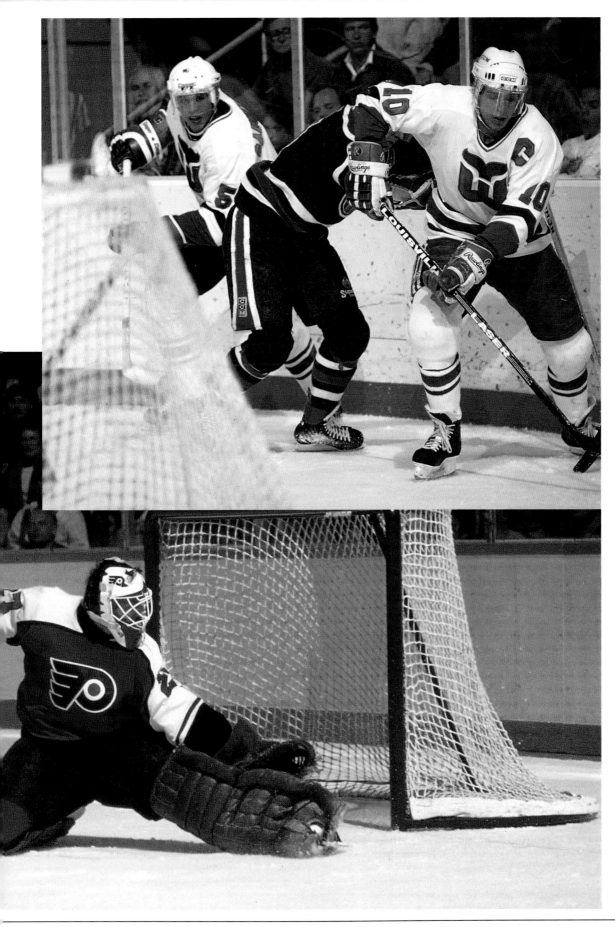

Hartford Whalers' captain Ron Francis is the club's all-time leader in goals (243), assists (502), and points (745).

edge after five games. Incredibly, in each of the three remaining games, Henderson dashed Soviet hopes for victory with dramatic tie-breaking goals. The final game saw Henderson rap his own rebound past a fallen Soviet netminder Vladislav Tretiak with only 34 seconds remaining, to win the series for Canada. Leftwinger Henderson played 13 NHL seasons for Detroit, Toronto and Atlanta and five WHA seasons for Toronto and Birmingham.

Henry, Camille

b. Quebec City, Quebec, 31 January 1933.
Nicknamed "The Eel" because of his elusiveness around the opposition's goal, Henry was under 150 pounds but made up for his small size with an instinct for scoring goals. He joined the New York Rangers in 1953-54 and was used mostly on the power play. He specialized in deflections and wound up with 24 goals, enough to win him the Calder Trophy as the league's top rookie. After a 50-goal season with Providence of the AHL, he rejoined the Rangers in 1956-57. He earned a second team all-star selection and won the Lady Byng Trophy in 1958. He was the Rangers' top scorer on three occasions before being traded to Chicago during the 1963-64 season. He returned to the Rangers in 1967-68 and then closed his playing days with St. Louis from 1968 to 1970. He later coached in the WHA.

Hern, Riley

b. St. Mary's, Ontario, 5 December 1880; d. 24 June 1929. Hall of Fame: 1962
Riley Hern played in goal for Doc Gibson's famous Portage Lakes team in the International (Pro) League in 1904. He had played junior, intermediate and senior hockey in Ontario before turning pro and returned to Canada to join the Montreal Wanderers in 1906. He was instrumental in the Wanderers' Stanley Cup victory that season and again in 1907-08 and 1909-10. Making Montreal his home, he retired as an active player in 1911 but remained active in the city's hockey scene as a referee and goal judge.

Hewitson, Bobby

b. Toronto, Ontario, 23 January 1892; d. 9 January 1969. Hall of Fame: Referee, 1963
Bobby Hewitson became a referee prior to 1920, handling games not only in hockey but in lacrosse and football as well. He went on to officiate 10 years in the NHL. He was also secretary of the Canadian Rugby Union for almost 25 years, was closely associated with horse racing and was a expert commentator on

hockey broadcasts. He became the first curator of both the Hockey Hall of Fame and Canada's Sports Hall of Fame, retiring in 1967.

Hewitt, Foster,

b. Toronto, Ontario, 21 November 1902; d. 21 April 1985. Hall of Fame: Builder, 1965
Beginning in March of 1923, when he broadcast a hockey game from the Mutual Street Arena in Toronto, Foster Hewitt became the eyes and ears of radio listeners and, later, television viewers across Canada. He described thousands of hockey games, including national, world and Olympic championships in Canada, the United States and in Europe. His distinctive voice perfectly mirrored the emotions and flow of the game for almost 50 years, up to and including the 1972 Canada-Soviet series. His father, W.A. Hewitt, is also a member of the Hockey Hall of Fame.

Hewitt, W.A.

b. Cobourg, Ontario, 15 May 1875; d. 8 September 1966. Hall of Fame: Builder, 1947
W.A. Hewitt enjoyed a 60-year association with hockey. He was sports editor of the Toronto Star for 32 years and was secretary of the Ontario Hockey Association from 1903 to 1961. He was also registrar and treasurer of the Canadian AHA for 39 years and manager of three champion Canadian teams in Olympic Hockey. He is credited with inventing the first goal net when he draped a fish net over the goal posts in an attempt to end disputes on whether the puck had gone in. He later served as the first attractions manager of Maple Leaf Gardens when the new building opened in 1931.

Hextall Family

The Hextalls are a three-generation NHL family. The original, and perhaps greatest was Bryan, Sr. A strong right wing, Bryan was schooled in the New York Rangers' farm system and became the linchpin of one of the greatest hockey teams in New York City history. The Rangers, in the period from 1939-42, ranked among the foremost NHL powers with Hextall leading the way on offense. His son Bryan, Jr. also played for the Rangers and several other NHL teams. Bryan, Jr.'s son Ron became one of the NHL's top goaltenders, starring for the Philadelphia Flyers in the late 1980s and into the new decade.

Hextall, Ron

b. Winnipeg, Manitoba, 3 May 1964.
Philadelphia's Ron Hextall is one of a small number of goaltenders who have changed the

way the position is played. Hextall built on Jacques Plante's innovation of leaving his net to corral loose pucks by adding the ability to make fast, accurate passes to his defensemen or forwards. Hextall also could shoot the puck like a forward and became the first goalie to fire the puck from one end of the rink into the opposition's empty net for a goal. Hextall's stick skills have occasionally landed him in trouble as well. His willingness to wield his stick against opposing players has earned him several suspensions.

High Stick

A player is not allowed to carry his stick above the normal height of the shoulder. A puck batted down with a high stick results in a stoppage in play. A goal scored by a high stick is illegal, unless it goes off the high stick of a defending player. If a player raises his stick while checking an opponent, he can be penalized for high-sticking. A referee can assess a minor or, if an injury has occurred, a major plus game misconduct penalty for a high-sticking infraction.

Above: **Though Foster Hewitt was not the first man to broadcast a hockey game, he was the first man to broadcast a televised game coast to coast across Canada on 1 November 1952. Hewitt was also the broadcast voice for the first radio coverage of the IIHF World Championships on 6 March 1955, when the Penticton V's downed the Soviet Union 5–0.**

Left: **The new Hockey Hall of Fame is scheduled to open in 1992, coinciding with the NHL's 75th anniversary season (1991–92) and the centennial of the Stanley Cup (1992–93).**

Hockey Hall of Fame

In 1943, a group of veteran hockey men, led by Captain John Sutherland, assembled to discuss the idea of establishing a Hall of Fame for the sport of ice hockey. Member inductions began in 1945, but the first permanent home for the Hall was not constructed until 1961. Located on the Canadian National Exhibition grounds in Toronto, this first Hall of Fame Building will be replaced by a new facility in downtown Toronto scheduled to open in 1992. Honored members of the Hall of Fame are inducted into one of three categories: players, builders and referees/linesmen. As of January 1, 1990 membership in the Hall of Fame totalled 275 (190 players, 74 builders, 11 referees/linesmen). To be eligible for selection, players, referees and linesmen must have completed their careers for a minimum of three seasons.

Hockey Night in Canada

The television program seen by millions of Canadians coast to coast each week during the course of a hockey season. Foster Hewitt's radio broadcasts from Toronto's Maple Leaf Gardens began using the title in 1935. The first televised Hockey Night in Canada broadcast aired (in French) on Radio-Canada, the French service of the Canadian Broadcasting Corporation (CBC) from the Montreal Forum on October 11, 1952, when the Detroit Red Wings visited the Montreal Canadiens. The first English broadcast emanated from Toronto's Maple Leaf Gardens on November 1, 1952, when the Toronto Maple Leafs hosted the Boston Bruins. Color telecasts were initiated in 1966 and proved to be a resounding success. Innovations such as the first use of instant replays and interesting on-air personalities such as Foster Hewitt, Jack Dennett, Bill Hewitt, Danny Gallivan, Howie Meeker, Brian MacFarlane, Dick Irvin, Dave Hodge and Don Cherry have helped make Hockey Night in Canada a Canadian institution for more than 50 years.

Holmes, Harry (Hap)

b. Aurora, Ontario, 24 November 1889; d. 1940
Hall of Fame: 1972

Hap Holmes was a top goaltender in five pro leagues: the NHA, PCHA, WCHL, WHL and NHL. He turned pro with the new Toronto franchise in the NHA in 1912-13 and went on to play 15 years with teams in Toronto, Seattle, Victoria and Detroit. He played on seven championship teams and four Stanley Cup winners. Holmes had a goals-against average of 2.90 in 405 league games. His Cup teams included Toronto in 1913-14 and 1917-18, Seattle in 1916-17 and Victoria in 1924-25. Holmes registered 41 league shutouts and another six in playoff competition. His memory is perpetuated through the Harry Holmes Memorial Trophy, awarded annually since 1941 to the leading goalie in the AHL.

Holmgren, Paul

b. St. Paul, Minnesota, 2 December 1955.

A tall, rangy forward, Paul Holmgren succeeded Dave Schultz as the 'policeman' of the tough Philadelphia Flyers. Holmgren later became coach of the Flyers and piloted them to upset playoff series wins over both the Washington Capitals and Pittsburgh Penguins in the opening rounds of the 1988-89 playoffs. Though his club lost the next round of the playoffs, Holmgren gained considerable respect for his handling of the injury-riddled Flyers' lineup against the powerful Montreal Canadiens.

Horner, Red

b. Lynden, Ontario, 28 May 1909.
Hall of Fame: 1965

Defenseman Red Horner is one of the few members of the Hall of Fame who was known during his playing days as one of the NHL's 'badmen'. Horner led the NHL in penalties for eight straight seasons – 1932-33 through 1939-40. He set a league record for penalties in a single season, spending 167 minutes in the box in 43 games during 1935-36, a mark which stood for 20 years. Horner moved to the Leafs directly from the Marlboro juniors in the 1928-29 season. He became the Leafs' captain in 1937-38. Red scored 42 goals and added 110 assists, and his play was an inspiration to the Toronto teams of the 1930s. His former manager, the late Conn Smythe, said: "He was one of the best drawing cards in the League. Truly, he helped establish the NHL as a popular attraction."

Horton, Tim

b. Cochrane, Ontario, 12 January 1930; d. 21 February 1974.
Hall of Fame: 1977

From the time defenseman Tim Horton accepted a hockey scholarship at St. Michael's College, he was recognized as a potential star. After three American Hockey League seasons, he became an NHLer with the Maple Leafs in 1952-53. He played almost 18 full seasons with Toronto, one each with New York and Pittsburgh, and then two with Buffalo until he died in a car accident. An excellent skater, Horton was noted for his rushing ability and powerful slap shot, as well as for his tremendous strength and self-restraint. He had a reputation as a peacemaker, flinging bodies out of piles during altercations and deterring over-eager opposing battlers. Tim played on four Stanley Cup winners with Toronto, and was named six times to all-star teams. Said team-mate Allan Stanley, "He was the finest man I ever knew."

Howe, Gordie

b. Floral, Saskatchewan, 31 May 1928.
Hall of Fame: 1972

When he first retired from the NHL in 1971 after 25 glorious seasons, rightwinger Gordie Howe said, "Say 'retired,' not 'quit.' I don't like the word quit." And that's one thing he never did during his brilliant career with the Detroit Red Wings, Houston Aeros, and New England and Hartford Whalers. In all, he played 32 big-league seasons in five different decades, establishing himself as one of the sport's greatest-ever talents. Gordie joined Detroit for the 1946-47 season. His effortless skating style and deceptive speed com-

Brett Hull eludes a check from the L.A. Kings' Ken Baumgartner. Hull, who became only the sixth NHL player to score 70 goals in a season, was nominated for both the Hart Trophy and the Lady Byng Trophy following his outstanding 1989–90 campaign.

Gordie Howe, below, scored his 801st and final NHL goal in his last regular-season game with the Hartford Whalers on 6 April 1980. Howe and his sons Marty and Mark joined the Whalers in 1977, when the New England team was still in the WHA. When the Whalers joined the NHL in 1979, Howe fulfilled his life-long dream of playing in the NHL with his sons.

bined with his tremendous strength and ability to shoot with equal dexterity from either side made him a difficult man to stop. He was tough, but not in a bullying way. By his final retirement in 1980, Howe had established more records than any other NHL player. These included most seasons (26), most games (1,767), most goals (801), most assists (1,049) and most points (1,850). He also holds the record for most selections to NHL all-star teams: 21, 12 of which were to the first team.

Howe, Mark

b. Detroit, Michigan, 28 May 1955.
Once regarded as one of the most gifted young forwards in North America, Mark Howe is the second – and youngest – of Gordie Howe's sons to play major-league hockey. He won a silver

medal as a member of the 1972 American Olympic team and with his older brother Marty, was a vital member of the OHA Toronto Marlboros in 1972-73. Both Howe brothers were signed as 18-year olds by the WHA's Houston Aeros in 1973-74 and joined their father who came out of retirement to play with his boys. He joined the New England Whalers in 1977 and stayed with that club when it joined the NHL as Hartford in 1979-80. Traded to Philadelphia in 1982-83, Howe was shifted to defense, winning the first of three first all-star team selections at the position. He remained one of the NHL's top defensemen throughout the 1980s.

Syd Howe only played a few games for the Maple Leafs in the 1931-32 season, spending the majority of the season with the Syracuse Stars. Howe was on loan to Toronto from the Ottawa Senators, and he returned to the nation's capital the following season.

Howe, Syd

b. Ottawa, Ontario, 28 September 1911; d. 20 May 1976. Hall of Fame: 1965

Howe was an unselfish player who played center, wing and defense during his 16 NHL seasons. He starred at both public and high school levels in Ottawa, and was a member of the first Ottawa team to play in the Memorial Cup finals. In 1930, he turned pro with the NHL's Ottawa Senators. He was loaned to the Philadelphia Quakers and the Toronto Maple Leafs before returning to Ottawa in 1932. Syd was with the Senators when they transferred to St. Louis, and it was from there that he was purchased by the Red Wings. He set a modern record on 3 February 1944, when he scored six goals in one game against the Rangers. During his NHL career, Howe scored 237 goals and had 291 assists.

Howell, Harry

b. Hamilton, Ontario, 28 December 1932. Hall of Fame: 1979

Howell appeared in more games than any defenseman in the history of major league hockey: 1,581 – 1,411 in the NHL and 170 in the World Hockey Association. He turned pro with the New York Rangers in 1952, and retired as a player in 1975. He missed only 17 games during his first 16 years in New York, setting team attendance records. Though he never played on a Stanley Cup winner, Howell was a first team all-star and Norris Trophy winner as the NHL's best defenseman in 1966-67. He later played for and coached WHA teams in New York, New Jersey, San Diego and Calgary.

Hull, Bobby

b. Pointe Anne, Ontario, 3 January 1939. Hall of Fame: 1983

As early as age 10, leftwinger Bobby Hull was tagged as a sure-fire NHL player; he didn't disappoint the experts. He earned a permanent spot with the Chicago Blackhawks in 1957-58. Although he didn't invent the slap shot, Bobby's blurring speed combined with his booming blast to make goalies cower. He led the NHL in goals seven times, and scored 610 goals and 560 assists in 16 NHL seasons. He added 62 goals and 67 assists in Stanley Cup play. He was the first to score more than 50 goals in a season, won the scoring title three times, the Hart Trophy as MVP twice, and the Lady Byng for gentlemanly play once. He was a 10-time first team all-star, and twice a second team selection. Hull was in the vanguard of players who helped launch the World Hockey Association, and his signing with

Bobby Hull, left, and Jack Evans pose with the Stanley Cup following the Chicago Blackhawks' Cup victory in 1961. Hull started his career wearing number 16 in 1958, but later changed first to number 7 and then to number 9. When he finished his playing days with Hartford in 1980, he reverted to number 16. Nine was already being used by fellow-Whaler Gordie Howe.

the Winnipeg Jets gave the new league much needed credibility.

Hull, Brett

b. Belleville, Ontario, 9 September 1964.

In scoring 105 goals in 56 games for Penticton of the British Columbia Junior Hockey League at age 19, Brett Hull served notice that indeed he was a chip off the old block of Hall of Famer Bobby Hull. Although his figures were not quite as spectacular at the University of Minnesota-Duluth, he did score 84 goals in 90 games over the course of two seasons and was voted to the WCHA first all-star team in 1985-86. Drafted by Calgary, he played primarily at Moncton of the AHL in 1986-87 where he scored 50 goals; won the Dudley 'Red' Garrett Memorial Trophy as rookie of the year; and was named to the first all-star team. By March of the 1987-88 season he had scored 26 goals and 50 points for the Flames when they traded him to St. Louis. With the Blues he had 41 goals and 43 assists in 1988-89, and in

1989-90 he became the sixth player in NHL history to score 70 goals in a single season.

Hyland, Harry

b. Montreal, Quebec, 2 January 1889; d. 8 August 1969. Hall of Fame: 1962

Few athletes can claim to have played on two national championship teams in the same season, but rightwinger Harry Hyland could support that boast. In 1909-10 his Montreal Wanderers won the Stanley Cup, and his New Westminster Salmonbellies captured the Minto Cup, symbolic of Canadian professional lacrosse supremacy. Hyland first played pro hockey with the Shamrocks in 1908, shifted to the Wanderers and then moved to New Westminster of the Pacific Coast Hockey Association in 1911. He rejoined his former Montreal team in 1913, and on January 27 of that year scored eight goals in the Wanderers' 10-6 win over Quebec. He remained with the Wanderers until 1918 when he joined Ottawa and finished his career.

Icing

When a player of a team at full strength shoots or deflects the puck from his side of the center red line to a point beyond the goal line (excluding the goal crease) of the opposing team, he is said to have iced the puck, resulting in a faceoff in the offending player's defensive zone. A player on a team that is short-handed may ice the puck with no stoppage in play.

Imlach, Punch

b. Toronto, Ontario, 15 March 1918; d. 1 December 1987. Hall of Fame: Builder, 1984

George (Punch) Imlach turned to coaching and managing when a badly broken wrist ended his playing career. He played four seasons – two as playing coach – with the Quebec Aces of the Quebec Senior League, taking on the job of general manager at age 31. He became assistant g.m. of the Toronto Maple Leafs, taking over as coach and g.m. part way through the 1958-59 season. With the Leafs, Imlach won four Stanley

Cups, making the playoffs in 10 of 11 seasons. He became coach and g.m. of the expansion Buffalo Sabres in 1970, staying with the franchise until the end of 1978. He rejoined the Leafs the next year, but continuing heart problems forced him from the game. Throughout his career he demanded and usually got the best from his players.

Influenza Epidemic of 1919

In nearly 100 years of competition, the Stanley Cup has been awarded every year except 1919 due to an outbreak of Spanish Influenza which reached epidemic proportions in Seattle, Washington, where the Cup final was played. The Montreal Canadians and Seattle Metropolitans, tied after five games with two wins each and a tie, abandoned further play when Montreal's Joe Hall died in hospital from complications arising from flu and fever. No Cup winner was declared.

International Ice Hockey Federation (IIHF)

Headquartered in Vienna, Austria, the International Ice Hockey Federation (IIHF) is the ruling body of international amateur hockey and is responsible for supervising World Championship, World Junior and Olympic ice hockey competitions. Formed in 1908, France was the

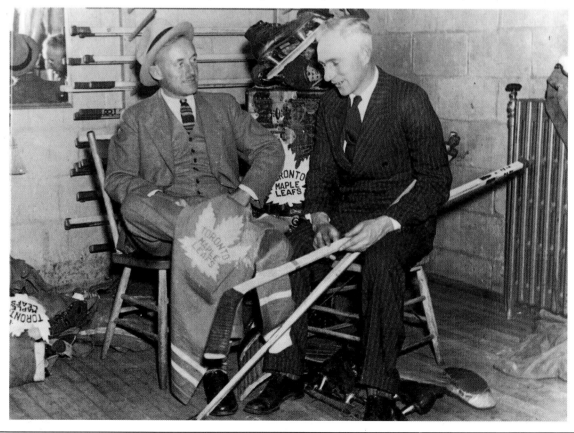

As a coach, Dick Irvin, right, led his teams (the Blackhawks, Leafs and Canadiens) into the Stanley Cup finals a record 16 times, but he also holds the record for most Cup losses, ending up the bridesmaid on 12 occasions. Conn Smythe, left, was the manager who built the Leafs into an NHL powerhouse.

first country to become a member. The first championship event occurred in 1920 when Canada captured the gold medal at Antwerp, Belgium. Annual tournaments have been held since 1930 with the exception 1940 to 1946 when play was interrupted because of World War II. The Soviet Union has won the World Championship or Olympic gold medal on 23 occasions. Canada stands second with 19 wins or gold medals. Currently, World Championship tournaments are held annually in the spring with teams being divided into four pools designated A, B, C, and D with A being the highest level of competition. Eight teams are entered in each pool based on their standing in the previous year's tournament. The winner of A is recognized as the world champion. The winner of B qualifies for the A the following year. Conversely, the eighth-place finisher in A drops down to B for the following year. The winner and second-place finishers in both C and D pools all move up one category while the seventh and eighth-place finishers in both B and C drop down one category. The IIHF selects 12 countries to compete in the Olympic Games based on their performance in the previous year's World Championships. Membership in the IIHF numbers 37 and includes nations such as Brazil, Kuwait, Luxembourg and Mexico.

International Professional Hockey League (1903-1907)

The International Professional Hockey League was the first outright professional hockey league. Dr. J.L. Gibson, a dental surgeon from Ontario, organized the league in 1903. The league operated teams in Portage Lake, Calumet, Pittsburgh and the American Sault. Offering good money, it was able to attract some top Canadian talent, resulting in some excellent hockey teams. The top team in the circuit, the Portage Lakers, offered challenges to Stanley Cup holders in Ottawa and Montreal, but on both occasions the trustees of the Cup refused the challenge.

International Hockey League (IHL)

Established in 1945, the IHL has evolved from a semi-pro industrial circuit to become a fully professional league made up of clubs affiliated with NHL franchises. In 1989-90, the IHL consisted of nine teams playing in two divisions: Kalamazoo, Muskegon, Flint and Fort Wayne in the east and Indianapolis, Salt Lake, Milwaukee, Peoria and Phoenix in the west. IHL games tied after overtime are decided by a shootout, resulting in no tied games. The team that loses in overtime or in a shootout receives one point in the standings. The winner receives two. The IHL playoff champion receives the Turner Cup.

Ion, Mickey

b. Paris, Ontario, 25 February 1886; d. 26 October 1964. Hall of Fame: Referee, 1961

Mickey Ion became a hockey referee in 1913, handling his first professional game in New Westminster, British Columbia. King Clancy, referring to Ion's grace under pressure, said, "There's nothing but ice-water running through his veins." He became a top official of the Pacific Coast Hockey Association, but when it folded moved east and joined the NHL staff. He refereed the memorable Howie Morenz memorial game, played in the Montreal Forum in 1937, and continued as an NHL official until 1941.

Ironmen

'Ironmen' are hockey players who are able to play extended periods without missing a game. Andy Hebenton played nine consecutive 70-game seasons with the Rangers and Bruins from 1955-56 through 1963-64. Johnny Wilson played 580 consecutive games with Detroit, Chicago and Toronto from 1952 to 1960. Ironmen in more recent eras include Garry Unger, who played 914 consecutive games with Toronto, Detroit, St.Louis and Atlanta from 1968 to 1979, and Craig Ramsay who played 776 games for Buffalo from 1973 to 1983. The league's leading ironman is Doug Jarvis who broke in with the Montreal Canadiens in 1975-76, and never missed a game with the Habs through 1981-82. He was traded to Washington in 1982-83 and Hartford in 1985-86, finally ending his ironman stint at 962 consecutive games on 5 April 1987.

Irvin, Dick Sr.

b. Limestone Ridge, Ontario, 19 July 1892; d. 16 May 1957. Hall of Fame: 1958

Forward Dick Irvin moved to Winnipeg in 1899 and it was there he embarked on his hockey career. He joined the senior Monarchs in 1912 as an emergency replacement, and scored six goals in two games of the Allan Cup final. In a 1914 exhibition, Irvin scored all nine goals in a 9-1 Monarchs' victory and the club went on to win the Allan Cup in 1915. He turned pro with the Portland Rosebuds next season and, after World War I, played four years with Regina before returning to Portland. He moved to Chicago of the NHL in 1926 and was the Blackhawks' first captain, finishing second in the scoring race. He fractured his skull in the twelfth game of the next season, ending his playing career. After coaching Chicago, he moved to Toronto in 1931 for a Stanley Cup-winning season. He also coached the Montreal Canadiens from 1940-1955, winning three Cups.

Ivan, Tommy

b. Toronto, Ontario, 31 January 1911.
Hall of Fame: Builder, 1974

Tommy Ivan's rise to the top of the NHL's coaching ranks began with a scouting job in the Detroit organization. He went on to coach in Omaha and Indianapolis before becoming coach of the Red Wings in 1947-48. In Detroit, Ivan coached six straight NHL championship teams and three Stanley Cups winners, leaving in 1954-55 to join the Chicago Blackhawks as general manager. He played a vital role in rebuilding the Hawks into a successful organization with a fine farm system. In 1960-61 with Ivan as g.m., the Hawks won their first Stanley Cup title in 23 years.

Izvestia Tournament

A prestigious invitational hockey tournament hosted by the Soviet Union's national team and held in Moscow. Named after the Russian newspaper 'Izvestia' (which donated the cup presented to the winning club), the tournament has been held annually since 1967 during mid-December and is seen as a major preparatory step for teams heading to the World Championships. The Soviet Union's national team has prevailed as tournament winners on 18 occasions. Canada's national team, in a major upset, won the 1987 event for its only tournament win in 13 appearances.

Jackson, Harvey (Busher)

b. Toronto, Ontario, 19 January 1911; d. 25 June 1966. Hall of Fame: 1971

An excellent leftwinger, Jackson collected 241 goals and 234 assists in 633 NHL games. In playoff competition, he had 18 goals and 12 assists in 72 games. Jackson signed with the Leafs in 1930, and played on three league championship and one Stanley Cup-winning team. He led the league in scoring in 1932-33, and was a five-time NHL all-star (four times on the first team). He injured his shoulder in the 1938-39 season final against Boston in what proved to be his last appearance for Toronto; he was dealt with three other players to the New York Americans for Sweeney Schriner. He went to the Bruins in 1942, ending his playing career in 1943-44.

Jennings, Bill

b. 14 December 1920; d. 17 August 1981. Hall of Fame: Builder, 1975

Bill Jennings became president of the Rangers in 1962. As an NHL governor, Jennings was an advocate of expansion and did much of the groundwork to overcome objections to what eventually became the six to 12-team expansion of 1967. Jennings also was an originator of the Lester Patrick Award for persons who have rendered "outstanding service to hockey in the United States," receiving the award himself in 1971.

Johnson, Ernest (Moose)

b. Montreal, Quebec, 26 February 1886; d. 25 March 1963. Hall of Fame: 1952

Leftwinger/defenseman Moose Johnson turned professional with the Montreal Wanderers and played with them on four Stanley Cup championship winners. He joined the New Westminster Royals of the Pacific Coast Hockey Association in 1912. Johnson later played with Victoria,

---

Aurel Joliat starred in the 1920s and made his final appearance in a Montreal Canadiens' uniform in January of 1985 when the club made him an honorary member of its 75th anniversary "dream team". Joliat proved he still had a bit of magic left even at the age of 84, when he broke in alone on Jacques Plante, pulled a clever deke, and scored.

Los Angeles and other teams of the Western Hockey League until retirement in 1931. Johnson became known as the player with the longest reach in hockey history – his reach, fully extended and with stick, was 99 inches.

Johnson, Ivan (Ching)

b. Winnipeg, Manitoba, 7 December 1897; d. 16 June 1969. Hall of Fame: 1958

Johnson stood out as one of the most colorful, hard-hitting defensemen in hockey. After returning from military service in 1919, Johnson played in Winnipeg, Eveleth (Minnesota) and Minneapolis. Although he was 28 years old at the time, the New York Rangers purchased his contract when that club was formed in 1926. He spent 11 years with the Rangers, and was named a first team all-star three times and a second team selection twice. His career ended with the New York Americans in 1937-38. He played 463 games and acquired 969 penalty minutes.

Johnson, Tom

b. Baldur, Manitoba, 18 February 1928. Hall of Fame: 1970

Johnson didn't play in a covered arena until he was 18, when he joined the junior Winnipeg Monarchs. Claimed by Montreal, he was sent to Buffalo for the 1947-48 season; he joined the Canadiens the next year. Johnson played 15 NHL seasons, scoring 51 goals and 213 assists in 978 games. His best season was 1958-59, when he won the Norris Trophy as the NHL's best defenseman. He frequently played center when his team needed a goal late in the game. Johnson won six Stanley Cups while with the Canadiens. A leg injury suffered after he had been acquired by Boston ended his career.

Johnston, Ed

b. Montreal, Quebec, 24 November 1935.

There have been few NHL goaltenders as consistent as Ed Johnston, who starred for the Bruins in the late 1960s and into the 1970s. Following his playing career, Johnston emerged as a well-liked front-office executive. He was general manager of the Pittsburgh Penguins when the club acquired Mario Lemieux, remaining with the team through the 1988-89 season. At the start of the 1989-90 campaign he was general manager of the Hartford Whalers and hired Rick Ley as his coach.

Joliat, Aurel

b. Ottawa, Ontario, 29 August 1901; d. 2 June 1986. Hall of Fame: 1947

Joliat was called the Mighty Atom or the Little

Giant, and spent 16 seasons with the Montreal Canadiens. He played his early hockey in Ottawa and Iroquois Falls, Ontario. He went west on a harvest excursion train and played for the Saskatoon Sheiks. His first season in Montreal was 1922-23, and Joliat went on to become one of the greatest leftwingers in NHL history. Despite six shoulder separations, three broken ribs and a nose broken five times, Joliat scored 270 goals. He played on three Stanley Cup-winning teams, was a four-time all-star and won the Hart Trophy as the league's MVP in 1934.

Juckes, Gordon

b. Watrous, Saskatchewan, 20 June 1914. Hall of Fame: Builder, 1979

A newspaperman and soldier, Gordon Juckes began his career as a hockey administrator as president of his local senior club in Melville,

Ivan Johnson, who received the nickname "Ching" as a youth, was known by the other monikers as well. The greatest proponent of the "clutch and grab" style of his day, Johnson was often called the "The Holding Corporation" and "The Great Wall of China" by opponents who tried to sneak past his post on the Rangers' blueline.

Saskatchewan. He went on to serve as president of the Saskatchewan AHA in 1953-54 and later assumed the presidency of the Canadian AHA. He was appointed secretary-manager and, later, executive director, of the CAHA in 1960 and served the cause of amateur hockey until his retirement in 1978. At the time of his election to the Hockey Hall of Fame, he sat on the boards of Hockey Canada and the Canadian Olympic Association.

Junior Hockey

An amateur hockey division designated by age. Age limits in hockey were introduced in Canada in 1899, 'Junior' being specified as any player who is under the age of 20 on the first day of the year in which the season begins. There was one Junior division until part way through the 1933-34 season, when Junior 'A' and Junior 'B' divisions were established. These sections within the Junior ranks are based on caliber and skill levels. A Junior 'C' level was created in 1937 and a Junior 'D' grouping initiated in 1948. Another skill level was established in 1970, with the creation of 'Major Junior A', comprising the three major junior leagues located in Ontario (OHL), Western Canada (WHL) and Quebec (QMJHL). The CAHA also decided that only these three leagues would play for the Memorial Cup. The remaining Junior 'A' teams and leagues not at the major level compete for the Centennial Cup.

Kansas City Scouts

The Kansas City Scouts joined the NHL for the 1974-75 campaign along with the Washington Capitals. They played their home games at the Kemper Arena and posted a 15-54-11 record, good for 41 points. Unfortunately, the team failed to attract sufficient fans to inspire ownership to continue in Kansas City beyond the 1975-76 season. The franchise was renamed the Colorado Rockies and shifted to Denver in 1976.

Keenan, Mike

b. Toronto, Ontario, 21 October 1949.
Mike Keenan captained the St. Lawrence University hockey team and, in 1973-74, was voted most valuable player of the Southern Hockey League while a member of the Roanoke Valley Rebels. But his greatest successes have come through coaching. He began by winning two

junior B championships before taking the Peterborough Petes of the OHL to the Memorial Cup finals in 1978-79. He coached the Rochester Americans to a Calder Cup victory in the AHL before returning to the amateur ranks to guide the University of Toronto to the CIAU championship in 1983-84. Keenan was hired as head coach by the Philadelphia Flyers in 1984-85. In his four seasons with the Flyers he took them to the Stanley Cup finals on two occasions and registered 190 regular-season wins. He won the Jack Adams Trophy in 1985 and was the winning coach of Team Canada in the 1987 Canada Cup. In June of 1988 he became the 28th coach in the history of the Chicago Blackhawks. Although he finished with an sub-.500 record for the first time in his NHL career in 1988-89, the Blackhawks finished strongly in the Norris Division and then jelled in the playoffs, going to the Campbell Conference finals before losing to Calgary.

Jari Kurri (number 17) has led the NHL in goals scored during the playoffs on four occasions, and in each of those years, the Oilers went on to win the Stanley Cup. He and Wayne Gretzky are the NHL's all-time playoff goal-scoring leaders.

Kelly, Red

b. Simcoe, Ontario, 9 July 1927.
Hall of Fame: 1969

Kelly graduated to the NHL at 19 from St. Michael's Majors. He played with the Red Wings for 12½ seasons as a standout defenseman. During that time he was a four-time Lady Byng Trophy winner, and was the first winner of the Norris Trophy. He was traded to the Maple Leafs and finished his career as a center. Kelly played on eight Stanley Cup-winning teams, was a six-time first team all-star, playing in 1,316 regular season games. He retired as a player in 1967, accepting a coaching post with the expansion Los Angeles Kings. He became coach of Pittsburgh in 1969 and Toronto in 1973. He was a member of parliament while still playing, serving in government from 1962 to 1965. His opponent in a 1963 election, Alan Eagleson, went on to become executive director of the National Hockey League Players Association.

Kennedy, Ted (Teeder)

b. Humbertstone, Ontario, 12 December 1925.
Hall of Fame: 1966

Kennedy's bulldog tenacity and competitive spirit made him one of the outstanding centers and leaders in the game's history. He sparked the Toronto Maple Leafs to five Stanley Cup triumphs during a 12-year NHL career, and in his final season (1954-55) was awarded the Hart Trophy as the league's MVP. Originally property of the Canadiens, Kennedy attended their training camp at the age of 16 but was so homesick he left. The Leafs traded for his rights and he broke into the NHL at 18. In 696 games, he scored 231 goals and added 329 assists.

Kenora Thistles

The Kenora (Ontario) Thistles won the Stanley Cup in 1907. Playing in the Manitoba and Northwestern Ontario League, they first challenged for the Cup in 1903 as the Rat Portage Thistles (Rat Portage was an early name for Kenora). In 1905, while playing in the Manitoba Hockey League, they again challenged for the Cup without success. The 1907 Cup-winning team included Art Ross, Si Griffis, Tom Hooper and Tom Phillips.

Dave Keon spent only 117 minutes in the penalty box in his lengthy NHL career. This total includes only one major penalty, courtesy of a clash with Boston's Gregg Sheppard in the final game of the 1974 season.

Keon, Dave

b. Noranda, Quebec, 22 March 1940.
Hall of Fame: 1986

Keon spent 22 seasons in professional hockey, 18 in the NHL and four in the World Hockey Association. In over 1,800 professional games, he picked up only 151 penalty minutes. Keon was one of the most fastidious checking centers in the game's history. He joined the Leafs from St. Michael's in 1960-61, and was named the NHL's rookie of the year. He won the Lady Byng Trophy twice, and captured the Conn Smythe in 1967. He was a member of four Stanley Cup teams. After 15 NHL seasons with Toronto, Keon shifted to the WHA in 1975 and played for Minnesota, Indianapolis and New England before returning to the NHL with the Whalers. He retired in 1982.

Kilpatrick, J.R.

b. 15 June 1889; d. 7 May 1960.
Hall of Fame: Builder, 1960

General John Reed Kilpatrick was an outstanding athlete in many sports, but claimed that hockey was his favorite sport to watch. As president of Madison Square Garden and the New York Rangers for 22 years, he saw a lot of games and demonstrated considerable skills as an executive. He was an original director of the NHL Players' Pension Society which was established in 1946 and remained on its board until his death. He was elected an NHL governor in 1936 and during his years with the Rangers twice watched them win the Stanley Cup. He is credited with throwing football's first overhand forward pass for Yale against Princeton in 1907.

Kurri, Jari

b. Helsinki, Finland, 18 May 1960.

Finnish star Jari Kurri signed with the Edmonton Oilers at age 19 in 1980-81. Teamed with Wayne Gretzky, he scored more than 30 goals in his first two seasons and upped his totals to 34, 52 and 71 in the next three. His developing defensive skills were recognized in 1982-83 when he was runner-up to Bobby Clarke for the Selke Trophy. In 1985 when his 71 goals set an NHL record for rightwingers, he won the Lady Byng Trophy and was named to the first all-star team. He was also a first all-star in 1987 and a second team selection in 1984 and 1986. Kurri led all playoff goal scorers in the years that the Oilers won the Stanley Cup: 1984, 1985, 1987 and 1988. He is the highest playoff scorer in NHL history.

Lach, Elmer

b. Nokomis, Saskatchewan, 22 January 1918.
Hall of Fame: 1966

Lach brought great skills to the NHL – an unusual gift for playmaking, blinding speed, courage, intelligence and determination. He turned pro with the Canadiens in 1940-41, playing 646 regular-season and 76 playoff games; he amassed 215 goals and 408 assists, adding 19 goals and 45 assists in the playoffs. A five-time all-star, he made the first team in 1944-45 – when he had 80 points in 50 games. He was voted the Hart Trophy winner that year. Lach centered the Canadiens' great Punch Line between Maurice Richard and Toe Blake.

Lafleur, Guy

b. Thurso, Quebec, 20 September 1951.
Hall of Fame: 1988

Guy Lafleur was the NHL's most exciting scorer in the second half of the 1970s. He was an acclaimed junior, scoring 209 points in his final season with the Quebec Remparts and was selected first overall by the Montreal Canadiens in the 1971 Amateur Draft. His promise was fulfilled in 1974-75, when he recorded the first of six consecutive 50-goal seasons, earning six first all-star selections at right wing, three scoring championships and two Hart Trophies as the NHL's MVP. The Canadiens won four consecutive Stanley Cups during this stretch as Lafleur's dazzling array of moves, hard shot and superior skating ability made him the most compelling player in the league. He retired early in 1984-85, but came back to play with the New York Rangers in 1988-89 and the Quebec Nordiques in 1989-90.

LaFontaine, Pat

b. St. Louis, Missouri, 22 February 1965.

Pat LaFontaine learned his hockey in a suburb of Detroit and eventually made his way to Montreal where he became a junior hockey star. LaFontaine was one of the top players on the 1984 U.S. Olympic Team. After the Games he was signed by the New York Islanders and played in the 1984 playoffs. His most memorable goal was scored against the Washington Capitals on Easter Sunday morning in the fourth overtime period at the Capital Centre. LaFontaine took a pass from Gord Dineen, wheeled and fired the puck past goalie Bob Mason. The time was 1:46 a.m., at 8:47 of the fourth overtime period and the goal clinched the series for the Isles. LaFontaine was one of the NHL's top goal scorers in 1989-90.

Lalonde, Edouard (Newsy)

b. Cornwall, Ontario, 31 October 1887; d. 21 November 1971. Hall of Fame: 1950

As a youth, center Newsy Lalonde worked in a newsprint plant – hence his nickname. Lalonde began a somewhat riotous professional hockey career in Cornwall in 1905, and he was a dominant figure for almost 30 seasons. He played for Toronto, Woodstock, Sault Ste. Marie, Renfrew (all in Ontario), Vancouver, Saskatoon, the New York Americans and the Montreal Canadiens. He completed his active connection with the game as coach of the Canadiens. A brilliant goal scorer, he was also known as one of the roughest players of his day. Newsy scored 441 goals in 365 games and was a five-time league scoring champion in the National Hockey Association, Pacific Coast Hockey Association and NHL. An outstanding athlete, Lalonde was named the lacrosse athlete of the half-century in 1950.

Lamoriello, Lou

b. Providence, Rhode Island, 21 October 1942.
Long before he made his NHL debut as president and g.m. of the New Jersey Devils in 1987, Lou Lamoriello had been a successful collegiate coach at Providence College. In his first year, the Devils reached the playoffs for the first time since the club moved to New Jersey. He also made headlines in the summer of 1989 after a series of trips to Moscow enabled the Devils to sign Soviet stars Viacheslav Fetisov and Sergei Starikov. Later in the 1989-90 season, he added Russian defenseman Alexei Kasatonov to his squad.

When Guy Lafleur came out of retirement to join the New York Rangers in 1988, he became only the third player to return to active duty after being elected to the Hall of Fame. Gordie Howe returned to the NHL with Hartford after retiring in 1971, and Dit Clapper suited up for the Bruins as a player-coach after his election to the Hall in 1946.

St. Louis-born Pat LaFontaine slips the puck past Pittsburgh goalie Wendel Young for one of the 54 goals he scored during the 1989–90 season. LaFontaine was nominated for the Lady Byng Trophy after picking up just 38 minutes in penalties.

Langway, Rod

b. Formosa, Taiwan, 3 May 1957.

Raised in New England, Rod Langway played for the University of New Hampshire and turned pro with the Hampton (Virginia) Gulls in 1977-78. During the season, however, he joined the Birmingham Bulls of the WHA for 52 games as one of their youthful crop of 'Baby Bulls.' In 1978-79 he made his debut with the Montreal Canadiens, adding muscle to the team in its successful defense of the Stanley Cup. Traded to the Washington Capitals before 1982-83, Langway became the anchor of the Capitals' defense and eventually was named team captain. He

became the first American player to win the Norris Trophy in 1983; won it again 1984; and was also voted to the first all-star team in both those years. He captained Team USA in the 1987 Canada Cup. Langway is one of the few helmetless players in the NHL. His lifetime statistics through the 1988-89 season are 50-250-300 with 744 penalty minutes in 795 games.

Laperriere, Jacques

b. Rouyn, Quebec, 22 November 1941.
Hall of Fame: 1987

Laperriere continued the Montreal Canadiens tradition of recruiting big, mobile and talented

Rod Langway has been a fixture on the Washington Capitals defense for the past eight seasons. With Langway's leadership and spirited play, the Capitals won their first Patrick Division crown after downing the Rangers in the 1990 playoffs.

Brian Leetch has established himself as one of the Rangers' top defenseman after only two seasons on the New York blueline. He suffered a season-ending ankle injury in a game against Toronto near the end of the 1989–90 campaign, and his absence from the Rangers' lineup spelled an early exit from the post-season for the Broadway Blues.

defensemen. He played with the Junior Cana-diens before joining Montreal's Eastern Profes-sional Hockey League affiliate. He joined the Canadiens in 1963, after four EPHL seasons, and was named the NHL's top rookie. He also earned the first of four all-star selections. Laperriere was awarded the Norris Trophy as the NHL's top defender in 1966, and also won six Stanley Cups. He played his entire NHL career with Montreal, retiring in 1974 because of a serious knee injury.

Laviolette, Jack

b. Belleville, Ontario, 27 July 1879; d. 10 January 1960. Hall of Fame: 1962

Laviolette, with financial backing from T.C. Hare and Ambrose O'Brien, was the founder of the Montreal Canadiens. Laviolette moved to Quebec at a young age, and he played his early hockey there. He joined a team in Sault Ste. Marie, Michigan, and was named an all-star. When he formed the Canadiens, Laviolette played point (defense) but later moved to forward. Jack had great speed and played on a Stanley Cup winner in 1916. He retired in 1918.

LeBel, Bob

b. Quebec, Quebec, 21 September 1905. Hall of Fame: Builder, 1970

Robert LeBel is one of the most respected hockey executives in Quebec. He served as president of the Interprovincial Senior League (1944-47), the Quebec Amateur Hockey League (1955-57), the CAHA (1957-59), and the IIHF (1960-62). He was the first French-Canadian to hold the latter two offices.

Leetch, Brian

b. Corpus Christi, Texas, 3 March 1968.

Defenseman Brian Leetch played one year of NCAA hockey with Boston College in 1986-87, winning all-American honors. He played for the 1988 U.S. Olympic team before joining the New York Rangers. In his first full NHL season in 1988-89, he won the Calder Trophy as NHL rookie of the year and was named to the all-rookie team. He played 68 games for the Rangers, scoring 23 goals and 48 assists for 71 points, and helped the Rangers to a playoff

Leagues, Associations and Governing Bodies

Early (Defunct) Senior Organizations/Leagues

AHA	Amateur Hockey Association (1886-98)
CAHL	Canadian Amateur Hockey League (1898-1905)
CHA	Canadian Hockey Association (1909)
ECAHA	Eastern Canada Amateur Hockey Association (1905-08)
ECHA	Eastern Canada Hockey Association (1909)
FAHL	Federal Amateur Hockey League (1903-07)
I(P)HL	International Professional Hockey League (1903-07)
NHA	National Hockey Association (1909-17)
OPHL	Ontario Professional Hockey League (1908-11)
PCHA	Pacific Coast Hockey Association (1911-24)
WCHL	Western Canada Hockey League (1922-25)
WHL	Western Hockey League (1926)

Defunct Leagues

ACHL	Atlantic Coast Hockey League
CHL	Central Hockey League
EAHL	Eastern Amateur Hockey League
EHL	Eastern Hockey League
EPHL	Eastern Professional Hockey League
NAHL	North American Hockey League
PCHL	Pacific Coast Hockey League
SHL	Southern Hockey League
USHL	United States Hockey League
WHA	World Hockey Association
WHL	Western Hockey League (minor pro)

Active Organizations

AHAUS	Amateur Hockey Association of the United States
AHL	American Hockey League
CAHA	Canadian Amateur Hockey Association
CCHA	Central Collegiate Hockey Association
CIAU	Canadian Intercollegiate Athletic Union
ECAC	Eastern Collegiate Athletic Conference
ECHL	East Coast Hockey League
H.E.	Hockey East
IHL	International Hockey League
IIHL	International Ice Hockey Federation
MTHL	Metro Toronto Hockey League
NCAA	National Collegiate Athletic Association
NHL	National Hockey League
OHL	Ontario Hockey League (junior)
QMJHL	Quebec Major Junior Hockey League
WCHA	Western Collegiate Hockey Association
WHL	Western Hockey League (junior)

berth. Leetch quickly established himself as one of the league's finer offensive defensemen and was compared favorably to Hall of Famer Doug Harvey.

Lehman, Hughie

b. Pembroke, Ontario, 27 October 1885; d. 8 April 1961. Hall of Fame: 1958

A 21-year pro goaltender, Hughie Lehman played with Sault Ste. Marie, in the International Professional League before joining Berlin in the OPHL in 1909. When the Pacific Coast Hockey Association was formed in 1911-12, Lehman joined the New Westminster Royals and stayed with them for three season before becoming a member of the Vancouver Millionaires in 1914-15. He played with that team until the league was disbanded after the 1925-26 season. Lehman joined Chicago of the NHL in 1926-27 and retired to coach the club after 1927-28. He played on eight Stanley Cup challengers but was successful only once, with Vancouver in 1914-15.

Lemaire, Jacques

b. LaSalle, Quebec, 7 September 1945. Hall of Fame: 1984

The definition of a two-way hockey player, center Jacques Lemaire played 12 brilliant seasons with Montreal and was an integral part of eight Stanley Cup championships. In 145 Cup games, he scored 61 goals and had 139 points. He is one of only five players to twice score the Cup-winning goal. Lemaire joined the Canadiens in 1967-68, played with Montreal for his entire career, and retired in 1979. He scored 366 goals and 835 points in 853 regular season games, while accumulating only 217 penalty minutes. He returned to the Canadiens in 1983-84 as a member of the coaching staff, taking over as head coach midway through the schedule.

Lemieux, Mario

b. Montreal, Quebec, 5 October 1965.

Mario Lemieux combines skill and size as the NHL's most dangerous scoring threat. The 6-4, 200-pound center with a long reach was drafted number one by the Pittsburgh Penguins in 1984 after three seasons in the QMJHL. In the NHL he began by scoring 100 points; being named to the all-rookie team; and winning the Calder Trophy in 1984-85. He was named to the second all-star team in 1985-86 and 1986-87 and to the first team in 1987-88 and 1988-89. His awards include the Lester Pearson Trophy in 1986 and 1988; the Hart Trophy in 1988; and the Art Ross Trophy in 1988 and 1989. His 85 goals in 1988-89 is the third-highest total in NHL history, and with 199 points in that same season, he came within one point of

being only the second player to reach the 200 mark, leading the Penguins to their first playoff appearance since 1982. His 13 short-handed goals in 1988-89 set a league record and his 47-game scoring streak in 1989-90 was the second-longest in NHL history. If one man can he said to have revitalized a franchise it is Lemieux in Pittsburgh. He figures to be a dominant force in the 1990s.

LeSueur, Percy

b. Quebec City, Quebec, 18 November 1881; d. 27 January 1962. Hall of Fame: 1961

The hockey career of Percy LeSueur spanned 50 years, but he gained his fame as the goaltender of the Ottawa Senators from 1906 to 1913. He won two Stanley Cups in Ottawa, served as captain for three years and manager and coach for part of the 1913-14 season. He was traded to Toronto in 1914, playing until he joined the armed services in 1916. He remained involved with hockey as a referee, arena manager, broadcaster and columnist. LeSueur is credited with inventing the gauntlet-type goaltender's glove and the net used by the NHA and NHL from 1912 to 1925.

Lewis, Herbie

b. Calgary, Alberta, 17 April 1907. Hall of Fame: 1989

Leftwinger Herbie Lewis was known as the "Duke of Duluth" because of four high-scoring seasons with the Duluth Hornets of the AHL. He joined the Detroit Cougars (later to become the Red Wings) in 1928, bringing his stylish, high-speed brand of hockey to the NHL. He played on a superb two-way forward line with Cooney Weiland and Larry Aurie, becoming the Red Wings' captain in 1933. He and Aurie played in the NHL's first all-star game in 1934. Marty Barry replaced Weiland on Lewis' line in 1935-36, and the Red Wings rebounded from last place to win the first of two consecutive Stanley Cups. Lewis had 37 and 32 points in these years, adding 12 more in 17 playoff encounters. He retired in 1939 after 11 productive seasons in Detroit.

Ley, Rick

b. Orillia, Ontario, 2 November 1948.
Rick Ley, a short, rugged defenseman, began his NHL career in 1968-69 as part of the Toronto Maple Leafs' "Kiddie Korps" backline that included Jim Dorey and Brad Selwood. He played four seasons with the Leafs before jumping to the New England (later Hartford) Whalers in the WHA's inaugural season of 1972-73. He played 559 games for the franchise, including the first two seasons Hartford was a member of the NHL.

For six seasons Ley captained the Whalers and, in 1978-79, won top defenseman honors in the WHA. Ley was named an assistant coach of the Whalers but in 1982-83 became coach of the Binghamton Whalers of the AHL. In 1983-84 he left the Whalers' organization to coach Mohawk Valley of the ACHL. Then, in 1984-85, he became affiliated with the Pittsburgh Penguins' farm club at Muskegon in the IHL, coaching them to four consecutive first-place divisional finishes. After coaching the Milwaukee Admirals of the IHL to a winning season in 1988-89, Ley finally was given a chance to lead an NHL club when the Whalers signed him in June of 1989.

Linden, Trevor

b. Medicine Hat, Alberta, 11 April 1970.
Many Vancouver fans believed that Trevor Linden deserved to win the rookie of the year award in 1988-89. The center was the second overall choice in the 1988 Entry Draft. He played all 80 games for the Canucks in 1988-89, scoring 30 goals with 29 assists for a total of 59 points. In the playoffs he played seven games, scoring three goals and four assists for seven points.

Toronto's "Kid Line" of Charlie Conacher, Joe Primeau and Busher Jackson were leading playoff scorers en route to the 1932 Stanley Cup and earned all-star team selections in the 1930s.

Lindsay, Ted

b. Renfrew, Ontario, 29 July 1925.
Hall of Fame: 1966
Ted Lindsay was a remarkable hockey player and one of the greatest leftwingers of all time. He joined the Detroit Red Wings from Oshawa's Memorial Cup-winning team in 1944, and quickly established himself as a leader. Lindsay played on the great Production Line with Sid Abel and Gordie Howe, and that line played a major role in the phenomenal success of the Wings between 1949 and 1955, when they won seven league titles and four Stanley Cups. Ted played 13 seasons with Detroit, before being traded to Chicago in 1957. He retired in 1960, but made a remarkable comeback with Detroit in 1964-65. Lindsay scored 379 goals in 17 NHL seasons, and was a nine-time all-star – eight times a first team selection.

Line Change

The term line change refers to all player changes, not just those involving the forward line. Players may be changed at any time during

the game from the players' bench, and such changes are usually dictated by the coach or assistant coach. The player or players leaving the ice must be within five feet of the players' bench and out of the play before a change is made. If a player enters the game before a proper change is made, a minor penalty for too many men on the ice is called.

Boston's famed "Kraut Line" of from left to right, Woody Dumart, Bobby Bauer and Milt Schmidt was one of the most dynamic forward combinations of all time, helping the Bruins win the Stanley Cups in 1939 and 1941.

Lines

Throughout hockey's history, top forward lines have been given nicknames. One of the most famous was Montreal's Punch line of the late 1940s featuring Maurice Richard, Toe Blake, and Elmer Lach. An earlier trio which gained considerable attention for the Toronto Maple Leafs in the 1930s was the Kid Line made up of Charlie Conacher, Joe Primeau and Harvey Jackson. The Maple Leafs boasted a Kid Line II in the late

The Los Angeles Kings continued their tradition of post-season upsets when they downed the defending Cup champion Calgary Flames in six games during the first round of the 1990 Stanley Cup playoffs. The Kings ran out of magic against the Edmonton Oilers, who swept the injury-plagued Kings in four straight games.

1940s with Ted Kennedy, Howie Meeker, and Vic Lynn. One of the best nicknamed units was Montreal's Razzle-Dazzle Line of the early 1940s featuring Pete Morin, Gerry Heffernan and Buddy O'Conner. Detroit's most famous trio was the Production Line whose headliners were Gordie Howe, Ted Lindsay, and Sid Abel which reached its peak at the start of the 1950s. The Rangers G-A-G or Goal-A-Game Line was no laugh to enemy goalies. This unit was comprised of Rod Gilbert, Vic Hadfield, and Jean Ratelle. Another appropriately named group was the Blackhawks' Scooter Line led by Stan Mikita, who was flanked by speedster Ken Wharram and Ab McDonald. They were a cornerstone of Chicago's 1961 Stanley Cup winners. Easily the best triumvirate in the Blackhawks' history was the Pony line of Max Bentley flanked by brother Doug Bentley and Bill Mosienko. One of Boston's favorites was the Kraut line. All of German descent, the Krauts included Milt Schmidt, Bobby Bauer, and Woody Dumart. They led the Bruins to a Stanley Cup in 1939 and again in 1941. Among the more recent colorful units was the Los Angeles Kings' Triple Crown Line with Marcel Dionne centering Dave Taylor and Charlie Simmer and the Soviet Union's high-flying KLM line with Igor Larionov between Vladimir Krutov and Sergei Makarov.

Linesman

One of two on-ice officials who assist the referee during a hockey game. Linesmen supervise the calling of off-sides and icing infractions, stop action when the puck leaves the ice surface, handle most of the face-offs, break up skirmishes and altercations and watch for too many men on the ice violations. Although linesmen do not call regular penalties, they do report stick infractions and other fouls to the referee.

Lockhart, Tommy

b. 21 March 1892; d. 18 May 1979.
Hall of Fame: Builder, 1965

Tommy Lockhart was instrumental in setting up competitive amateur hockey in New York City. In 1932 he organized and promoted amateur hockey at Madison Square Garden. He later organized the Eastern Amateur Hockey League, becoming its president in 1935. In 1937, he helped set up and became the first president of the Amateur Hockey Association of the United States. And, between 1932 and 1952, he super-vised the Metropolitan Amateur League in New York, and, at various times, coached and man-aged the New York Rovers. He was also business manager of the New York Rangers from 1946 to 1952.

Los Angeles Kings

The Los Angeles Kings first skated into the NHL in the fall of 1967 with Red Kelly as coach and a 38-year old Terry Sawchuk in goal. The club finished the 1967-68 season with the best record against the established clubs of all the expansion franchises. Second in the West Division, they took the quarter-final series against the Minnesota North Stars to the full seven games, before losing 9-4, in the final contest. The Kings made the playoffs in their second season, but then fell on hard times until goaltender Rogie Vachon and young superstar Marcel Dionne revitalized the team in the mid-1970s. Dionne blossomed into a superstar with the Kings who became a distinct Stanley Cup threat in the late 1970's and late 1980's. Dionne, Dave Taylor, and Charlie Simmer formed the Triple Crown Line which was one of the league's best. Bruce McNall took over ownership of the Kings in 1988 and stunned the hockey world when he obtained Wayne Gretzky from the Edmonton Oilers in August of that year. The Gretzky-McNall duet immediately kindled hockey interest in California and the Kings responded by defeating the Edmonton Oilers in the 1989 playoffs. By 1990, the Kings had become one of the most popular franchises in the NHL.

CUMULATIVE RECORD	GP	Won	Lost	Tied	Pct
Regular Season	1818	698	854	266	.457
Playoffs	100	34	66	0	.340
Series: 22 W6 L16					
TOTALS	1918	732	920	266	.451

Harry Lumley played for all of the "Original Six" teams except the Montreal Canadiens in his 16 year NHL career. He established a modern day record for shutouts in 1954 with 13 zeros, a mark that lasted until Tony Esposito bettered it in 1971.

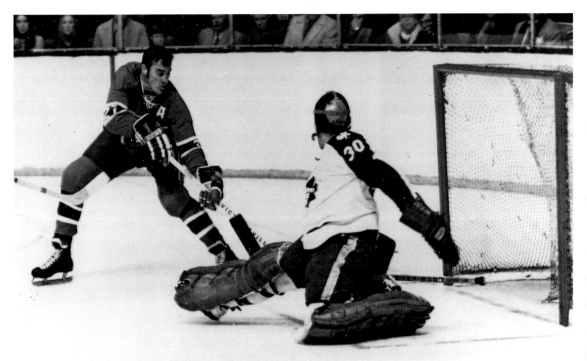

Lowe, Kevin

b. Lachute, Quebec, 15 April 1959.

If the NHL ever presented an award to the league's best defensive defenseman, Kevin Lowe would have won it several times in the 1980s. One of the original NHL Oilers, Lowe joined the team in 1979-80 and was as important to the club's development into a champion as teammates Wayne Gretzky, Mark Messier and Grant Fuhr. Lowe was most effective in critical games, and more than most, was able to shake off injuries. During the 1988 Stanley Cup playoffs, Lowe played every contest despite broken ribs and a severe hand injury. Following the trade of Paul Coffey to the Pittsburgh Penguins, Lowe became the dominant Edmonton defenseman and was essential in holding the team together after the trade of Wayne Gretzky from Edmonton to Los Angeles.

Lumley, Harry

b. Owen Sound, Ontario, 11 November 1926.
Hall of Fame: 1980

Harry Lumley signed with the Detroit Red Wings at the age of 16 and within a couple of years was with the Wings to stay. He played six full seasons with Detroit, winning a Stanley Cup in 1950. After two seasons with Chicago, he was traded to Toronto where he won the Vezina Trophy in 1953-54, recording 13 shutouts. Lumley completed his NHL career with the Boston Bruins, wrapping up a three-year stint in 1959-60. He played 15 full seasons in the NHL, posting a goals-against per game average of 2.75.

MacInnis, Al

b. Inverness, Nova Scotia, 11 July 1963.

Defenseman Al MacInnis was drafted by the Calgary Flames out of Kitchener of the OHL. He began the 1983-84 season at Colorado of the Central League but, after 19 games, was called up to the Flames for good. As one of the premier pointmen in the NHL, he possesses one of the hardest and fastest shots in hockey. He was named to the second all-star team in 1987 and 1989. With seven goals and playoff-leading 24 assists and 31 points, MacInnis was a major factor in the Flames' Stanley Cup win in 1989, and was awarded the Conn Smythe Trophy as playoff MVP.

MacKay, Duncan (Mickey)

b. Chesley, Ontario, 21 May 1894; d. 21 May 1940.
Hall of Fame: 1952

Often called "The Wee Scot," center Mickey MacKay was a big star during professional hockey's formative years. Said Frank Patrick (for whom MacKay played), "He was outstanding in every way." Though a junior, MacKay played senior hockey at Edmonton and in British Columbia until Patrick hired him to play for the Vancouver Millionaires of the Pacific Coast

Hockey Association. MacKay scored 33 goals in his rookie season, missing the scoring title by one point. He played with Vancouver for 242 games, during which time he won three scoring titles and one Stanley Cup. He moved to Chicago in 1926, and was the team's leading scorer during 1927-28. In 1928-29, he played half a season with Pittsburgh, but joined Boston in time to help them win the Cup. He retired after the start of the next season, finishing the year as Boston's business manager.

Mahovlich, Frank

b. Timmins, Ontario, 10 January 1938.
Hall of Fame: 1981

Leftwinger Frank Mahovlich won the Calder Trophy in 1958 and did just about everything a player could be expected to do, but it was always felt he could have been even greater. Mahovlich played on six Stanley Cup winners (four with Toronto and two with Montreal), and was a nine-time all-star. He was an important and productive player for three teams: Toronto, Montreal and Detroit. He played four seasons in the WHA for Toronto and Birmingham. His swooping style earned him 533 goals and 1,103 points in 1,181 regular season games; he added 51 goals and 118 points in 137 playoff games.

Major Junior Hockey

The highest level of amateur hockey in North America and the primary source of young talent selected by National Hockey League clubs during the annual NHL Entry Draft. Players generally range in age from 16 to 20, though rules do exist to to allow a small number of 21-year-olds per club. In special circumstances players who show extraordinary ability may be accepted into the league before age 16. The Ontario Hockey League (OHL), Quebec Major Junior Hockey League (QMJHL) and the Western Hockey League (WHL) are the leagues which oversee the 40 teams (to end of 1989-90 season) deemed eligible to compete for junior hockey's highest award, the Memorial Cup.

Makarov, Sergei

b. Chelyabinsk, Soviet Union, 19 June 1958.
When Soviet players arrived in the NHL in 1989-90, many predicted that that the player who would make the greatest impact was Sergei Makarov who had been signed by the Calgary Flames. A 10-time Soviet all-star and three-time Soviet player of the year, the tough rightwinger demonstrated extensive stickhandling, skating, and passing skills in NHL game conditions. Makarov fitted in neatly with the Flames and though he did not score in abundance, was

extremely creative and proved to be one of the top forwards on the team.

Malone, Joe

b. Quebec City, Quebec, 28 February 1890;
d. 15 May 1969. Hall of Fame: 1950

Center Joe Malone was a remarkable marksman who performed scoring miracles in both the National Hockey Association and the NHL – he is credited with 379 goals as a pro, from 1909-10 until retirement in 1923-24. In his eight biggest seasons (five with Quebec, two with Hamilton and one with the Montreal Canadiens), he scored 280 goals in 172 games. Malone topped the NHL in its first season, 1917-18, with 44 goals in 20 games. Some of his outstanding single-game performances include: nine goals against the Sydney Millionaires in 1913; eight against the Montreal Wanderers in 1917, and an NHL-record seven goals against Toronto in 1920. He retired in 1923-24 after playing a few home games for the Canadiens.

The jungle cat goalie mask of Gilles "Grattoonie the Loonie" Gratton was one of the most colorful face protectors to be worn in the NHL. It didn't scare off too many NHL sharpshooters however, as Gratton won only 13 games in his NHL career.

Mantha, Sylvio

b. Montreal, Quebec, 14 April 1903; d. 7 August 1974. Hall of Fame: 1960

Mantha played 14 NHL seasons as a hard-as-rock defenseman, playing for nine first-place teams and three Stanley Cup winners. He joined the Montreal Canadiens in 1923-24, the first NHL year they won the Cup. Mantha scored 63 goals and earned 72 assists for 135 career points in the NHL, and was twice named a second team all-star. He played for the Notre Dame de Grace (Quebec) juniors in 1918-19, and the Montreal Nationals in Quebec Senior League before becoming a professional. Although a forward as an amateur, Mantha was converted into a defenseman in his first season with the Canadiens. He became a player-coach for Montreal in 1935-36, then moved to the Boston Bruins where he finished his career the following season. Mantha later was a linesman in the NHL and a referee in the American Hockey League.

Gilles Gratton's Mask (1976-77)
This colorful mask allowed Montreal Gratton to live up to his equally colorful nickname, "Gratoony the Loony."

Mariucci, John

b. Eveleth, Minnesota, 8 May 1916; d. 23 March 1987. Hall of Fame: Builder, 1985

John Mariucci was a varsity All-American with the University of Minnesota hockey team in 1940 and went on to play defense for the Chicago Blackhawks. In 1952, he became coach at the University of Minnesota. He encouraged the growth of high school hockey throughout the state and insisted on recruiting U.S.-born players instead of importing Canadians. He produced a dozen all-Americans and coached the U.S. Olympic club to a silver medal at Cortina in 1956. In 1967, he returned to the NHL as assistant to the general manager of the Minnesota North Stars, a position he held at the time of his election to the Hall of Fame.

Masks

In 1929 Clint Benedict, then the goaltender of the Montreal Maroons, donned a primitive leather device for a few games to protect his injured nose, but the use of facial shields for goaltenders really began when Jacques Plante of the Canadiens had his nose and cheek gashed by an Andy Bathgate backhander on November 1, 1959. Plante, who had suffered two fractured cheekbones in unrelated warm-up and practice incidents, had already begun wearing a plastic mask during Montreal's workouts. Coach Toe Blake would not allow Plante to use it in a game, but he refused to return to the nets without it after being hit by Bathgate's shot. The Canadiens went on to win the game, 3-1, and the era of the mask commenced. Soon Terry Sawchuk began wearing a molded model and others followed suit. Gerry Cheevers of the Bruins decorated his protector with facsimile stitch marks where he claimed the real stitches would have been if he played unprotected. This started a trend and, by the end of the 1970s, all manner of colorful designs were displayed, from team logos to animals, buildings and fanciful faces. Next came the combination helmet with "bird-cage" attached favored by the Europeans, perhaps popularized by the highly-respected Soviet goaltender Vladislav Tretiak. Later models combined a molded mask with a smaller cage, and "cow catchers" were dangled from the mask's chin rim to cover the vulnerable neck area.

McCammon, Bob

b. Kenora, Ontario, 14 April 1941.

Bob McCammon played for 11 years with the Port Huron Flags of the IHL. He went behind the bench in 1972-73, coaching through 1976-77. In 1977-78 he became part of the Philadelphia organization as coach of the Maine Mariners of the AHL. His team won the Calder Cup and he was named coach of the year. After coaching 50 games with the Flyers in 1978-79, he returned to Maine where the Mariners won more than 40 games for three seasons in a row. At the tail-end of the 1981-82 season he once more was installed as head coach of the Flyers. In 1983-84 he also took on the job of general manager. In each of those seasons the Flyers finished the regular season with a winning percentage of over .600 but won only one out of a total of ten games in the playoffs. After serving as an assistant coach with Edmonton Oilers in 1985-86 he became their head of player development. He was named head coach of the Vancouver Canucks in 1987 and, in his second season, 1988-89, delivered a 15-point improvement as the Canucks finished at 33-39-8 and came within a hair of defeating the Calgary Flames in overtime of seventh game of the Smythe Division semi-final.

Lanny McDonald was a crowd favorite in Toronto, where he bagan his NHL career. His overtime goal against Chico Resch of the New York Islanders in game seven of the 1978 quarter-finals gave the Leafs their only visit to the semi-finals since 1967.

McDonald, Lanny

b. Hanna, Alberta, 16 February 1953.
Lanny McDonald, a WHL all-star with the Medicine Hat Tigers in 1972-73, broke in with the Toronto Maple Leafs the following season. He became one of the premier rightwingers in the NHL, topping 90 points twice and 40 goals three times with the Leafs through the 1978-79 season. The next season he also scored 40 but was traded mid-campaign to the Colorado Rockies. Two years later he was dealt again, joining the Calgary Flames where the popular winger with the prodigious, orange moustache finished his career in 1988-89 by scoring his 500th goal and netting an important goal in the game that gave the Flames their Stanley Cup championship triumph over Montreal. McDonald was a second team all-star in 1977 and 1983; won the Bill Masterton Trophy in 1983; and the King Clancy Memorial Trophy in 1988. His best season came in 1982-83 when he recorded 66 goals for the Flames.

McGee, Frank

b. 1890; d. 16 September 1916.
Hall of Fame: 1945
McGee's name was written into the record book in 1905 with one spectacular scoring splurge. On January 16, 1905, McGee scored 14 goals in a Stanley Cup game as Ottawa trounced a team from Dawson City, Yukon, 23-2. McGee played center and rover for the Ottawa Silver Seven between 1903 and 1906 and, although he had lost the sight of one eye prior to joining the club, became one of the best forwards in the game. He combined exciting speed with extraordinary stickhandling ability to average almost three goals per game. He finished his career with 71 goals in 23 games, and had another 65 in 23 playoff encounters. He was killed in action during World War I.

McLaughlin, Frederic

b. Chicago, Illinois, 27 June 1877; d. 17 December 1944. Hall of Fame: Builder, 1963
Major Frederic McLaughlin was a hockey pioneer in Chicago. In 1926, when Lester and Frank Patrick sold six Western Canada League teams to the owners of teams in an expanding NHL, McLaughlin was president of the group that brought the Blackhawks to Chicago. Attendance was poor when games were played in the Chicago Coliseum and eventually McLaughlin purchased controlling interest. The club moved to the new Chicago Stadium in December, 1929, and soon its attendance was among the league's highest. McLaughlin's Blackhawks won the Stanley Cup in 1934 and 1938.

Meehan, Gerry

b. Toronto, Ontario, 3 September 1946.
Gerry Meehan saw limited duty with both Toronto and Philadelphia in 1968-69 before joining the Buffalo Sabres in their first season of 1970-71. A center, Meehan played with Buffalo through 1973-74 and finished his career in 1978-79 having also worn the uniforms of the Vancouver Canucks, Atlanta Flames and Washington Capitals. In 670 games he scored 180 goals and 243 assists for 423 regular-season points. Despite the fact that he no longer played for the Sabres after 1974, Meehan remained in the Buffalo area during the off-season, graduating from Canisius College and earning a law degree from the University of Buffalo. He practised law in Buffalo before becoming assistant general manager of the Sabres in 1984-85. The first former Sabres' player to move into the front office, he was promoted to general manager midway through in the 1986-87 season.

Memorial Cup

Awarded annually to the top major junior hockey team in North America by the Canadian Amateur Hockey Association. The trophy was donated in 1919 by the province of Ontario to honor Ontario hockey players who died as Canadian soldiers in World War I. There are currently 40 teams eligible to compete for the Memorial Cup, with four located in the United States. The cup is classified as Tier I, and is the highest level of competition for junior hockey in Canada. The OHL, WHL and QMJHL champions compete for the trophy annually.

Messier, Mark

b. Edmonton, Alberta, 18 January 1961.
Center Mark Messier combines power, speed, toughness and determination like few players before him. His professional debut with Indianapolis and Cincinnati of the WHA in 1978-79 was undistinguished but he began to blossom with the Edmonton Oilers in their first NHL season of 1979-80. From 1981-82, when he scored 50 goals, he failed only once – when injuries reduced his games played to only 55 out of 80 in 1984-85 – to score more than 30 goals per season. He was named to the first all-star team in 1982 and 1983; and the second team in 1984. He has played on all five of Edmonton's Stanley Cup champions, winning the Conn Smythe Trophy in 1984. At the end of the 1988-89 season, Messier had 841 points in 719 regular-season games plus 169 points in 126 playoff matches. He was named Oilers' captain at the start of the 1988-89 season and won the 1989-90 Art Ross Trophy.

Mikita, Stan

b. Skolce, Czechoslovakia, 20 May 1940.
Hall of Fame: 1983
Center Stan Mikita arrived in Canada in 1949. He played 20 full seasons, plus parts of two others, after joining the Chicago Blackhawks in 1958. His intelligence made him a respected leader and an integral part of the Chicago team which won the 1961 Stanley Cup. He was an eight-time all-star and six times a first team member. He was the first player to win the Ross, Hart and Lady Byng trophies in the same season and achieved this impressive feat in consecutive seasons – 1967 and 1968. Mikita won two other scoring titles, as well as the Lester Patrick Trophy for outstanding contributions to U.S. hockey. He played 1,394 regular-season games, scoring 541 goals and 926 assists.

Milbury, Mike

Brighton, Massachusetts, 17 June 1952.
Signed out of Colgate University as a free agent in November of 1974, Mike Milbury has spent his entire professional life in the Boston Bruins' organization. He began his distinguished career on the Bruins' blueline in 1975-76 and, with one interruption, played through the 1986-87 season. He first retired after the 1984-85 season and became Boston's assistant coach under Butch Goring. Late in 1985-86, injuries to the Bruins' defensive corps forced him back into uniform. He won his first game as co-coach with Terry O'Reilly on November 7, 1986, and was appointed playing assistant coach on November 14 when O'Reilly became head coach. His second retirement came in July 1987 when he was hired to coach the Maine Mariners of the AHL, where he also served as g.m. In his first season, the Mariners won a division championship and Milbury was named co-winner of coach of the year honors. In May of 1989 he was named coach and assistant general manager of the Bruins.

Milford, Jake

b. Charlottetown, Prince Edward Island, 29 July 1914; d. 24 December 1984.
Hall of Fame: Builder, 1984
Jake Milford was talented minor pro player who went on to make his mark as a coach and manager. He worked in the Rangers' system for 14 years, and finally reached the NHL as general manager of the Los Angeles Kings in late 1973, guiding the club to three strong second-place finishes behind the Canadiens. Milford became g.m. of the Vancouver Canucks of the NHL in 1977, gradually improving the team until the club reached the Stanley Cup finals in 1982.

Minnesota North Stars

In the expansion of 1967 the NHL granted a franchise to the Twin Cities area which was known as the Minnesota North Stars. The club was a success during its early years and would make the playoffs five of its first six seasons in the league. Players like Cesare Maniago, Bill Goldsworthy, Danny Grant, J.P. Parise and Gump Worsley contributed to the early success of the Stars. On the downside, Bill Masterton died midway through the team's first season following a head injury sustained in a game, the only on-ice fatality in the history of the NHL. From 1973-74 to 1978-79 the North Stars made the playoffs only once and fan interest was declining, but a merger with the Cleveland Barons following the 1977-78 added key players and depth. A playoff upset over the defending Stanley Cup champion Montreal Canadiens in 1980 and the maturing of young draft picks like Bobby Smith, Steve Payne, Craig Hartsburg and

The Minnesota North Stars finished fourth in the Norris Division in 1989-90 led by Brian Bellows (number 23), who fired a career-high 55 goals in the regular season. In the playoffs, the North Stars forced Chicago to a seventh game before bowing out in postseason play.

Opposite page, bottom: Swede Mats Naslund returned to play in Europe after eight seasons with the Montreal Canadiens. His best season in the NHL was 1985–86 when he finished with 110 points and was part of a Cup winner. *Top:* Mark Messier earned an MVP nomination during the 1989–90 season, finishing in second place in the scoring race with career-high totals in assists (84) and points (129).

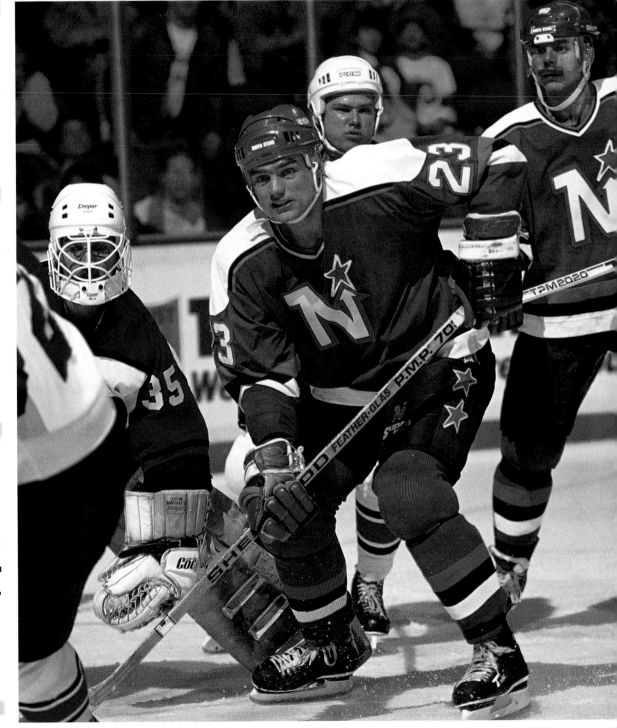

Dino Ciccarelli gave the North Stars the confidence and talent to compete with the best. They reached the Stanley Cup finals in 1981 but lost to the New York Islanders in five games. In 1982-83 they reached their highest point total in team history, finishing with 96.

CUMULATIVE RECORD	GP	Won	Lost	Tied	Pct
Regular Season	1818	663	851	304	.448
Playoffs	136	63	73	0	.463
Series: 26 W11 L15					
TOTALS	1954	726	924	304	.449

Minor hockey

There are seven designated age-levels for minor amateur hockey, under the auspices of the Canadian Amateur Hockey Association, as follows:

Tyke –   for players eight years old.

Novice –   for players nine years old.

Atom –   for players 11 years of age. Minor atom refers to players 10 years old.

Pee Wee –   for players 13 years old. Minor pee wee refers to players 12 years old.

Bantam –   for players 15 years old. Minor bantam refers to players 14 years old.

Midget –   for players 17 years old. Minor midget refers to players 16 years old.

Juvenile –   for players 18 or 19 years old. Some players who are 17 will also be grouped in this classification.

Minor Officials

Minor or off-ice officials present at each NHL game include two goal judges, a game timekeeper, penalty timekeeper, official scorer and statistician, all of whom are under the supervision of the game referee.

Miracle on Ice

In the winter of 1980 the U.S. Olympic hockey team accomplished what has come to be known as the 'Miracle on Ice', winning the gold medal over a highly favored team from the Soviet Union. The U.S. team had the benefit of an outstanding coach in Herb Brooks, effective skaters like Mark Johnson, Ken Morrow, Dave Christian and Neil Broten and inspirational leadership from captain Mike Eruzione who scored a pivotal goal in the critical match against the Soviets. The Americans also received world-class goaltending from Jim Craig who stonewalled the Soviets en route to a colossal upset.

Misconduct Penalty

This 10-minute penalty with fine is usually assessed for unsportsmanlike conduct. It can also be given as a game misconduct, suspending the player for the balance of the game.

Mogilny, Alexander

b. Khabaravosk, Soviet Union, 18 February 1969.
Twenty-year old leftwinger Alexander Mogilny was one of the Soviet Union's leading junior players when he defected to the U.S. and signed with the Buffalo Sabres for the 1989-90 season. Considerably younger than the other Soviets making their NHL debuts, Mogilny had speed and finesse that impressed fans in Buffalo and

The Montreal AAA, were not only the first winners of the Stanley Cup, they were also the first team to repeat as champions, capturing the Cup in 1893 and 1894. The AAA are one of six Montreal teams to win the trophy; the Shamrocks, Victorias, Wanderers, Maroons and Canadiens are the others.

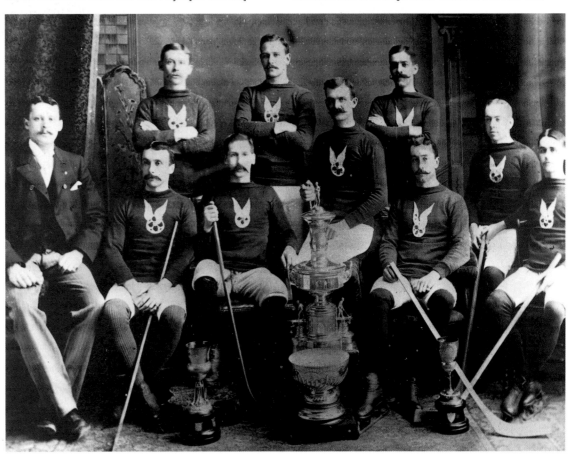

throughout the NHL. He contributed to the Sabres' fast start and though he has had some problems adapting to the pressures of NHL play and the travel that is part of modern hockey, has demonstrated that he has the tools to enjoy a long and successful NHL career.

Molson, Hartland

b. Montreal, Quebec, 29 May 1907.
Hall of Fame: Builder, 1973

Senator Hartland Molson's father was a founder of the Canadian Arena Company, owner of the Montreal Forum and the Canadiens. Senator Molson was president and, following that, chairman of the Canadian Arena Company and Les Canadiens Hockey Club from 1957-68. As a member of the NHL's finance committee, he played a vital role in strengthening owner-player relations.

Montreal Amateur Athletic Association

The Montreal AAA organization formed a hockey club as early as 1884. The club was one of the top teams of its day, winning then the Senior Championship Trophy (AHA) from 1888 to 1894. It became the first team to have its name inscribed on the Stanley Cup. The AAA competed in Cup-deciding matches six times and was victorious in four outings. Men who made a difference on this club include Haviland Routh, Billy Barlow and Jack Marshall.

Montreal Canadiens

The Montreal Canadiens are the most successful franchise in professional sport. Winners of 23 Stanley Cup championships since 1909 and 18 since World War II, the Canadiens have always inspired fierce loyalty from their fans. From their inception, the Canadiens displayed exceptional speed and elan, and soon were dubbed 'the Flying Frenchmen.' Even a partial list of the team's stars reads like a chronological 'who's who' in hockey: Jack Laviolette, Didier Pitre, Newsy Lalonde, Georges Vezina, Aurel Joliat, Howie Morenz, Toe Blake, Rocket Richard, Doug Harvey, Boom-Boom Geoffrion, Jean Beliveau, Jacques Plante, Henri Richard, Yvan Cournoyer, Guy Lafleur, Serge Savard and Larry Robinson. In post-War years, the franchise has enjoyed several overlapping dynasties.

Led by Rocket Richard, the Canadiens established an unequalled mark, winning five consecutive cups beginning in 1956 and appearing in ten consecutive Stanley Cup final series from 1951 to 1960. The club won four of five Cup titles in the late 1960s with a team built around the speed of Yvan Cournoyer and Henri Richard and the skills of Jean Beliveau. Montreal also

won four straight Stanley Cups beginning in 1976, dominating the NHL both offensively and defensively. With Guy Lafleur leading the way, the club posted regular-season totals of 127, 132 and 129. No other club has surpassed 120.

In addition to a glittering scorer, each of these dynasties featured one of the top goaltenders: Jacques Plante (1950s), Gump Worsley (1960s), and Ken Dryden (1970s). Also known as the 'Habs', the Canadiens continue to be one of the top teams in the NHL, last winning the Stanley Cup in 1986 and reaching the finals in 1989.

CUMULATIVE RECORD	GP	Won	Lost	Tied	Pct
Regular Season	4432	2352	1385	695	.609
Playoffs	566	344	214	8	.615
Series: 121 W78 L42					
TOTALS	4998	2696	1599	703	.610

An American announcer summed up the feelings of millions of hockey fans when he asked "Do you believe in miracles?" The United States hockey team certainly did, for after defeating the Soviet Union and Finland, they had pulled off one of sports' greatest upsets by winning the gold medal at the 1980 Lake Placid Olympics.

Montreal Maroons

In the early National Hockey League, two teams competed for the hearts and minds of Montrealers. While the Canadiens were the team of the French-Canadians, it was the Maroons who skated for the English-speaking population. The Maroons joined the NHL in 1924. They captured the Stanley Cup in 1926 and 1935, and finished in first place in 1930 and 1936. The club ceased operations after the 1937-38 season. Outstanding contributors to the team include Babe Siebert, Hooley Smith and Nels Stewart, as well as Lionel Conacher and King Clancy, who coached them in their last year.

Montreal Rules

On March 3 of 1875, at the Crystal Ice Rink in Montreal, a set of rules devised by J.G.H. Creighton was used to play a game of ice hockey. This is considered the first organized game played under rules that can be traced to the current rules of hockey. The Montreal Rules, which included nine-man sides, no forward passing, and two periods of thirty minutes each, were very soon altered to accommodate seven men. The Montreal Rules are generally regarded as those agreed upon by the founders of the Amateur Hockey Association of Canada in 1868.

Montreal Shamrocks

When the Amateur Hockey Association was born in 1886 it included a team known as the Crystals. In 1896, this team became the Shamrocks Hockey Club of Montreal. Though the franchise was responsible for innovations in the game and for a 'scientific' approach to playmaking, they won the Stanley Cup on only one occasion, 1911. The most famous line from this team was composed of Art Farrell, Harry Trihey and Fred Scanlan, all Hockey Hall of Famers.

Montreal Victorias

The Montreal Victorias club was one of the first to play the game. As a founding member of the Amateur Hockey Association in 1886, the Victorias hold an important place in the history of the game, winning the Stanley Cup on five occasions from 1895 to 1899. Included in the Victorias' roster were two Hall of Famers: Mike Grant and Graham Drinkwater.

Montreal Wanderers

The Wanderers of Montreal first appeared as a franchise in the Federal Amateur Hockey League in 1903. Having attracted most of the talent from the AAA team, they took the league title and challenged Ottawa's Silver Seven for the Stanley Cup. A dispute resulted in the Ottawa club retaining the Cup following a tie game, but the Wanderers did manage to win the trophy in 1906, 1907, 1908 and 1910. The great Lester Patrick got his first taste of big-league hockey with this club in 1906. When the NHL formed in 1917, the Wanderers were one of the league's charter members. The team was forced to withdraw after only six regular-season games as its home arena was destroyed by fire. Great players of the Wanderers include Pud Glass, Art Ross, Walter Smail, Lester Patrick, Cecil Blachford, Ernie Russell and Riley Hern.

Moore, Dickie

b. Montreal, Quebec, 6 January 1931.
Hall of Fame: 1974

To his final game, rightwinger Dickie Moore's aggressive play drew praise from all who saw him in action. Moore played significant roles in

Memorial Cup triumphs by two Montreal junior teams. Moore was called up to the Montreal Canadiens from the Royals of the Quebec Senior League in 1951-52, and played for Montreal until retiring in 1963. He came out of retirement twice, playing 38 games with Toronto in 1964-65 and 27 games with St. Louis in 1967-68. Although plagued with injuries throughout his career, Moore twice led the NHL in scoring and he set an NHL scoring record in 1958-59 with 96 points. A three-time all-star, Moore scored 261 goals and 608 points in 719 NHL games. He won six Stanley Cups during his 12 years with Montreal.

Moran, Paddy

b. Quebec City, Quebec, 11 March 1877;
d. 14 January 1966. Hall of Fame: 1958

Paddy Moran was one of the best goaltenders of the standup era. He began his pro career with the Quebec Bulldogs in 1901-02 and except for

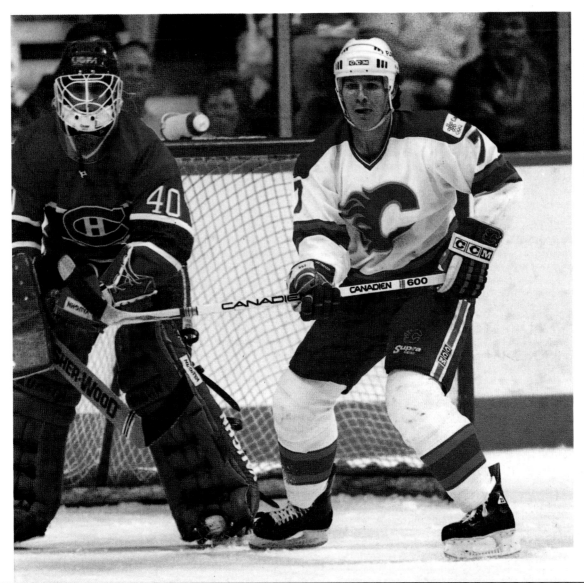

Joe Mullen failed to reach the 40-goal mark for the first time in seven seasons during the 1989–90 schedule. After a slow start, he rebounded to end the campaign with 36 goals and appeared in his second all-star game.

one season with Haileybury, Ontario, in 1909-10, remained with that team throughout his 16-year career. Although he never had an outstanding goals-against average – 5.40 for 201 games – Moran's stick-stopping abilities were an important part of Quebec's consecutive Stanley Cup wins in 1911-12 and 1912-13.

Morenz, Howie

b. Mitchell, Ontario, 21 September 1902; d. 8 March 1937. Hall of Fame: 1945

He had color in every motion and his brilliance stood out in an era of colorful and brilliant players. Center Howie Morenz was the runaway leader in a 1950 Canadian Press poll to select the outstanding hockey player of the half-century. Signed by the Montreal Canadiens, he joined the club in 1923-24. His reckless speed set turnstiles clicking wherever the Canadiens played, and he was nicknamed "The Babe Ruth of Hockey" by U.S. sportswriters. He performed in the NHL for 14 seasons playing for Montreal, Chicago and the New York Rangers. He returned to the Canadiens for the 1936-37 season, breaking his leg in a game on 28 January 1937 [n] leading to his death. He scored 270 goals and won the Hart Trophy three times.

Mosienko, Bill

b. Winnipeg, Manitoba, 2 November 1921. Hall of Fame: 1965

During a 14-year NHL stay, rightwinger Bill Mosienko scored 258 goals and 540 points in 711 games. He spent 20 years in professional hockey, playing in 1,030 games, while accumulating only 129 penalty minutes. He turned pro with the Blackhawks' organization at 18, joining the parent club in 1942; he remained with them until retiring in 1955. Mosienko won the Lady Byng Trophy in 1945, and was a two-time second team all-star. He set an NHL record by scoring three goals in 21 seconds against the New York Rangers on 23 March 1952.

Muckler, John

b. Paris, Ontario, 13 April 1934.

After seven years as the assistant coach of the Edmonton Oilers, John Muckler was named head coach in 1989, replacing Glen Sather who moved up to be full-time president-general manager. Muckler joined the Oilers in 1981 when he was hired to coach their Central Hockey League affiliate, the Wichita Wind. He was named an assistant coach in 1982 and then promoted to co-coach in the 1985-86 season. Muckler's coaching career began in 1959 with the Long Island Ducks of the EHL. In 1966 he joined the Rangers as director of player person-

nel and later served as g.m. for various clubs in the Minnesota system. He also coached Providence of the AHL and Dallas of the CHL. He led three teams to championships: Long Island, 1963-64; Providence, 1974-75; and Dallas 1978-79. He also coached the North Stars for 35 games in 1968-69.

Mullen, Joe

b. New York, New York, 26 February 1957.

Joe Mullen grew up playing roller hockey on the streets of a midtown Manhattan neighborhood known as Hell's Kitchen, not far from the old Madison Square Garden where his father drove the Zamboni. He graduated to ice hockey and starred in the Metropolitan Junior Hockey Association where he once scored 110 goals in 40 games. He was a first team all-star at Boston College in 1978 and 1979; rookie of the year in the Central League at Salt Lake City in 1979-80; scoring leader and league MVP in 1980-81. The following season he joined the St. Louis Blues in mid-campaign and became the first player to score at least 20 goals in both the minors and the NHL in one season. Traded to the Calgary Flames during the 1985-86 season, Mullen won the Lady Byng Trophy in 1986-87 and has scored 40 or more goals in his last six seasons. The right-handed shooting right wing is of small stature but a true sniper. He was selected as a first team all-star in 1988-89, a season in which he set a record for most points (110) by a U.S.-born player. His 16 goals in the playoffs led all scorers and set a Flames' record. Younger brother Brian plays for the New York Rangers.

Muller, Kirk

b. Kingston, Ontario, 8 February 1966.

Selected second overall in the 1984 Entry Draft by the New Jersey Devils, Kirk Muller is an hard-working player who is strong both offensively and defensively. When the Devils advanced to the Wales Conference finals in 1988, it was captain Muller who was a driving force through the first three playoff rounds. Although primarily a center, Muller was switched to left wing by coach John Cunniff during the 1989-90 season. Muller worked with center Mark Johnson and rightwinger Sylvain Turgeon to comprise an effective scoring unit.

Murdoch, Bob

b. Kirkland Lake, Ontario, 20 November 1946.

A graduate of the University of Waterloo in Ontario, Bob Murdoch joined the Montreal Canadiens for the 1970-71 season and was a member of a Stanley Cup-winner in 1971 and 1973. Traded to Los Angeles the following season, he played defense for the Kings until the 1978-79 when he moved on to the Atlanta Flames. He was with the Flames for three years as a player and five as an assistant coach in both Atlanta and Calgary. He became head coach of the Chicago Blackhawks for the 1987-88 season but was replaced by Mike Keenan after posting a 30-41-9 record and failing to lead his team past the first playoff round. His capabilities as teacher, communicator and motivator were recognized by the Winnipeg Jets who signed him to coach their club for 1989-90.

Murray, Brian

b. Shawville, Quebec, 5 December 1942.
Brian Murray coached the Washington Capitals for eight full seasons before being replaced by his brother Terry midway through the 1989-90 season. Murray started his professional coaching career in the American League, leading the 1980-81 Hershey Bears to their best record in 40 years. After the 1983-84 season, when the Capitals broke 100 points for the first time in franchise history, Murray was awarded the Jack Adams Award as the coach of the year. The Capitals played winning hockey under Murray (325-222-79) for a .582 winning percentage over eight regular seasons.

Murray, Terry

b. Shawville, Quebec, 20 July 1950.
Terry Murray's playing career spanned a dozen seasons and was divided equally between the AHL and NHL. He won the Eddie Shore Plaque as the AHL's top defenseman in two successive seasons when he was part of the Calder Cup champion Maine Mariners in 1978 and 1979. He became an assistant coach of the Washington Capitals in 1982, serving under his brother Bryan. He stayed in the Caps' organization, taking over as head coach of their AHL farm club the Baltimore Skipjacks in June of 1988. He was promoted to the head coaching job in Washington early in 1990, replacing his brother in the position.

National Collegiate Athletic Association (NCAA)

The National Collegiate Athletic Association is the governing body of American college hockey and has operated a national championship prog-

ram since 1947 when the University of Michigan Wolverines captured the crown. Modern U.S. college hockey is organized in three divisions with the top hockey schools playing in Division I. In addition to independent Division I schools, the top teams play in four conferences: the Central Collegiate Hockey Association (CCHA); Eastern Collegiate Athletic Conference (ECAC), Hockey East (H.E.) and Western Collegiate Athletic Association (WCHA).

Neely, Cam

b. Comox, British Columbia, 6 June 1965.
Acquired in a trade from the Vancouver Canucks, Boston Bruins' rightwinger Cam Neely has developed into one of the top forwards in the NHL. He scored 36 goals in 1986-87, his first year with Boston, increasing this total to 42 en route to a second team all-star selection in 1987-88. He had nine goals in postseason play as the Bruins reached the Stanley Cup finals in 1988 and reached the 50-goal plateau in 1989-90 as Boston again reached the Stanley Cup final.

Although Howie Morenz was known throughout his career as the Stratford Streak, he was actually born in Mitchell, Ontario. Folks from that small Ontario hamlet preferred to call Morenz by his other well-known moniker; the Mitchell Meteor.

Kirk Muller continued his fine play throughout 1989–90, leading the Devils in scoring with 86 points and appearing in his fourth all-star game. The Devils made the playoffs for only the second time in the 1980s, but were defeated by the Washington Capitals in the first round.

Neilson, Roger

b. Toronto, Ontario, 16 June 1934.

Named coach of the New York Rangers in 1989, Neilson established a reputation as an innovator during 10 successful seasons with Peterborough of the OHA beginning in 1966. Neilson got his chance in the NHL with Toronto in 1977-78. His Leafs finished with 92 points and then upset the favored New York Islanders in a seven-game playoff series. He joined Scotty Bowman in Buffalo in 1979 and was part of an innovative 'multi-coach' system. He later coached in Vancouver and Los Angeles and worked as an advance or special assignment scout for Chicago. He was one of the first coaches to adopt the now common practice of using edited videotape to analyze play, earning him the nickname "Captain Video".

New Jersey Devils

The New Jersey Devils began play in 1982-83. The franchise was originally granted to Kansas City in 1974 and shifted to Colorado in 1976 before being moved east. The Devils struggled in the NHL's tough Patrick Division until 1987-88. New general manager Lou Lamoriello changed coaches late in the season, hiring Jim Schoenfeld to oversee a late-season rally that enabled the Devils to catch a playoff berth on the last night of the season. The Devils then shocked the first-

Cam Neely put all aspects of his game together during the 1989–90 season, combining his aggressive checking with a sniper's accuracy to become the offensive leader for the Boston Bruins.

place Islanders, beating them four games to two and then edged the favored Washington Capitals in a seven-game Patrick Division final. They were beaten in the Wales Conference finals by Boston, but only after the Bruins were extended to seven games.

CUMULATIVE RECORD	GP	Won	Lost	Tied	Pct
Regular Season	1280	355	749	176	.346
Playoffs	28	13	15	0	.464
Series: 5 W2 L3					
TOTALS	1308	368	764	176	.349

New York Americans

The NHL's New York Americans were one of the most colorful hockey teams of all time. Their owner was bootlegger "Big Bill" Dwyer, who bought the Hamilton Tigers franchise for $75,000 in 1925, despite never having heard of ice hockey. Tommy Gorman was the first manager of the 'Amerks', as they were nicknamed, and players included the Green brothers, Shorty and Red, who flanked center Billy Burch, giving the Amerks a line of extraordinary ability; forward "Bullet" Joe Simpson, who had a shot as good as Bobby Orr's; and defenseman "Big Leo" Reise (whose son was later to play with the Rangers), Alec McKinnon, and Lionel "Big Train" Conacher, voted Canada's Athlete of the Half-Century. As netminder, the Amerks had Roy "Shrimp" Worters, who emerged as one of the better diminutive goaltenders of the time. The

team finished out of the running more often than not and when owner Dwyer went to jail, the team was financed by the father of defenseman Red Dutton who had a contracting business in western Canada. Despite this support, the team was losing fans to the New York Rangers. An attempt to create a separate identity resulted in the team being known as the Brooklyn Americans in 1941-42, but dwindling support forced the team to fold in the spring of 1942.

New York Islanders

After paying a $6 million franchise fee and a $5 million indemnity to the New York Rangers, the dream of a second team in the New York metropolitan area became a reality in 1972-73. Known as the New York Islanders because of its Long Island home base, the club won just 12 games in its first year. This last-place finish allowed the Isles to pick first in the 1973 draft and they promptly selected junior standout Denis Potvin. The team quickly matured and by their third season the Islanders were playoff bound. That year the Islanders defeated their cross-town rival Rangers in the first round and despite losing the first three games of the next series, defeated Pittsburgh in the quarter-finals. Playoff losses to Cup-winner Montreal in 1976 and 1977 were not nearly as disappointing as those to the Maple Leafs in 1978 and the Rangers in 1979. By 1980 with the likes of Bryan Trottier,

The first New York Americans team outside the old Madison Square Garden in October, 1925. After the team folded in 1942, Red Dutton tried to revive the franchise in Brooklyn, and despite having the backing to build a new arena for the team, he was thwarted in his attempts by League officials.

Billy Smith, Mike Bossy, Potvin and coach Al Arbour leading the way, the Islanders set upon a determined course that would result in four consecutive Stanley Cup championships. They would fall one short of the all-time record of five straight when the Edmonton Oilers defeated them in the 1984 finals. In the 1990's, the Islanders are again looking to maturing youngsters such as Pat LaFontaine to be the cornerstones of another winning tradition.

CUMULATIVE RECORD	GP	Won	Lost	Tied	Pct
Regular Season	1436	697	526	213	.560
Playoffs	196	119	77	0	.607
Series: 39 W28 L11					
TOTALS	1632	816	603	213	.565

New York Rangers

In 1920 Tex Rickard, a rambunctious fight promoter, noticed that an insurance company was foreclosing the mortgage on New York City's old Madison Square Garden. Rickard formed a corporation to build a new Garden and one of his associates, Colonel John S. Hammond, suggested that hockey be played in the new arena. An ice-making plant was installed in the new building and Rickard leased the new Garden to the New York Americans. Soon after, Rickard hired Conn Smythe to manage a team that Rickard would control. This new club was to be called the Rangers. Smythe was soon replaced by Lester 'the Silver Fox' Patrick, a former player and manager from the Pacific Coast Hockey Association. The young team, which included stars Frank Boucher and the Cook brothers, Bun and Bill, took first place in its division in 1926-27 and won the Cup in 1927-28. The 1932-33 season brought another Cup to New York and a third followed in 1939-40 after Frank Boucher had taken over as coach. During the 1950s and 1960s, the club's farm system produced such talented players as Andy Bathgate, Harry Howell, Dean Prentice and Rod Gilbert, but the team could never win in the playoffs. Through the 1970s and 1980s, the club hired a succession of g.m.s and coaches including Emile Francis, John Ferguson, Fred Shero, Craig Patrick, Herb Brooks, Phil Esposito, Ted Sator, Tom Webster and Michel Bergeron. Neil Smith took over as g.m. in 1989, hiring Roger Neilson as coach. The emergence of defenseman Brian Leetch and a mid-season trade for high-scoring Bernie Nicholls put the Rangers into the thick of the NHL's extremely competitive Patrick Division.

CUMULATIVE RECORD	GP	Won	Lost	Tied	Pct
Regular Season	4206	1743	1786	677	.495
Playoffs	308	141	159	8	.473
Series: 72 W33 L39					
TOTALS	4514	1884	1945	685	.493

National Hockey Association (1909-1917)

The National Hockey Association was formed on December 2, 1909. The league was born out of a dispute within the ECHA, which dissolved and reformed as the CHA having excluded the Wanderers of Montreal. The Wanderers joined with interests in the Temiskaming league in northeastern Ontario to form the new league with franchises in Renfrew, Cobalt, Haileybury and Montreal. Very early in the season, the NHA amalgamated with several teams from the CHA, and the season continued with the addition of Ottawa, Shamrocks and Canadiens. In November of 1917 the National Hockey Association voted itself out of existence, and its former members formed the National Hockey League.

NHL Official Guide & Record Book

Often called, "the bible of hockey", the *NHL Official Guide & Record Book* is the league's annual statistical guide. Once used only by reporters, broadcasters, coaches, scouts and general managers throughout the hockey world, each year's *Guide* is now widely read by hockey fans in Canada, the United States and Europe. It contains historical and contemporary information and photos about the NHL and brings together player records from NHL, minor pro, European, junior and college hockey.

National Hockey League Players' Association (NHLPA)

The NHLPA is an organization that was formed in the spring of 1967 to represent NHL players in

The National Hockey Association originally awarded the O'Brien Trophy to its champion when the league was formed in 1910. The NHL took possession of the trophy in 1917 and continued to award it until it was replaced by the Prince of Wales Trophy in 1924. When the NHL went to two divisions in 1928, the O'Brien was awarded to the champion of the Canadian Division. Beginning in 1939 when the League reverted to a single division, it was awarded to the team finishing second in regular-season play. The O'Brien Trophy was retired following the 1949–50 season.

their negotiations with club owners. The NHLPA's executive board is made up of player representatives from each NHL team in addition to a president and four vice-presidents. The board meets with a committee of owners twice a year in order to discuss concerns or grievances. Association members are provided with life insurance, disability insurance, full medical and dental insurance coverage and an extensive pension plan. An additional benefit provides a lump sum payment of $250,000 at age 55 for every player who plays 400 NHL games during his career. Bob Goodenow has been appointed to succeed Alan Eagleson as executive director of the Association following the negotiation of a new collective bargaining agreement with the NHL in 1991.

Opposite page: Bernie Nicholls had another outstanding season in 1989–90, finishing in sixth place on the NHL scoring ladder. His trade to the New York Rangers gave the squad the offensive leader they needed to finish in first place in the Patrick Division.

Nicholls, Bernie

b. Haliburton, Ontario, 24 June 1961.

Bernie Nicholls joined the Los Angeles Kings for the 1981-82 season and soon began to display exceptional skating and shooting skills that would make him one of the most popular players in Los Angeles' history. Nicholls reached his peak in California in 1988-89, scoring 70 goals and emerging as one of the NHL's true superstars. He was off to another superb season in 1989-90 when, in mid-campaign, he was traded to the New York Rangers for Tomas Sandstrom and Tony Granato. Initially shocked by the trade, Nicholls went to work for the Rangers, contributing greatly to the club's upward swing in the tight Patrick Division.

Nighbor, Frank

b. Pembroke, Ontario, 1893; d. 13 April 1966.
Hall of Fame: 1947

Center Frank Nighbor was a slick 160-pound package of stickhandling ability. He was a 60-minute center with the Ottawa Senators from 1915 to 1929, and was one of the game's great exponents of the pokecheck. He turned professional with Toronto in 1913, and won his first Stanley Cup with the Vancouver Millionaires in 1915. He returned to Ottawa next season and remained with the Senators until the last half of 1928-29 (his final season as a player), when he played for Toronto. While with the Senators, Nighbor won four more Stanley Cups. He was also the initial winner of two of the NHL's great trophies, the Hart (MVP) and the Lady Byng (sportsmanship).

Noble, Reginald (Reg)

b. Collingwood, Ontario, 23 June 1895;
d. 19 January 1962. Hall of Fame: 1962
Championships followed Reg Noble wherever

he went. After helping his junior and senior teams to group and league titles, Noble joined the Toronto Arenas in 1917; they won the Stanley Cup, and Noble scored 28 goals in 22 games that season. He added two more Cups during his career, with Toronto again in 1920, and with the Montreal Maroons in 1926. Traded to the Detroit Cougars where he played five years as a defenseman, Noble returned to the Maroons early in 1933. He finished his NHL career with 170 goals. Noble played one more season for Cleveland of the International League. He refereed in the NHL for two seasons.

Norris, Bruce

b. Chicago, Illinois, 19 February 1924;
d. 1 January 1986.
Hall of Fame: Builder, 1969

Bruce Norris was named president of the Detroit Red Wings in 1955 at age 31. He succeeded his

sister in the position, continuing Norris family ownership of the team begun by his father in 1933. He carried out an arena expansion program costing more than $2.5 million that made Detroit's Olympia one of the finest arenas in the NHL.

Norris, James Sr.

b. St. Catherines, Ontario, 10 December 1879; d. 4 December 1952.
Hall of Fame: Builder, 1958

James Norris formed his life-long love of hockey growing up in Montreal. When his grain business interest took him to Chicago, he purchased the Chicago Shamrocks of the American Hockey Association in 1930 and three years later, with his son James D., bought Detroit's Olympia and its NHL franchise. They changed the team name from the Falcons to the Red Wings and immediately set out in pursuit of the Stanley Cup by

building a strong farm system. Two years later, the Red Wings won, repeating in the following season of 1936-37 and again in 1942-43 under the Norris banner. At one time, Norris and his three children also owned Chicago Stadium and a majority interest in the Madison Square Garden Corporation, which owned the New York Rangers.

Norris, James D.

b. 6 November 1906; d. 25 February 1966.
Hall of Fame: Builder, 1962

Along with his father James Sr., James D. Norris acquired the Detroit Red Wings and the Olympia in 1933. Detroit went on to win three Stanley Cups: 1935-36, 1936-37 and 1942-43 and, during these years, James D. signed or helped develop NHL stars Sid Abel, Ted Lindsay, Jack Stewart, Red Kelly and Gordie Howe. In 1946, James D. and partner Arthur Wirtz assumed ownership of the Chicago Blackhawks, last-place finishers in the NHL in each of the previous three seasons. Following the same formula that had worked in Detroit, they rebuilt the Hawks into a successful franchise and winner of the Stanley Cup in 1961.

Northey, William

b. Leeds, Quebec, 19 April 1872; d. 9 April 1963. Hall of Fame: Builder, 1947

William M. Northey was president of the Montreal Amateur Athletic Association, the first winner of the Stanley Cup. He helped supervise construction of the original Montreal Forum and was for many years managing director of the building. A supporter of amateur hockey, it was Northey who prevailed upon Sir Montagu Allan to present the Allan Cup when the Stanley Cup became a professionals' trophy in 1908.

Notre Dame Hounds

Hockey team formed by Father Athol Murray in 1928 at Notre Dame College in Wilcox, Saskatchewan. The college began with an enrollment of 15 students, but from these humble beginnings Father Murray built a powerhouse hockey team. Despite having a limited student population, Murray and his Hounds competed with and often beat junior teams from across Canada. The tenacity and fair play exhibited by the team made them crowd favorites, and helped raise well-needed funds for the impoverished college. The Hounds' roster over the years includes such names from the past as Garth Boesch, Nick and Don Metz from the Cup-winning Leaf teams of the 1940's to present stars Wendel Clark, Russ Courtnall and Gary Leeman.

Oakland Seals

In November of the 1967-68 season the owners of the California Seals changed the team's name from 'California' to 'Oakland' Seals so that fans in the Oakland area where the club was based could more readily identify with the first-year NHL team. The Seals made the playoffs in 1968-69 when they finished second in the West and in 1969-70 when they finished in the tie for fourth with Philadelphia but were winners on the basis of more victories. They were renamed the California Golden Seals in 1970-71.

O'Brien, J. Ambrose

b. Renfrew, Ontario, 27 May 1885; d. 25 April 1968. Hall of Fame: Builder, 1962

When Renfrew, Ontario, was unable to gain admission to the professional Eastern Canada Association in 1909, J. Ambrose O'Brien set out to organize a rival league. O'Brien's new league, the National Hockey Association, included four teams financed by his father, M.J. O'Brien, but Ambrose O'Brien concentrated his efforts on the Renfrew Creamery Kings, signing stars like Lester and Frank Patrick, Fred Whitcoft and Cyclone Taylor. He also helped launch what would eventually become one of the most famous teams in NHL history, the Montreal Canadiens.

O'Connor, Buddy

b. Montreal, Quebec, 21 June 1916; d. 24 August 1977. Hall of Fame: 1988

Center Buddy O'Connor played 10 NHL seasons with the Canadiens and Rangers, recording 140 goals and 157 assists in 509 regular-season games. He played senior hockey with the Montreal Royals, moving up to the Canadiens in 1941-42. He joined the Rangers in 1947-48 and had his best season, finishing with 24 goals and 36 assists for 60 points in as many games, earning the Hart Trophy as MVP and the Lady Byng Trophy as most gentlemanly player. Throughout his career, O'Connor had only 34 penalty minutes.

Offside

There are two types of offside violation:

1) Players of the attacking team must not precede the puck over the blueline into the offensive zone. Failure to do so results in play being stopped with a faceoff in the neutral zone.

2) Passes from a player's defensive zone picked up by a teammate skating on the other side of the center red line result in a two-line offside and a faceoff in the defensive zone.

It is the position of the player's skates, and not his stick, which determines an offside. Both skates must be completely over the outer edge of the blueline or redline line involved in the play.

Oliver, Harold (Harry)

b. Selkirk, Manitoba, 26 October 1898; d. 16 June 1985. Hall of Fame: 1967

Rightwinger Harry Oliver went on to greatness with the Boston Bruins and the New York Americans in an NHL career that spanned 11 seasons. He moved with the speed and grace of a thoroughbred, and his on-and-off-ice deport-

ment was exemplary. In his entire career, Oliver never spent more than 24 minutes in the penalty box in any one season. He moved to Calgary in 1920 to play in the Western League, remaining there until he was sold to the Bruins in 1926. He played on a Stanley Cup winner in 1928-29, and was traded to the Americans in 1934, where he remained three more years.

Olmstead, Bert

b. Scepter, Saskatchewan, 4 September 1926.
Hall of Fame: 1985

Leftwinger Bert Olmstead broke into the NHL with the Chicago Blackhawks during the 1948-49 season and went on to play 13 full seasons in the NHL, establishing a reputation as one of the game's hard-nosed players. He played junior hockey with Moose Jaw before turning pro with Kansas City of the U.S. League. After a full season with Chicago in 1949-50, he was traded first to Detroit and then to Montreal in 1950-51 – where he became an integral part of four Canadiens' Stanley Cup wins. The Toronto Maple Leafs claimed him in 1958, and he won another Cup with Toronto in 1962. He retired after that season. In 848 games, Olmstead scored 181 goals and added 541 assists. He was the first coach at Oakland, following NHL expansion in 1967.

Olympic Hockey

Competition sanctioned by both the International Olympic Committee (IOC) and the International Ice Hockey Federation (IIHF) and held every four years at the site of the Winter Olympic Games. The first official Olympic hockey tournament took place in 1924 at Chamonix, France, with Canada winning the gold medal. Today, the IIHF selects 12 teams for the competition based on the previous year's World Championship standings. List of Olympic Hockey Champions:

Olympic Hockey Gold Medal Winners

1988 – USSR	1964 – USSR	1940 – (no competition)
1984 – USSR	1960 – USA	
1980 – USA	1956 – USSR	1936 – Great Britain
1976 – USSR	1952 – Canada	
1972 – USSR	1948 – Canada	1932 – Canada
1968 – USSR	1944 – (no competition)	1928 – Canada
		1924 – Canada

Orr, Bobby

b. Parry Sound, Ontario, 20 March 1948.
Hall of Fame: 1979

He played only nine full NHL seasons, but Orr's achievements rank among the greatest in the

Bobby Orr, left, puts the grab on Henri Richard in this Bruins-Habs match-up. One of the highlights of Orr's career was his performance in the 1976 Canada Cup, when Orr was elected to the tournament all-star team and was named MVP for the series.

game. With Boston, he was named the NHL's top rookie in 1967, and held a monopoly on the Norris Trophy as the league's best defenseman winning the award in each of the next eight seasons. He was also named a first team all-star in that time. Orr won the league's MVP honors three times and became the first defenseman to lead the league in scoring. He was the MVP in the playoffs in 1970 and 1972, winning Stanley Cups both years. The dominant player in the NHL, Orr controlled the pace of every game in which he played. After six knee operations and an unsuccessful comeback attempt with Chicago, he retired in 1978. In 657 games he scored 270 goals and collected 645 assists.

Ottawa Senators

The Ottawa Senators had their roots in the Ottawa City Hockey Club, organized around 1884. In that year they played in the Montreal Winter Carnival series, the first such exhibition series known. Before joining the NHL in 1917, the Senators, or their predecessors, successfully challenged for or defended the Stanley Cup 15 times. As a member of the NHL, the Ottawa Senators won Stanley Cups five times before shifting to St. Louis in 1934. 20 Stanley Cup victories is second on the all-time record list. The Senators played 18 NHL seasons, and were first-place finishers nine times.

Ottawa Silver Seven

The Silver Seven is the name given to the Ottawa Hockey Club between the years 1903 and 1906. The origin of the sobriquet is obscure, though the "silver" is said to refer to the money paid to the seven men on the squad. The Silver Seven, who played in the days of point, cover-point and rover, first won the Stanley Cup in 1903, and held it against nine successive challenges, the best run of defenses in the Cup's history, before giving it up in March of 1906. The team was built around the talents of Bouse Hutton, Harvey Pulford, the Gilmour brothers, Harry "Rat" Westwick, Frank McGee and Alf Smith.

Overtime

In NHL regular-season play since 1983-84 (after a break of 41 seasons), if the score is tied at the end of the regulation three periods, one additional overtime period lasting five minutes or until the first goal is scored is played. The overtime period begins after a two-minute rest with players remaining on the ice or on their respective benches. In the playoffs, tie games are determined by means of unlimited sudden-death overtime played in 20-minute periods. The longest overtime game in the NHL lasted 116 minutes (almost six full periods) of extra time and ended when Mud Bruneteau scored for the Detroit Red Wings to defeat the Montreal Maroons 1-0 in a game that began on 24 March 1936.

Pacific Coast Hockey Association (PCHA)

The PCHA was organized by Frank, Lester and Joseph Patrick in 1911. The key executives had played for Stanley Cup contending teams, and offered contracts to outstanding eastern players. In this way, and through innovations for which the Patricks became famous, they built a league which played hockey on a level which rivaled the best in the east. By 1914, the PCHA had established an east vs. west annual challenge for the Stanley Cup, a situation which brought American-based teams into Cup competition. In 1916, the Portland Rosebuds were defeated by the Montreal Canadiens for the Cup, but the following year another American team defeated the Habs and became the first U.S.-based team to win the Cup. By 1921 the fortunes of the league were in decline, and its club owners agreed to play the Western Hockey League champions for a spot in the Stanley Cup playoffs against the NHL champions. In 1924, the remaining PCHA teams joined the Western Hockey League, and finally, after the 1926 season, the remaining teams and many of the players were sold to eastern NHL interests.

Page, Pierre

b. St. Hermas, Quebec, 30 April 1948.
Colorful Pierre Page is often compared to his older rival Jacques Demers. Both men paid their dues in the lower ranks before finally getting a

chance to coach in the NHL. Page worked in the Calgary organization for eight years, serving as assistant coach under Al MacNeil and Bob Johnson. He also was coach and g.m. of the Flames' minor league affiliates in Denver and Moncton. He was hired as head coach of the Minnesota North Stars in 1987-88.

Parent, Bernie

b. Montreal, Quebec, 3 April 1945.
Hall of Fame: 1984

Goaltender Bernie Parent turned pro in 1965, playing 57 games with Boston before being claimed by Philadelphia in the 1967 expansion draft. He left the Flyers to play 65 games with Toronto of the NHL and 63 with Philadelphia of the WHA, coming back to the Spectrum to stay in 1972. With Parent in goal, Philadelphia was a defensive powerhouse, winning the Stanley Cup in 1974 and 1975. Parent won the Conn Smythe Trophy as playoff MVP each of those two years. He shared the Vezina Trophy with Tony Esposito in 1974 and won it outright in 1975. An eye injury ended his career in 1979.

Park, Brad

b. Toronto, Ontario, 6 July 1948.
Hall of Fame: 1988

Brad Park was one of the NHL top defensemen throughout a 17-year career that began with the New York Rangers in 1968. He was a fine skater with a heavy shot, graduating from the Toronto Marlboros juniors to become the Rangers' first choice in the 1966 Amateur Draft. His best NHL season was 1973-74 when he had 25 goals and 57 assists with the Rangers. He joined Boston in 1975-76 and went on to finish his career in Detroit from 1983 to 1985. A seven-time all-star, he was part of the defense corps for Team Canada in the historic 4-3-1 series win over the Soviet national team in 1972.

Patrick, Craig

b. Detroit, Michigan, 20 May 1946.

The NHL has had a member of the famed Patrick family as part of its structure ever since Lester Patrick took over the New York Rangers in 1926-27 as coach and manager. Craig, Lester's grandson, played eight seasons in the NHL, scoring 163 points (72 goals, 91 assists), in a total of 401 games. He played with California, St. Louis, Kansas City, and Washington before retiring following the 1978-79 season. He served as assistant manager and assistant coach of the U.S. Olympic team that captured the gold medal at Lake Placid in February, 1980, and was hired as Ranger g.m. that same year. He held this post for one season and then became athletic direc-

tor of the University of Denver. He became g.m. of the Pittsburgh Penguins in January of 1990 and also agreed to coach the team until he found a suitable candidate for the job.

Patrick Family

No single family has had a more profound impact on the development of the professional game than the Patricks. Brothers Lester and Frank Patrick were great players, hockey entrepreneurs and innovators. Founders of the Pacific Coast Hockey Association, Frank and Lester later transferred many of that league's top players to the newly-expanded NHL in 1926. Lester was called to New York to help organize the Rangers, delivering a a Cup champion in the franchise's second season. Frank Patrick later became an executive with Boston. Lester's sons Lynn and Murray (Muzz) Patrick played for the Rangers in the late 1930s and starred on their 1940 Stanley Cup championship team. Both went on to coach and serve as general managers in the NHL. Muzz's son Dick eventually became president of the Washington Capitals after a distinguished career as a high school and college player. Lynn's sons Craig and Glenn both played in the NHL during the 1970s. Craig continued in the game after his playing days as manager of the 1980 U.S. Olympic team and later as general manager and occasional coach of the New York Rangers in the 1980s. He became coach and g.m. of the Pittsburgh Penguins early in the 1989-90 season.

Pete Stemkowski, left, of the New York Rangers checks Brad Park of the Boston Bruins. Park holds the NHL record for consecutive appearances in the playoffs, but despite playing in the postseason in 17 straight years, was never on a Stanley Cup winner.

In one of hockey's greatest bits of folklore, coach Lester Patrick, then aged 44, donned the pads to replace an injured Lorne Chabot in goal on 7 April 1928 during the Stanley Cup finals against the Montreal Maroons. Patrick allowed only one goal as the Rangers won the game in overtime and went on to win their first Stanley Cup.

Patrick, Frank

b. Ottawa, Ontario, 21 December 1885; d. 29 June 1960. Hall of Fame: Builder, 1958

Frank Patrick was responsible for many innovations in hockey including the origination of the blueline. He played with his brother Lester for the Renfrew Creamery Kings but felt big-time hockey could grow on the Pacific coast. The Patricks moved west, building the first artificial rinks in Canada including a 10,000-seat facility in Vancouver. Frank became president of the Pacific Coast Hockey Association when it was formed in 1911, owned, managed and coached the Vancouver club and played defense. In 1926, he engineered the biggest deal in hockey to that time, selling the entire league to eastern interests. He later served as managing-director of the NHL, as a coach with Boston and manager with the Canadiens.

Patrick, Lester

b. Drummondville, Quebec, 31 December 1883; d. 1 June 1960. Hall of Fame: 1947

Patrick was one of hockey's greats and is identified with many of the major developments in style of play, organization and expansion of the game. He was one of the first rushing defensemen in hockey, inaugurated hockey's first major farm system and created the playoff system in use today. He broke into pro hockey as a defenseman with Brandon, Manitoba, in 1903 and joined the Montreal Wanderers in 1905, where he won two successive Stanley Cups. Along with brother Frank, he built arenas in Vancouver and Victoria, British Columbia, and formed the Pacific Coast Hockey Association. Lester became manager of the New York Rangers in 1926, and the Rangers won all three of their Stanley Cups under his guidance.

Patrick, Lynn

b. Victoria, British Columbia, 3 February 1912; d. 26 January 1980. Hall of Fame: 1980

Though his father Lester was a Hockey Hall of Famer, leftwinger Lynn Patrick's youth was spent in a non-hockey environment; he didn't play organized hockey until he joined a senior Montreal club. Fearing charges of nepotism, Lester (who was managing the Rangers) wouldn't give Lynn a chance with the club until warned by another manager, "either put him on your list, or I'll put him on ours." Lynn twice led the Rangers in scoring, played for the Rangers' Cup-winning team in 1940, and was a two-time all-star. He scored 145 goals and 190 assists in 455 games. He coached five seasons in Boston, his Bruins never missing the playoffs, and then spent the next 10 years in the front office. He became general manager of the St. Louis Blues in 1966, retiring as senior vice-president in 1977.

Pavelich, Matt

b. Park Hill Gold Mines, Ontario, 12 March 1934. Hockey Hall of Fame: Linesman, 1987

Matt Pavelich was the first linesman to be inducted into the Hall of Fame. He worked his first NHL game in Boston on October 11, 1956, and called his first playoff game that same season. The brother of former Red Wing Marty Pavelich, Matt worked his 1,727th and final regular-season game on April 8, 1979. A member of the Sault Ste. Marie Hockey Hall of Fame, Pavelich also officiated in 11 NHL all-star games.

Penalty Killing

When a team plays one or more players short as a result of a penalty, it attempts to kill the penalty

The infraction imposed on this St Louis player could be judged to be either tripping or hooking, but it seems certain the guilty party will spend two minutes in the "box" for this penalty.

time with good defensive play until the penalized players return to the ice. Certain players develop into accomplished penalty killers and are used as a 'specialty unit' for that purpose when a team is playing short-handed.

Penalty, Major

A five-minute penalty assessed for fighting or injury-related infractions. No substitutes are allowed for a player serving a major penalty, even if any goals are scored by the opposition during the term of the penalty. In the case of coincident major penalties, i.e. both teams receiving major penalties at the same time, substitutions are allowed.

Penalty, Match

This serious penalty results in the suspension of a player for the reminder of the game. If, in the judgement of the referee, the infraction resulted in an injury to an opponent, the penalized player's team must play a man short for ten minutes. If, in the judgement of the referee, an attempt was made to injure an opponent but no injury resulted, the penalized player's team must play a man short for five minutes.

Penalty, Minor

A two-minute penalty assessed for a number of minor infractions such as tripping, holding, hooking, roughing, etc. No substitutes are allowed for the player serving the penalty, but the player can return to the ice immediately if the opposing team scores a goal. In the case of coincident minor penalties, i.e. both teams receiving minor penalties at the same time, substitutions are allowed.

Penalty Shot

Awarded for infractions such as deliberately displacing a goal post during the course of a breakaway, interference, illegal entry into a game, throwing a stick, fouling a player from behind, falling on the puck in the goal crease, etc. Penalty shots occur very rarely, and even when one is taken the success rate is low. In 1989-90 there were 16 shots and 6 goals in the regular season and 4 shots and 1 goal in the playoffs. Depending on the nature of the penalty, the referee or the captain of the non-offending team will designate the player who will take the penalty shot from those that were on the ice

Below: The New York Islanders' penalty killers, wearing white in this photograph, try to set a four-man defensive box against the Los Angeles Kings. The Islanders' special teams were a key factor in the teams success in the early 1980's.

when the infraction was committed. The puck is then placed at center ice and players from both teams go to the side boards, except for the designated shooter and goalkeeper. At the referee's signal, the shooter then proceeds unopposed with the puck from center ice toward the opposition goal defended by the goalkeeper. Once the player takes a shot on net, the play is whistled dead, whether a goal has been scored or not. A goal scored on a rebound is not allowed. The game clock does not run during a penalty shot.

Penticton V's

Senior hockey team from Penticton, B.C., that won the 1955 World Championships. The team was born in 1951, and in the space of three years won the senior championship of western Canada twice before winning the Canadian senior championship and the Allan Cup in 1954. As Allan Cup winners, the V's were selected to represent Canada at the World Championships in 1955. Canada had lost the world title in 1954 to the Soviet Union, which at that time was making its first appearance in international play. The V's went undefeated in the tournament, allowing only six goals in eight games and shutting out the Soviets 5-0 in the decisive last match. The Penticton V's, Canadian heroes in 1955, folded in 1989 due to financial problems.

Periods

A hockey game usually consists of three 20-minute periods of actual play, with a rest intermission of 15 minutes between periods.

Perreault, Gilbert

b. Victoriaville, Quebec, 14 November 1950.
Chosen first overall By Buffalo in the 1970 Amateur Draft, center Gil Perreault won the Calder Trophy and almost immediately took over as leader of the Sabres. He won the Lady Byng Trophy in his third season and demonstrated scoring finesse that invited comparison with that of Jean Beliveau. His finest season was 1975-76, when he had 44 goals and 113 points, earning the first of two consecutive second team all-star selections. He was part of the French Connection line with Rene Robert and Richard Martin. He retired in 1986 having scored a franchise- record 512 goals and 814 assists. He later coached Victoriaville of the QMJHL.

Philadelphia Flyers

The Philadelphia Flyers joined the NHL in 1967 with 'Bud' Poile as general manager and Keith Allen as coach. The club drafted first-rate young

goaltenders Bernie Parent and Doug Favell in 1967, made the playoffs in its first season and then fell out of post-season contention until 1972-73. The new-look Flyers of the mid-1970s were the most colorful club in the NHL, replacing the 'Big, Bad Bruins' of the first part of the decade as the league's most intimidating opponent. The first expansion team to win big, the Flyers were Stanley Cup winners in 1974 and 1975, led by goaltender Parent, team captain Bobby Clarke and coach Fred Shero. The 1973-74 Flyers spent 1,750 minutes in the penalty box, astonishing considering that no other team had ever topped 1,400. The finesse-based Montreal Canadiens dethroned the Flyers in 1976, but despite numerous changes in personnel, the Flyers remained a competitive top-rank NHL club enjoying tremendous fan support. The club reached the Stanley Cup finals on three occasions in the 1980s.

CUMULATIVE RECORD	GP	Won	Lost	Tied	Pct
Regular Season	1818	920	604	294	.587
Playoffs	223	116	107	0	.520
Series: 43 W25 L18					
TOTALS	2041	1036	711	294	.580

Philadelphia Quakers

The Philadelphia Quakers played one year in the NHL. Following the unsuccessful attempt to maintain a franchise in Pittsburgh, the team was moved to Philadelphia where it finished the 1931-32 season with a 4-36-4 record. The team was coached by Cooper Smeaton, a future Hall of Fame referee.

Pilote, Pierre

b. Kenogami, Quebec, 11 December 1931.
Hall of Fame: 1975

Pilote was a premier rushing defenseman. He broke into the NHL with Chicago in 1956 and didn't miss a game during his first five full seasons; he was finally forced out with a shoulder separation in 1962. He was voted to all-star berths eight straight times, including five consecutive first team selections. He won three consecutive Norris Trophies as the NHL's top defenseman, and scored 80 goals and 418 assists in regular-season play. He captained the Hawks from 1963 to 1968, and won the Stanley Cup in 1961. Pilote didn't play organized hockey until age 16. He retired after the 1968-69 season.

Pilous, Rudy

b. Manitoba, 11 August 1914.
Hall of Fame: Builder, 1985

Rudy Pilous set up a junior club in St. Catharines, Ontario, in 1941-42, making the playoffs in each of the team's first three seasons. He moved up to

Buffalo in the AHL in 1946, and went on to work his magic as a promoter and trouble-shooter in Houston and San Diego in the late 1940s. He was manager and coach of Memorial Cup winners at St. Catharines in 1954 and 1969; coach of the Stanley Cup-winning Chicago Black Hawks in 1961; manager and coach of the Western Hockey League champion Denver Invaders in 1964; and manager of the WHA champion Winnipeg Jets in 1976 and 1978. Pilous later scouted for Detroit and Los Angeles and was general manager of Toronto's farm club at St. Catharines.

Pitre, Didier

b. Valleyfield, Quebec, 1 September 1883; d. 29 July 1934. Hall of Fame: 1962

Pitre was the idol of French-Canadian hockey followers in the early days of the game. A versatile player, he performed on defense, rover and rightwing during his career. He had a shot like a cannonball, and skated with tremendous speed. He entered big-league hockey as a defenseman with the Montreal Nationals of the FAHL. In 1909, Pitre played for Lester Patrick's team in Edmonton. When Jack Laviolette formed the Canadiens that same year, Pitre was the first player he signed. He remained with the team until his retirement in 1923 except for a stint with Vancouver during 1913-14. Pitre's biggest scoring year was 1915, when he scored 30 goals. He won a Stanley Cup with Montreal in 1915-16.

Pittsburgh Penguins

One of six franchises accepted into the National Hockey League in the 1967 expansion, the Penguins made the playoffs just once in their first six seasons, performing admirably in losing to the St. Louis Blues in a six-game semi-final in 1970. In 1974-75 the club finished with its highest point total in franchise history but squandered a 3-0 series lead to lose to the New York Islanders in the quarter-finals. In 1975-76, two Penguins' players, Pierre Larouche and Jean Prono[?] scored more than 50 goals. A poor finish i[?] 1983-84 enabled the club to select center [?] Lemieux first overall in the 1984 Entry Dra[?] Lemieux soon became a celebrity in Pittsb[?] and his popularity and success on the ice [?] translated into the Penguins becoming an [?] tion both at home and on the road. In 1988-[?] Lemieux led the Penguins to their first play[?] appearance in seven years while capturing [?] second consecutive Art Ross Trophy as the [?] NHL's leading point-getter.

CUMULATIVE RECORD	GP	Won	Lost	Tie[?]
Regular Season	1818	668	888	26[?]
Playoffs	62	28	34	
Series: 14 W4 L10				
TOTALS	1880	696	922	26[?]

Pittsburgh Pirates

The Pittsburgh Pirates grew out of a local Pittsburgh amateur team of the 1920's called the Yellow Jackets. Lionel Conacher, studying at Duquesne on a football scholarship, led the team to great success at the amateur level, and when an NHL franchise was offered to the city in 1925, Conacher and the Yellow Jackets jumped at the chance. The team made Stanley Cup play on two occasions, and coach Odie Cleghorn is given credit for perfecting player changes while play was ongoing. The franchise was shifted to Philadelphia for the 1930-31 season.

Pittsburgh Yellow Jackets

This amateur team won the United States Amateur Hockey Association in 1924 and 1925, and formed the nucleus of an NHL team, the

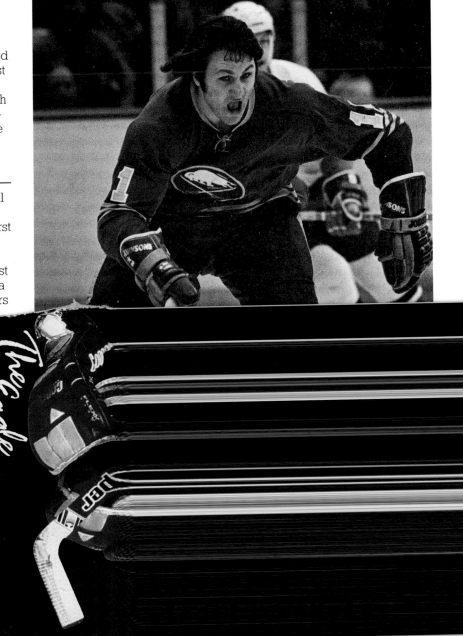

Opposite page:

Pittsburgh Penguins' goaltender Tom Barrasso. After going all the way to the Wales Conference finals in 1988–89, the Penguins missed the playoffs in 1989–90, finishing with a 32–40–8 record.

Philadelphia Flyers' star Rick Tocchet in full flight. Though the Flyers missed the playoffs in 1989–90, Tocchet remained one of the NHL's top forwards, finishing with 37 goals and 96 points.

Pittsburgh Pirates in 1926. The Yellow Jackets were coached by Dick Carroll, Cup-winning coach from Toronto, and were the testing ground for the Hall of Fame goalminder Roy 'Shrimp' Worters, who allowed less than a goal-a-game over two seasons between the pipes for the team.

Plante, Jacques

b. Shawinigan Falls, Quebec, 17 January 1929; d. 27 February 1986. Hall of Fame: 1978

Jacques Plante was a superb goaltender and a hockey innovator. He became a regular with the Canadiens in 1954-55 and was part of six Cup

winners in Montreal, winning an equal number of Vezina Trophies in the process. He won the Hart Trophy as MVP in 1962 before being traded to the New York Rangers where he played two more years before retiring. In 1968-69 he made a successful comeback at age 40, joining Glenn Hall to win the Vezina Trophy with the expansion St. Louis Blues. He later played in Toronto and Boston, retiring after the 1972-73 season. Plante's enthusiasm and his roving style made him a crowd favorite throughout his career. He also designed and built his own facemask and was the first goaltender to regularly use what is now a standard part of every goaltender's equipment.

Playoff Format

The system by which NHL teams compete against one another upon completion of the regular schedule in order to determine the winner of the Stanley Cup. After numerous changes over the years, the current arrangement – in place since 1986-87 – dictates that the first four teams in each division (Adams, Patrick, Smythe, Norris) earn playoff berths. In each division, the first-place team opposes the fourth-place team and the second-place team opposes the third-place team in a best-of-seven division semi-final series (DSF). In each division, the two winners of the DSF meet in a best-of-seven division final series (DF). The two winners of the DF meet in a best-of-seven conference final series (CF). In the Prince of Wales Conference, the Adams Division winner opposes the Patrick Division winner; in the Clarence Campbell Conference, the Smythe Division winner opposes the Norris Division winner. The two CF winners then meet in a best-of- seven Stanley Cup final series (F). In all cases the team with the most regular-season points is awarded home games for the first, second, fifth and seventh games.

Poile, David

b. Toronto, Ontario, 14 February 1949.
Hired as g.m. of the Washington Capitals in 1982, David Poile had served as assistant g.m. under Cliff Fletcher in Atlanta and Calgary. Poile, son of former NHLer Bud Poile, swung a major trade early in his tenure with the Capitals, acquiring Rod Langway, Doug Jarvis, Craig Laughlin, and Brian Engblom from Montreal for Ryan Walter

and Rick Green. Langway became not only the leader of the Washington Caps, but a franchise player who almost overnight turned the Capitals into contenders. Although Poile's Capitals never progressed beyond the Patrick Division in the playoffs, they were one of the NHL's better and more consistent teams in the 1980s.

Point (on the ice)

The point refers to those areas of the ice found close to the boards just inside the blueline closest to the opponent's goal. Many scoring plays, particularly when the attacking team has time to set up in its opponent's end of the ice, begin with a hard shot on net from the point. During a man advantage situation, the attacking team will usually set two good shooters on the points to direct hard shots toward the net for possible deflection into the goal.

Pollock, Sam

b. Montreal, Quebec, 15 December 1925.
Hall of Fame: Builder, 1978
Sam Pollock was one of hockey's most successful executives. He first became involved with the Canadiens as manager of the players' summer softball team. He also operated the organization's midget hockey team. In 1947, after six years in minor hockey, he had his first full-time job with the Canadiens and, in 1964, became vice-president and general manager. He was coach and/or g.m. of numerous championship teams at the junior or minor pro level as well as being part of nine Stanley Cups with the Canadiens. He also assembled Team Canada '76, winners of the Canada Cup.

Pucks are kept frozen until needed on the ice. Pucks used in NHL games have the NHL logo on one side and the home team logo on the other.

Potvin, Denis

b. Hull, Quebec, 29 October 1953.
Defenseman Denis Potvin came to the NHL as a can't-miss prospect from the Ottawa 67s of the OHA. Drafted first overall by the New York Islanders in 1973, he won the Calder Trophy as the NHL's top rookie at the age of 19 in 1973-74. He was selected to the first all-star team the following season and went to win a total of seven all-star berths in his career. On the ice Potvin was a hard hitter with great offensive skills. He orchestrated the Islanders' potent powerplay and was an integral part of four consecutive Stanley Cup winners beginning in 1980. He won the Norris Trophy as the NHL's top defender in 1976, 1978 and 1979. When he retired in 1988, his 310 goals, 742 assists and 1,052 points were all-time records for defensemen.

Power Failure Game

One of the most unusual playoff game postponements occurred on May 24, 1988, during the 1988 Stanley Cup finals between the Boston Bruins and Edmonton Oilers. In game four at Boston Garden, a power failure blacked out the arena midway through the second period with the score tied 3-3. Efforts to restore power were unsuccessful and the game was postponed. Edmonton won the next game to take the series and Cup four games to nil.

Powerplay

The powerplay is a manpower advantage that accrues to a team as a result of penalties called on its opponents. NHL teams average approximately one powerplay goal scored for every five manpower advantages.

Pratt, Walter (Babe)

b. Stoney Mountain, Manitoba, 7 January 1916; d. 16 December 1988. Hall of Fame: 1966
In tracing Pratt's record, it can be noted that almost invariably when he joined a team, that team quickly became a championship club. In a 26-year career that spanned juvenile hockey to Stanley Cup winners, Pratt played on 15 champions. He turned pro with Philadelphia, then a Rangers' farm club, and joined New York in 1936. He won a Stanley Cup with New York in 1940 when teamed with Ott Heller on defense, and was on the ice for only 17 goals-against in 48 games. He was traded to Toronto in November, 1942. With Toronto he won the Hart Trophy as the NHL's MVP and was twice named to all-star teams. In 1947, Pratt played for Hershey, New Westminster and Tacoma before retiring as a player.

Primeau, Joe

b. Lindsay, Ontario, 29 January 1906; d. 14 May 1989. Hall of Fame: 1963
Primeau was a great hockey player who achieved equal success as a coach. He was the only man to coach Memorial, Allan and Stanley Cup-winning teams. He first attracted attention as a center for the St. Michael's College juniors and Conn Smythe signed him to a professional contract with the Maple Leafs in 1927. He joined the Leafs as a regular in 1929-30, centering Toronto's famous 'Kid Line' between Charlie Conacher and Busher Jackson. Primeau's smooth passing made the line's exploits possible. He was a tenacious checker and extremely clean player, often referred to as 'Gentleman Joe.' Primeau twice finished second in NHL scoring, was a second team all-star, and won the Lady Byng Trophy for gentlemanly conduct in 1932.

Pronovost, Marcel

b. Lac la Tortue, Quebec, 15 June 1930. Hall of Fame: 1978
Defenseman Marcel Pronovost played 20 NHL seasons, 15 with Detroit and five with Toronto. He won four Stanley Cups with Detroit, and added another with the Leafs. He was a four-time all-star, and played a prominent role as a clubhouse leader. The respect he gained around the NHL was demonstrated in 1960 at the Montreal Forum, when admiring fans from his home province presented him with an automobile and his teammates gave him a diamond ring. Traded to Toronto in the 1965-66 season, he was a key man in an eight-player deal that helped bring the Leafs a Stanley Cup in 1967. He stayed with Toronto three more seasons, became a coach at Tulsa of the Central League, and retired from playing after 1969-70.

Puck

A flat, circular disk three inches in diameter and one inch thick made of six ounces of vulcanized rubber. The origin of the term is unknown, however researchers at the Hockey Hall of Fame speculate that early players, (most of whom were college educated) referred to the disk as 'puck' in reference to Shakespeare's sprite from 'A Midsummer Night's Dream' who appeared and disappeared without warning.

Pulford, Bob

b. Newton Robinson, Ontario, 31 March 1936.
Bob Pulford, a classy, two-way centerman, labored for sixteen seasons in the NHL with the Toronto Maple Leafs and the Los Angeles Kings. Never a flamboyant player, Pulford quietly and

efficiently got the job done, taking a regular shift, skating on the powerplay, and killing penalties. Pulford finished his active playing career in 1972, by retiring as the Kings' captain and stepping right into their coaching post. After molding the Los Angeles squad into one of the finest defensive units in the league, Pulford took over as general manager- coach of the Chicago Blackhawks in 1977. He gave up the coach's portfolio after two seasons, but took over again for parts of the 1981-82 and 1984-85 seasons as well as for 1985-86 and 1986-87.

Pulford, Harvey

b. Toronto, Ontario, 1875; d. 31 October 1940. Hall of Fame: 1945

Pulford is best remembered as a clean but hard-hitting defenseman who contributed to Ottawa's Stanley Cup victories over Kenora and Dawson City. A great all-around athlete, Pulford

spent most of his life in Ottawa where he won championships in virtually every sport he played. At various times, he held titles in squash, Canadian football, lacrosse, boxing and rowing. He starred for Ottawa's Silver Seven, and won three Stanley Cups.

Quebec Bulldogs

The city of Quebec is one of the oldest hockey centers in Canada, having joined the Amateur Hockey Association upon its formation in 1886. In 1911, the Quebec Bulldogs joined the National Hockey Association, assuming the former Cobalt franchise, and finished in last place in their first year of operation. The following year, Quebec stood first in the league, and took on the Moncton team from the Maritime Professional Hockey League, to become the Stanley Cup champions for 1912. The following year they soared to the top of the NHA again, and defeated a team from Sydney Mines and, later, the Victoria Cougars of the PCHA to win their second and last Stanley Cup. The Bulldogs entered the NHL in 1919-20, but gave up their franchise after a disastrous finish. Outstanding contributors to the Quebec Bulldogs include Joe Malone, Joe Hall, Harry Mummery, Jack Marks and Eddie Oatman.

Quebec Nordiques

The Quebec Nordiques were a charter member of the WHA and joined the NHL along with Edmonton, Winnipeg and Hartford in 1979-80. The Nords enjoyed some early success in the NHL largely due to the play of Peter and Anton Stastny and Michel Goulet. The club quickly developed into a playoff threat, fostering a superb rivalry with their provincial rivals the Montreal Canadiens. The two clubs have split four playoff series with the Canadiens winning their last meeting in seven games in 1987 and the Nordiques winning the encounter previous to that in seven games in 1985. Former Montreal superstar Guy Lafleur joined the Nordiques for the 1989-90 season.

CUMULATIVE RECORD	GP	Won	Lost	Tied	Pct
Regular Season (NHL)	880	350	419	111	·416
Playoffs	68	31	37	0	.456
Series: 13 W6 L7					
TOTALS	948	381	456	111	.460

The Quebec Nordiques' roster is dotted with promising youngsters like center Joe Sakic who finished with 102 points in 1989–90.

The Quebec Bulldogs of 1912–13 with, from left to right, the O'Brien Trophy, their canine mascot and the Stanley Cup. The Bulldogs were originally supposed to enter the NHL when that league was created in 1917, but withdrew before the season got under way.

Quinn, Pat

b. Hamilton, Ontario, 29 January 1943.

As a player Pat Quinn was a rugged defenseman with the Toronto Maple Leafs, Vancouver Canucks and Atlanta Flames, beginning in 1968-69 and ending more than 600 games later in 1976-77. Quinn began his coaching career with the Maine Mariners of the AHL at a time when the club was a Philadelphia farm team. He was given the head coaching job with Flyers in the 1978-79 season and next season won the Jack Adams Award as he led the Flyers to the Stanley Cup finals. He left the Flyers after 1981-82 and didn't re-emerge as a coach until 1984-85 when he took the helm of the Los Angeles Kings. In the interim he had started studying law, eventually earning a degree from Delaware Law School and the University of San Diego. During Quinn's time with the Kings he coached Team Canada to

a bronze medal in the 1986 World Championships. He left Los Angeles during 1986-87, having agreed to become general manager of the Canucks for the 1987-88 campaign.

Ratelle, Jean

b. Lac St. Jean, Quebec, 3 October 1940.
Hall of Fame: 1985

Ratelle ended his 20-year NHL career with the New York Rangers and Boston in 1981 as the league's sixth-leading scorer, with 1,267 points on 491 goals and 776 assists. In 1,281 games, this

ey club. In 1937 the company acquired the Canadiens and though the Depression forced the Maroons out of business, Raymond's support enabled the Canadiens – and professional hockey in Montreal – to survive. He remained president of the company until 1955 when he became chairman of the board.

Rayner, Chuck

b. Sutherland, Saskatchewan, 11 August 1920. Hall of Fame: 1973
Agile goaltender Chuck Rayner broke into the NHL in 1939-40, but military service postponed the continuation of his career until 1946-47 when he joined the New York Rangers. Despite the fact that the Rangers only made the playoffs twice in his seven seasons with the club, Rayner earned second team all-star selections in 1948-49, 1949-50 and 1950-51. He also won the Hart Trophy as the NHL's MVP in 1950-51, giving up just 2.83 goals per game on a team that missed the playoffs. He retired after the 1952-53 season with a lifetime goals-against per game average of 3.05.

Reardon, Kenny

b. Winnipeg, Manitoba, 1 April 1921. Hall of Fame: 1966
Defenseman Kenny Reardon had a headlong, fearless style of play which made him a favorite of fans around the League. He came to the Montreal Canadiens as a 19-year-old. During World War II he played for the Allan Cup-winning Ottawa Commandos in 1942-43. He rejoined the Canadiens in 1945-46 and for the next five seasons was named to either the first or second all-star team. He played on a Stanley Cup winner in 1945-46. He retired after the 1949-50 season, and became a successful executive in the Montreal organization.

Referee

On-ice official in full charge of all game action. The referee calls penalties for rule infractions and fouls, conducts face-offs after a goal and to start the game and periods, awards goals, and checks all equipment. The referee is also responsible for making oral and/or written reports to league officials on any game in which a game misconduct or gross misconduct has been called so further disciplinary action can be taken, if necessary. The referee will consult with the linesman in cases of stick fouls, too many men on the ice penalties or fight instigator fouls. In case of a dispute, the referee is the chief arbitrator, and his ruling is final.

classy centerman collected only 276 penalty minutes. He came up to the Rangers to stay in the 1964-65 season and spent 13 of his 20 seasons in New York, where he centered the 'Goal-A-Game' Line with Rod Gilbert and Vic Hadfield. He was traded to the Bruins in 1975. Ratelle won the Lady Byng Trophy for gentlemanly play in 1972 and 1976, the Lester B. Pearson Award in 1972 as players' choice for NHL MVP, and the Bill Masterton Trophy in 1971 for exemplifying the qualities of perseverance, sportsmanship and dedication to hockey.

Raymond, Donat

b. Montreal, Quebec, 3 January 1880; d. 5 June 1963. Hall of Fame: Builder, 1958
Senator Donat Raymond was president of the Canadian Arena Company that in 1923 built the Montreal Forum and formed the Maroons hock-

Rendez-Vous '87

Rendez-Vous '87 was a two game series played between the NHL All-Stars and the Soviet National team which took place in Quebec City during Winter Carnival week of 1987. The NHLers won game one 4-3 on February 11; the Russians won game two 5-3 on February 13. But in a sense, the hockey games were but a sidelight to the full scope of celebrations that made up the event. The brainchild of Marcel Aubut, president of the Quebec Nordiques, Rendez-Vous also included fashion shows, gourmet dinners, concerts and a huge exhibition of artifacts from the Hockey Hall of Fame.

Retired Numbers

Uniform numbers withdrawn from active use in order to acknowledge the outstanding achievements of players who wore those numbers. In some instances numbers have been retired because of a player's untimely death. National Hockey League teams have retired 40 numbers over the years with the Boston Bruins leading all clubs with seven. Gordie Howe and Bobby Hull have the unique distinction of having had their number nines retired by two NHL clubs; Howe with Detroit and Hartford and Hull with Chicago and Winnipeg.

Richard, Henri

b. Montreal, Quebec, 29 February 1936.
Hockey Hall of Fame: 1979

Richard achieved great success during an NHL career that spanned 20 years, despite predictions of a short stay in the league by many who thought he was too small. Stamina and toughness became trademarks of this extremely clever center; he was a four-time all-star. Henri broke into the NHL in 1955-56 with Montreal, and in 1,256 regular-season games scored 358 goals. He excelled as a playmaker, collecting 688 assists – twice leading the league in that category. Richard was also recognized for his sportsmanship, winning the Masterton Trophy (for perseverance and dedication to hockey) in 1974. He was a member of 11 Stanley Cup teams.

Richard, Maurice (The Rocket)

b. Montreal, Quebec, 4 August 1921.
Hall of Fame: 1961

Known as 'The Rocket' throughout his 18-year NHL career, rightwinger Maurice Richard scored 544 goals in 978 league games. He played for the Verdun juniors and Canadiens seniors before joining the NHL Canadiens in 1943-43. Richard was the first NHLer to score 50 goals in a season, reaching this total in 50 games

Maurice "Rocket" Richard, the NHL's most colorful and controversial superstar. Richard's competitive edge caused him to sometimes lose control on the ice, but he scored more important goals in spectacular fashion than any other player.

during 1944-45. He scored 83 game-winners and 28 game-tying goals in his career and had 82 goals and 44 assists in 133 playoff games. He was named to the NHL's first all-star team eight times, and the second team six times. A fiery player, Richard was once suspended from the playoffs for striking an official. This caused a riot in the downtown Montreal area that resulted in hundreds of thousands of dollars of damage. NHL President Clarence Campbell – the man who suspended him – said of Richard: "We all have a lesson to learn from this man . . . Never have I met a man with such singleness of purpose and so completely devoted to his profession."

Richard Riot

The series of events that has become known as the Richard Riot occurred on March 17 and 18, 1955. It stemmed from an altercation which

Patrick Roy of the Montreal Canadiens puts his best foot forward to make a key save for the Habs. Roy became a crowd favorite in Montreal with odd characteristics such as talking to his goalposts and bobbing his head in rooster-like fashion. He certainly ruffled the feathers of the opposition by being the NHL's best netminder in the late 1980s.

occurred four days earlier when Montreal Canadiens' star Maurice 'The Rocket' Richard high-sticked Boston Bruins' defenseman Hal Laycoe after Laycoe had opened a gash on Richard's scalp. In an attempt to get at Laycoe again, Richard struck linesman Cliff Thompson as he tried to intervene. Two days later NHL president Clarence Campbell, after hearing the story from all sides, suspended Richard for the remainder of the season and the playoffs. On March 17 the Canadiens hosted Detroit in a critical match-up which Campbell attended despite warnings from the city's mayor and police chief. Arriving in the midst of the first period, Campbell's entrance set off a chain of events that began with angry words from Canadiens' fans directed toward the NHL president. Soon a fan attempted to attack Campbell while he was seated. A barrage of debris, rotten fruit and vegetables then descended upon him. The release of a smoke bomb would follow, resulting in the

evacuation of the Forum and the forfeiting of the game to the Red Wings. The hysteria created inside the arena sent much of the crowd onto the streets in a state of frenzy. A mob of more than 10,000 went on a rampage for hours. Cab drivers were assaulted, newsstands were burned to the ground and rocks and bottles were thrown as windows were smashed and stores looted. By the time police were able to quell the riot, 37 people were injured, 70 arrested and an estimated $50,000 to $100,000 in damage was done.

Rink Dimensions

There are no set dimensions for actual ice surface size, although most North American arenas have ice surfaces measuring 200 feet long by 85 feet wide. Most European ice surfaces are 200 feet long by 100 feet wide. Regardless of size, the rink must have corners rounded in the arc of a circle, 28 feet in radius.

The playing surface is enclosed by sideboards, no more than 48 and no less than 42 inches high and surrounded by protective glass. The surface of the boards must be smooth but may have advertising signage affixed to it. All doors and gates leading to the ice must open inwards, and all supporting devices for the glass and other protective equipment must face away from the playing area.

Road hockey

Played by Canadian youths on the hard-packed snow of winter roads, road hockey is part of the lore of the game. Players usually wear rubber boots or moccasins instead of skates. Today's road hockey players favor a bald-headed tennis ball or a special hard plastic fluorescent orange hockey ball, but in the old days, the game featured 'road apples' or frozen horse droppings molded into pucks. Former New York Ranger Rod Gilbert noted, "You didn't want to be a goalie in the spring."

Roberts, Gordon

b. 5 September 1891; d. 2 September 1966. Hall of Fame: 1971

Roberts was a great leftwinger who played professional hockey while acquiring a medical degree at McGill University. Although he scored 203 goals in 166 regular-season games, Roberts never played for a championship team. He entered McGill in 1911, and played six seasons with the Montreal Wanderers, reaching the playoffs only once. He was a strong and tireless player with a tremendous shot. On graduation from McGill in 1916, Roberts signed with Vancouver and was sensational with the Millionaires. In 1917, he scored 43 goals in 23 games, an all-time record for the Pacific Coast Hockey Association. His hospital duties took him to Seattle the next year, but he returned to Vancouver in 1920, his last season in pro hockey.

Robertson, John Ross

b. 28 December 1841; d. 31 May 1918. Hall of Fame: Builder, 1947

John Ross Robertson was a founding father of the Ontario Hockey Association. He served as OHA president from 1898 to 1904 and donated three trophies for annual competition in the senior, intermediate and junior divisions. In his first speech to the OHA, Robertson stated: "A manly nation is always fond of manly sports. We want our boys to be strong, vigorous and self-reliant and must encourage athletics. Sport should be pursued for its own sake."

Art Ross in the redband uniform of the Montreal Wanderers. In addition to his career as player, Ross was also affiliated with the Boston Bruins as a coach and/or general manager from the birth of the franchise in 1924 until he retired in 1954.

ARTHUR ROSS

Robinson, Claude

b. Harrison, Ontario, 17 December 1881; d. 27 June 1976. Hall of Fame: Builder, 1947

Claude Robinson was an important member of the Stanley Cup-winning Winnipeg Victorias hockey club as a player and as an executive. He was instrumental in the formation of a national association to compete for amateur hockey championships and became the first secretary when the Canadian Amateur Hockey Association was formed in 1914. Robinson also managed the Canadian team at the 1932 Winter Olympic Games.

Robinson, Larry

b. Marvelville, Ontario, 2 June 1951.

Larry Robinson broke in on defense with the Montreal Canadiens in 1972-73. He won the Norris Trophy as the league's best defenseman with 85 points in 1977 and was voted playoff MVP in 1978. In 1976, when Montreal faced Philadelphia in the Stanley Cup finals, Robinson's efforts were considered pivotal in enabling Montreal to take the Cup. The Habs went on to retain the cup in 1977, 1978, and 1979, with Robinson the keystone of the defense corps. Nicknamed 'Big Bird,' Larry continued to excel through the 1980's – the Habs won another Cup in 1986 – until he broke his leg playing polo just before the 1987-88 season. Although his game slowed considerably, Robinson still took a regular turn on the Montreal defense through 1988-89 when the club reached the Stanley Cup finals against the Calgary Flames. He joined the Los Angeles Kings for the 1989-90 season.

Rodden, Mike

b. Mattawa, Ontario, 24 April 1891; d. 11 January 1978. Hall of Fame: Referee, 1962

Mike Rodden refereed 1,187 NHL games but was associated with many other aspects of sport as a player, coach and sportswriter. In hockey, he played for Queen's University, Haileybury and the Toronto St. Patrick's. In football, he was the guiding hand behind 27 championship teams. He was sports editor of the Toronto Globe from 1928 to 1936 and of the Kingston Whig-Standard from 1944 until his retirement in 1959.

Rookie

Any player in his first full year of competition in a league. In the NHL, each year's top rookie is awarded the Calder Memorial Trophy.

Ross, Art

b. Naughton, Ontario, 13 January 1886; d. 5 August 1964. Hall of Fame: 1945

Ross was many things to the game of hockey: pioneer, innovator, strategist, promoter, coach and outstanding player. Ross was a defenseman during a 14-year playing career that started with Westmount of the Canadian Amateur Hockey League in 1905. He led Kenora to a Stanley Cup victory in 1907, and his only other Cup win as a player came the next season with the Montreal Wanderers. He scored 85 goals in 167 games. Ross improved the design of both the puck and the goal used in the NHL, and the Art Ross Trophy is awarded annually to the NHL's scoring champion.

Ross, Philip

b. Montreal, Quebec, 1 January 1858; d. 7 July 1949. Hall of Fame: Builder, 1976

Philip Ross was one of the first trustees of the Stanley Cup, a position he held for 55 years. A superb all-round athlete, Ross played hockey for the Ottawa Rebels, a team which did much to popularize hockey in Ontario. One of his teammates was the son of Governor-General Lord Stanley who became intrigued by the game and donated the famous trophy that bears his name. Before his death Ross delegated to the NHL "full authority to determine and amend . . . conditions

of competition for the Stanley Cup . . . providing always that the winners . . . shall be acknowledged as the 'World's Professional Hockey Champions'."

Roy, Patrick

b. Quebec City, Quebec, 5 October 1965.

Patrick Roy broke in with the Granby Bisons of the QMJHL in 1982-83 and was drafted fourth by the Montreal Canadiens in 1984. After one more season at Granby he joined Montreal during the 1985-86 season which he capped by winning the Conn Smythe Trophy as the Canadiens won the Stanley Cup. Roy won 15 of 20 playoff games and compiled a 1.92 goals-against average. He made the all-rookie team that same season; shared the William Jennings Trophy with teammate Brian Hayward for the next three years; won the Vezina Trophy in 1989; and was named to all-star teams in 1988 and 1989.

Russell, Ernest

b. Montreal, Quebec, 21 October 1883; d. 23 February 1963. Hall of Fame: 1965

Russell was a fast skater and accomplished stickhandler, equally at home playing center or rover. He collected 180 goals in 98 league games. He is remembered in Montreal for scoring three goals in five consecutive games. In the Eastern Canada League schedule of 1907, he scored 42 goals in nine games. Russell was captain of the Sterling Juniors in 1903 when they won Canada's junior championship. He first appeared in senior hockey with the Winged Wheelers of 1905, but the remainder of his playing career was spent with the Montreal Wanderers with whom he won four Stanley Cups.

St. Louis Blues

The St. Louis Blues joined the NHL as part of the expansion of 1967. Lynn Patrick was hired as general manager-coach, assisted by Scotty Bowman. They set out to build a winning team, acquiring veterans such as Glenn Hall, Al Arbour, Ron Stewart and Jim Roberts. After a slow start, Bowman took over as behind the bench. The team made the playoffs and reached the Cup finals, losing to the Montreal Canadiens as goaltender Hall took home the Conn Smythe Trophy as the most valuable player in the Cup

Peter Zezel of the St. Louis Blues. The circled number 8 on Zezel's shoulder is in memory of Barclay Plager, an original Blues player and coach who died in 1988.

Opposite page: Denis Savard, the playmaking leader of the Chicago Blackhawks has scored more than 100 points five times. One of the NHL's craftiest centermen, he played a major role in helping the Chicago squad win its second consecutive Norris Division flag in the 1990 playoffs.

round. In 1969 and 1970, the Blues finished atop the West Division, reaching the Stanley Cup finals. On-ice performance declined in the 1970s and the team appeared to be in trouble. The appointment of Ron Caron as general manager and director of hockey operations in 1983 began the revitalization of the franchise, despite the fact that the team did not participate in the 1983 Entry Draft. Caron did wonders with the players available and molded the team into a contender in three years. By the end of the 1986-87 season, the Blues had captured the Norris Division title.

CUMULATIVE RECORD	GP	Won	Lost	Tied	Pct
Regular Season	1818	733	803	282	.481
Playoffs	176	78	98	0	.443
Series: 35 W15 L20					
TOTALS	1994	811	901	282	.477

St. Louis Eagles

The Eagles of St. Louis played in the National Hockey League for one season. In 1934-35, St. Louis interests purchased the Ottawa Senators franchise. Most of theOttawa players went to St. Louis as the new club took the Senators' place in

a very tough Canadian Division. They ended up in last place, with an 11-31-6 record. After the Eagles suspended operations, the remaining clubs in the NHL held a draft to distribute the St. Louis players.

Salming, Borje

b. Kiruna, Sweden, 17 April 1951.

The first of what was to become a strong representation of Swedish players in the NHL in the 1970s and into the next two decades, Borje Salming came from Brynas in the Swedish Elite League to the Toronto Maple Leafs in 1973-74. He played 15 seasons for the Leafs before being signed as a free agent by the Detroit Red Wings in June 1989. Salming, an outstanding two-way performer, made the first all-star team in 1976-77 and the second all-stars in 1978 through 1980. His 148 goals and 768 points are all-time marks for Toronto defensemen.

Sather, Glen

b. High River, Alberta, 2 September 1943.

Glen Sather was a serviceable, combative winger with Boston, New York Rangers, St. Louis, Montreal and Minnesota before jumping to the Edmonton Oilers of the WHA for the 1976-77 season. In 658 NHL games he scored 193 points and accumulated 724 penalty minutes. His best offensive year was with Edmonton when he had 19 goals and 34 assists. Sather was signed as coach of the Oilers in January of 1977 and, under him, they made it to the playoffs in 11 consecutive seasons in the WHA and NHL. When Edmonton joined the NHL in 1979-80, he added president and general manager to his titles. After leading the Oilers to six first-place finishes in the Smythe Division and four Stanley Cups, Sather turned the coaching reins over to John Muckler for 1989-90. Sather's NHL coaching record stands at 446-250-104 plus 89-37 in the playoffs. He won the Jack Adams Trophy in 1985-86.

Savard, Denis

b. Pointe Gatineau, Quebec, 4 February 1961.

From his rookie season with the Chicago Blackhawks in 1980-81, Denis Savard demonstrated that he could dipsy-doodle with the puck in a manner that no other player in the NHL could match. Savard's footwork and stickwork were not his only glittering attributes. He was also a gifted scorer. He earned a second all-star berth in 1982-83 when he recorded 35 goals, 86 assists and 121 points. In the 1985 playoffs he tallied 29 points on nine goals and 20 assists in 15 games. He had another superb season in 1987-88, when in 80 games he achieved a career high 131 points on 44 goals and 87 assists.

Savard, Serge

b. Montreal, Quebec, 22 January 1946.
Hall of Fame: 1986

Defenseman Serge Savard played 14 seasons in the NHL with the Montreal Canadiens,and two more with the Winnipeg Jets, totalling 1,040 regular season games. He won eight Stanley Cups with the Canadiens, and was a member of the 1972 Team Canada squad which defeated the Soviet Nationals in the first series between Soviets and the NHL's best. Savard retired from the Canadiens in 1981, but was persuaded to join Winnipeg. His achievements are all the more remarkable, given that his career almost ended during his fourth and fifth seasons when he twice suffered a badly broken leg. Savard joined the Canadiens, and earned the Conn Smythe Trophy as the playoff MVP, in 1969. He also won the Masterton Trophy, exemplifying sportsmanship, perseverance and dedication to hockey, in 1979. He was named managing director of the Canadiens in 1983.

Borje Salming, perhaps the finest European-trained defenseman to ever play in the NHL. Salming's 1,099 games played for the Toronto Maple Leafs ranks him third on that team's all-time list. He was released in 1990 by the Detroit Red Wings after one season on the Motown blueline.

Sawchuk, Terry

b. Winnipeg, Manitoba, 28 December 1929;
d. 31 May 1970. Hall of Fame: 1971

Terry Sawchuk played more seasons and more games, recording more shutouts than any other goalie in the history of the NHL. He played more than 20 NHL seasons, recording 103 shutouts and a lifetime goals-against per game average of 2.52. He was the league's top rookie with Detroit in 1950-51 and, although he played most of his career with the Red Wings, also played for Boston, Toronto, Los Angeles and the New York Rangers before retiring in 1970. He was at his most brilliant in the 1952 playoffs when he led Detroit to the Stanley Cup in the minimum eight games, collecting four shutouts and allowing only five goals-against. He played for three Cup winners in Detroit and another in Toronto, winning the Vezina Trophy on four occasions as well. He died suddenly just after the end of the 1969-70 season.

Schmidt, Milt

b. Kitchener, Ontario, 5 March 1918.
Hall of Fame: 1961

Schmidt centered one of the most potent forward lines in NHL history: the 'Kraut Line,' with Bobby Bauer and Woody Dumart. With the exception of three years in service during World War II, Schmidt played for Boston from 1936-37 until his retirement as a player midway through the 1954-55 season – when he gave up playing to become the team's coach. After sevens seasons of coaching, Schmidt became Boston's general manager. He was a powerful, hard-hitting center who scored 229 goals and 346 points in his career. Schmidt won the league scoring title in 1939-40, and was named the Hart Trophy winner as the player most valuable to his team in 1952. He played for two Stanley Cup-winning teams, and was a four-time all-star.

Schriner, Sweeney

b. Calgary, Alberta, 30 November 1911.
Hall of Fame: 1962

Leftwinger Sweeney Schriner divided his NHL career between the New York Americans and the Toronto Maple Leafs. He played all of his minor hockey in Calgary and turned professional with Syracuse in 1933-34. He moved to New York the following season, and won the Calder Trophy as the league's best rookie. While with the Americans, he was a two-time scoring champion. He remained with the Americans until the 1938-39 season, when he was traded to Toronto in exchange for five players. Schriner played on two Stanley Cup winners with Toronto, scoring 201 goals in 11 NHL campaigns.

Scoring

Scoring points are awarded for goals and assists, both of which are worth one point. The goal scorer is the last player on the team credited with the goal to touch the puck. Up to two assists can be awarded on each goal. These are credited to players on the scoring team who take part in the play immediately preceding the goal. The awarding of points is at the discretion of the game's official scorer. In the NHL, the top scorer each year is awarded the Art Ross Trophy. In the event two players are tied for the point-scoring lead at the end of the season, the player with the greatest number of goals is declared the scoring leader.

Screen Shot

When an attacking player obstructs the view of a goalkeeper as a shot is being directed to the goal by one of his teammates, he is screening the goalie. The shot is called a screen shot.

Seattle Metropolitans

The Seattle Metropolitans of the Pacific Coast Hockey Association won the Stanley Cup in 1917, becoming the first U.S.-based team to do so. The Mets joined the league for the 1915-16 season and included Bernie Morris (PCHA scoring leader), Jack Walker, Cully Wilson and Frank Foyston in the lineup. The following season, they clinched the PCHA title and went on to face the Canadiens in the east-west Cup final. Seattle lost the first game badly, but took the next three as

the Stanley Cup became truly an international symbol of hockey supremacy. The Seattle team continued to produce competitive hockey clubs until its demise in 1924.

Seibert, Earl

b. Berlin, Ontario, 7 December 1911; d. 20 May 1990. Hall of Fame: 1963

Seibert played 15½ NHL seasons, establishing himself as one of the game's all-time great defensemen; he was voted to 10 consecutive all-star teams. He was noted for his rushing ability and scored 89 goals and 276 points: His speed and strong bodychecking as a junior player caught the eye of several clubs, and he eventually turned pro with the Springfield Indians in 1929. He moved up to the New York Rangers in 1931-32, and became a defensive standout and adept shot-blocker. He was later traded to Chicago, and from Chicago to Detroit. His father, Oliver, was previously elected to the Hockey Hall of Fame, making them the first father-son combination so honored.

Seibert, Oliver

b. Berlin, Ontario, 18 March 1881; d. 15 May 1944. Hall of Fame: 1961

Starting as a goaltender for Berlin (later Kitchener), Ontario, the speedy Seibert switched to forward and starred for many years. He was one of the first Canadians to play on artificial ice when he competed in an exhibition game in St. Louis, and was also the first Berlin player to turn professional. After playing for the Berlin Rangers, champions of the Western Ontario Hockey Association for six straight seasons, Seibert turned pro with Houghton, Michigan. He also played professionally with London and Guelph in the Ontario Pro League, and with teams in the Northwestern Michigan League. He was the father of Earl Seibert, another Hall of Fame member.

Selke, Frank

b. Berlin, Ontario, 7 May 1893; d. 3 July 1985. Hall of Fame: Builder, 1960

Frank J. Selke served hockey as a coach, manager and executive for more than 60 years. After managing minor teams in his hometown, he moved to Toronto in 1918 where he became a friend and associate of Conn Smythe. He was part of the Leafs' front office through the team's early days and left Toronto in 1946 after being assistant general manager to Smythe for three Stanley Cup teams. He moved to Montreal where he managed six more Cup champions, retiring after 18 years as general manager of the Canadiens.

Eddie Shore during his playing days with the Boston Bruins. Shore went on to become the owner of the AHL's Springfield Indians, quickly establishing himself as a shrewd businessman. He was known to be as tough in the front office as he was on the blueline.

Senior Hockey

Age division in amateur hockey for any player over the age of twenty, and at one time, one of the most popular brands of hockey played in North America. Senior hockey champions in Canada are awarded the Allan Cup, which was donated by Sir Montagu Allan in 1909 when the Stanley Cup became a professional trophy. Until 1963, the Allan Cup winners often represented the country in the World Hockey Championships, winning 11 of Canada's 19 world titles. At the peak of its popularity in the late 1950's and early 1960's, every province had at least one senior hockey league and dozens of teams. Now there are only a couple of senior 'AAA' leagues left in Canada, leaving the future of the Allan Cup in jeopardy.

Seven-Man Hockey

While hockey's first rules stipulated nine men per side, seven-man hockey soon predominated. The seven men played the following positions: goal, point, cover-point, rover, and three forwards (sometimes referred to as right wing, center, and left wing). Seven-man hockey was played in eastern and central Canada until the 1911-12 season, and in the west (PCHA) until the 1922-23. William E. Northey of the Montreal Arena is credited with first suggesting the reduction of the sides from seven to six, and upon his suggestion in 1911, the six-man game was adopted. For the season of 1912-13, it was agreed to play the second half of the season under the old seven-man rules, but after eight games in February, the NHA agreed to leave the game at six men per side. The cover-point was a defensive position and the cover-point man played directly behind the rover, and in front of the point man. While the rover was the first defenseman an attacker would meet, the cover-point worked with the point man to stop any attack and send the puck back to the opposing zone. The point was also a defensive position and the point man played a position directly in front of the goaltender, and directly behind the cover-point man. His role was to intercept the play and return the puck to the offensive zone. It was highly unusual for the a defensive player to carry the puck into the forward zone. Most often he would loft the puck above the heads of his fellows and into the charge of the opposing squad. The real skill of the position involved breaking up the attack of the offensive side. The rover was a free-ranging position, as the title suggested, with both offensive and defensive responsibilities. The rover would act as an attacker when the play was in the offensive zone, and as a defenseman when the play shifted into home territory.

Shore, Eddie

b. Fort Qu.Appelle, Saskatchewan, 25 November 1902; d. 16 March 1985.
Hall of Fame: 1947

One of the NHL's most colorful players, Shore took a backseat to no one. He had an explosive temper and hockey ability to match. The defenseman picked up 1,047 minutes of penalties in 553 games. Shore broke into the NHL in 1926 with the Boston Bruins and came to personify the most vigorous aspects of a hard, rough and fast game. His great talent enabled him to take over the offense and set up plays, literally knocking down any opponent in his way. During his 13-year stay with the Bruins, Shore scored 105 goals and added 179 assists. He concluded his NHL career with the New York Americans in the 1939-40 season. He is the only defenseman to win the Hart Trophy as the league's MVP four times. Shore played on two Stanley Cup winners, and was an eight-time all-star.

Shot on Goal

A puck directed toward the opposing goal that either enters the net or would enter the net if not stopped by a member of the defending team is credited as a shot on goal. Shots that hit the posts or crossbar of the net are not counted as shots on goal. In most arenas both the home and visiting teams' shot totals are displayed on a separate scoreboard called a shot clock. Shots on goal are often a useful indicator of the flow of play in a game.

Siebert, Albert (Babe)

b. Plattsville, Ontario, 14 January 1904; d. 25 August 1939. Hockey Hall of Fame: 1964

Siebert was a broad-shouldered giant who played with cool confidence. Although still a junior, he moved up to play for the Niagara Falls seniors in 1924-25 and made the jump to the NHL with the Montreal Maroons the following season. He was an outstanding leftwinger and combined with Nels Stewart and Hooley Smith to form the Maroons' highly-rated 'S Line' which played effectively for five seasons. Siebert was later traded to Boston, and then returned to Montreal to play with the Canadiens in 1936. Although his speed was gone, Siebert developed into an outstanding defenseman – so good, in fact, that he was voted the Hart Trophy as the NHL's most valuable player to his team during that regular season. He was named a first team all-star on defense in three straight seasons, beginning in 1935-36. He retired after the 1938-39 season and had been appointed coach of the Canadiens when he lost his life in a drowning accident.

Officials' Signals

The Referee is responsible for almost all the signals during a hockey game. The only ones the Linesmen are responsible for are: Icing, Slow Whistle and Washout. When a goal is disallowed, it is the Referee who signals Washout.

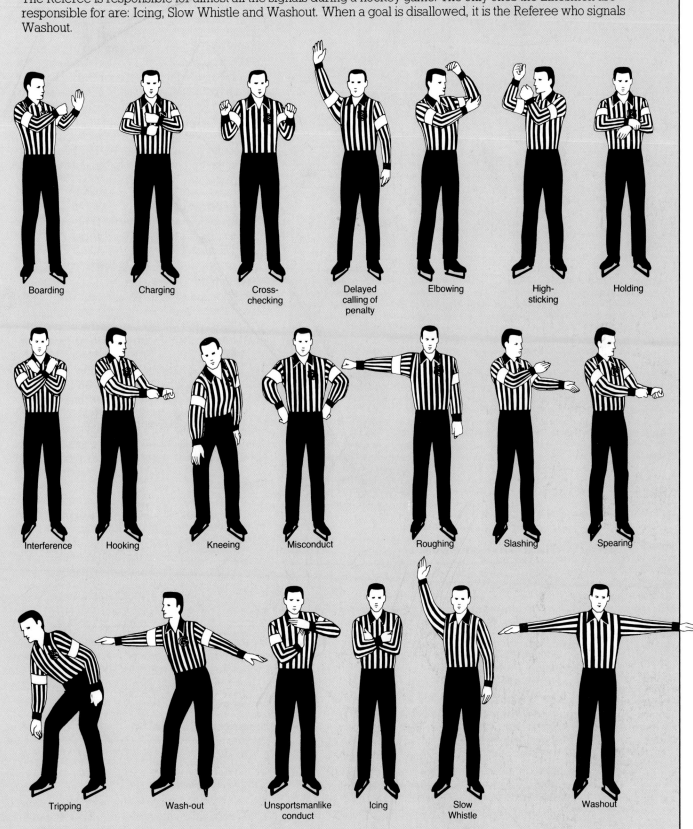

Boarding

Charging

Cross-checking

Delayed calling of penalty

Elbowing

High-sticking

Holding

Interference

Hooking

Kneeing

Misconduct

Roughing

Slashing

Spearing

Tripping

Wash-out

Unsportsmanlike conduct

Icing

Slow Whistle

Washout

**Harold "Bullet Joe"
Simpson in the uniform
of his only NHL squad,
the New York
Americans. Bullet Joe
came by his nickname
honestly; he was
injured twice during
World War I. He
survived these wounds
to become a star with
Edmonton in the WCHL
and a Hall of Fame
member.**

Simpson, Bullet Joe

*b. Selkirk, Manitoba, 13 August 1893; d. 26
December 1973. Hall of Fame: 1962*

In his prime, Simpson was described by Newsy
Lalonde as the "greatest living hockey player."
Not exceptionally big for a defenseman, Simpson had speed to burn, earning him his nickname. He won the Allan Cup with the Winnipeg
61st Battalion club. Returning to hockey following World War I, Simpson played a season with
the Selkirk Fishermen before joining the
Edmonton Eskimos in 1921-22 for four seasons
during which the Eskimos twice won the Western Canada Hockey League championship. Joe
joined the New York Americans of the NHL in
1925-26, remaining with that team as a player
until 1931. He managed the Americans from 1932
until 1935, and then managed New Haven and
Minneapolis before retiring from the game.

Sinden, Harry

*b. Collins Bay, Ontario, 14 September 1932.
Hall of Fame: Builder, 1983*

Harry Sinden was a fine senior player who was
captain of the Whitby Dunlops, IIHF world
champions in 1958. After working in the minors,
he became coach of the Boston Bruins in 1966.
The club made the playoffs for the first time in
nine years the following season and, two years
later, won its first Stanley Cup since 1940-41. He
went into private business the next season, but
returned to the game in 1972 as coach of Team
Canada for its memorable 4-3-1 series win
against the Soviet Union. He became general
manager of the Bruins in 1972-73.

Sittler, Darryl

*b. St. Jacobs, Ontario, 18 September 1950.
Hall of Fame: 1989*

Center Darryl Sittler played 15 NHL seasons,
working hard in every game. He began his
professional career in Toronto, playing 11 seasons with the Leafs. He was the team's top scorer
in six years and left Toronto as the club's all-time
goal scoring leader with 389. He had a dream
night in February of 1976, scoring six goals and
four assists for 10 points against the Boston
Bruins. He was a member of Team Canada later
that same year, scoring the overtime winner
against Czechoslovakia in the final game of the
first Canada Cup tournament. Sittler went on to
play in Philadelphia and Detroit, retiring with
484 goals and 637 assists for 1,121 points in 1985.

Slapshot

Refers to a hard shot made by a player who
literally slaps the puck with his stick, propelling
it at much greater speed than the conventional
wrist shot. Slapshots of the best professional
players are often timed at more than 90 miles
per hour.

Slot

A prime scoring area located directly in front of
the goal crease, between the two faceoff circles.
Proficient goal scorers often position themselves
in the slot to receive passes or corral rebounds
for a quick shot on net.

Smeaton, Cooper

*b. Carleton Place, Ontario, 22 July 1890;
d. 3 October 1978.
Hall of Fame: Referee, 1961*

Although he had more than one offer to become
a professional hockey player, J. Cooper Smeaton
instead became an outstanding referee. He

joined the staff of the NHA in 1913 and worked many Allan and Stanley Cup games. He managed the Philadelphia Quakers of the NHL in 1930-31, but returned to refereeing the following year when Philadelphia withdrew from the league. Smeaton was appointed head referee of the NHL and continued until his retirement in 1937. In 1946, he was appointed a trustee of the Stanley Cup, a position he held until his death in 1978.

Smith, Bill

b. Perth, Ontario, 12 December 1950.
Few goaltenders have come up with more clutch wins than Bill Smith who steered the Islanders to four consecutive Stanley Cup victories beginning in 1980. Claimed from Los Angeles in the 1972 expansion draft, Smith went through tough times with the fledgling Islanders. But by 1974-75, he played in 58 games, won 21, lost 18 and

tied 17. His goals-against average had dropped to 2.78. Smith continued to improve, and for some time shared goaltending duties with Glenn 'Chico' Resch. In 1979-80, the Islanders reached the Stanley Cup finals and Smith was designated the number one goalie. He played in 20 playoff games, winning 15. He continued starring for the Islanders from that point on, and finally retired at the conclusion of the 1988-89 season. His association with the New York team continued, and in 1989-90 he worked with the team's young goaltenders.

Smith, Bobby

b. North Sydney, Nova Scotia, 2 February 1958.
From his rookie year with the Minnesota North Stars (1978-79) to the present, center Bobby Smith has been one of the most dangerous shooters in the league. He scored 69 goals and had 123 assists in his last year of junior hockey

Darryl Sittler had a career year in 1976. He scored a NHL record 10 points in a game against the Boston Bruins, set an NHL playoff record with five goals against the Philadelphia Flyers and scored the winning goal in overtime for Team Canada in the 1976 Canada Cup.

but started slowly in the NHL. He came on late in the season to lead the North Stars in scoring with 30 goals and 74 points, earning him the Calder Trophy. He tallied 114 points in 1981-82, his best year, and was traded to Montreal for Keith Acton, Mark Napier, and a future draft choice early in the 1983-84 season. A major asset to the Canadiens, in 1985-86 he helped them to a Stanley Cup win and, in 1987-88, totaled 93 points.

Smith, Floyd

b. Perth, Ontario, 16 May 1935.

Throughout his eleven-year NHL career, Floyd Smith was a model of the steady, unspectacular defensive forward. He became coach of the Buffalo Sabres in May of 1974, leading the team to the Stanley Cup final that season. Two years later, Smith was moved to a scouting position and finally returned to coaching in 1978-79 with the Cincinnati Stingers of the WHA. He returned to the NHL the following season with Toronto,

and stayed with the Leafs throughout the 1980s, serving in different capacities. He became interim general manager in 1989 after the resignation of Gord Stellick and continued to hold down the g.m.'s portfolio in 1989-90.

Smith, Mike

b. Potsdam, New York, 31 August 1945.

Mike Smith's first NHL job was as assistant to the conditioning coach of the New York Rangers in 1976. He later became an assistant coach in New York and moved to Colorado as an assistant with the Rockies. He later moved to the Winnipeg organization as g.m. of the club's CHL farm club in Tulsa. He also wrote several hockey coaching manuals and a book entitled 'Life After Hockey' about former NHLers' adjustments to civilian life. He became Winnipeg's director of recruiting in 1981-82 and remained in that position until December of 1988 when he replaced John Ferguson as general manager.

Smith, Neil

b. Toronto, Ontario, 9 January 1954.

Named general manager of the New York Rangers on July 17, 1989, Neil Smith had spent a lifetime in hockey, first as a young player in Toronto, and then as an all-American defense-man with Western Michigan University. Drafted in 1974 by the New York Islanders, Smith stayed in college, receiving degrees in communications and business. He played two seasons in the IHL and then moved into the administrative side of the game when he was hired by the New York Islanders' Jimmy Devellano. He followed Devallano to Detroit as a scout and g.m. of the club.s Adirondack farm team, later moving to the Rangers as g.m.

Smith, Reginald (Hooley)

b. Toronto, Ontario 7 January 1903; d. 24 August 1963. Hall of Fame: 1972

Smith was a standout member of the Granites, winners of the Olympic hockey championship for Canada in 1924. He turned professional with Ottawa the following year, playing right wing. The Senators won the Stanley Cup in 1926-27. He was dealt to the Montreal Maroons the next season, and it was there that he combined with Nels Stewart and Babe Siebert to form the 'S Line' – a trio that combined scoring punch with aggressive play. The Maroons won the Stanley Cup in 1935; Smith, captain of the team, was named first team all-star center the next season. He was traded to Boston in 1936-37 and after one season joined the New York Americans, where he completed his career with his 200th goal in 1940-41.

Reginald "Hooley" Smith in his days with the Montreal Maroons. Smith wanted to play with Toronto, but when they couldn't meet his salary demands, he brashly named a couple of players the team could get rid of so they could pay him the salary he wanted. The St. Pats refused Smith's proposal, so he signed with Ottawa. He later played for the Maroons, Bruins and Americans.

Smith, Thomas

b. Ottawa, Ontario, 27 September 1885;
d. 1 August 1966. Hall of Fame: 1973

At 5-4 and 150 pounds, center/leftwinger Tommy Smith was known as a little bulldog of a player. He moved up to senior hockey with the Ottawa Victorias of the Federal Amateur Hockey League in 1906, leading the league in scoring. He joined Pittsburgh of the International League in 1907, leading his team with 23 goals in 22 games, and, in 1909, led all scorers in the Ontario Professional Hockey League. Smith played for Quebec in 1913, winning a Stanley Cup. He was dealt to the Canadiens in 1917, retiring from hockey when the National Hockey Association dissolved the next year. He came back to play 10 scoreless games for Quebec in 1919, finally retiring at age 35. He scored 239 goals in 171 recorded league games.

Vladimir Krutov in action during the 1987 Canada Cup. Krutov was part of the first Soviet "Airlift" to the NHL in 1989-90, joining Vancouver.

Snider, Ed

b. Washington, D.C., 6 January 1933.
Hall of Fame: Builder, 1988

Ed Snider was instrumental in bringing the Flyers to Philadelphia as part of the 1967 NHL expansion. He was part of the group that built the Spectrum in 1966 and, under his leadership as team president, the Flyers became an exemplary organization from front office to dressing room. In 1973-74 they became the first of the expansion teams to register 100 points in the regular season and win the Stanley Cup, a feat they repeated the following year. The Flyers remain a model sports franchise, making a strong contribution to their community. Philadelphia hosted the 1990-91 All-Star game.

Soviet Union (USSR)

An IIHF member since 1952, the Soviet Union quickly established itself as a major hockey power. Having been first introduced to hockey in 1932, the Soviets used the skills acquired in a traditional ice and ball game called bandy to form their own style of hockey. Emphasizing speed, passing and teamwork, the Soviet Union, after eight intense years of training, entered its first World Championships in 1954. The team's hard work paid off as the Soviets won. From that time forward the Soviets have proven themselves to be the dominant power in Olympic and World Championship competitions. As of January 1, 1990, the Soviet Union has won 23 World or Olympic titles. On the home front, the Soviet Union's first division consists of 14 clubs. By the end of the 1980s, Soviet players began to appear in the NHL.

The canny Conn Smythe giving some spectators a few pointers. When Smythe turned over control of the Leafs to his son Stafford in 1957, the younger Smythe appointed a group known as the "Silver Seven" to run the operation. This prompted Toronto scribes to muse that it took at least that many men to replace the man known as "The Major".

Smythe, Conn

b. Toronto, Ontario, 1 February, 1895;
d. 18 November 1980.
Hall of Fame: Builder, 1958

Conn Smythe was a natural leader and the man who made professional hockey a first-rank attraction in Toronto. A former captain of the University of Toronto Varsity team that won the Ontario championship in 1915, he coached the Varsity seniors to the 1927 Allan Cup and, playing as the Varsity Grads, to the 1928 Olympic title as well. He was hired by the newly-established NHL New York Rangers, but was released after assembling the team that won the 1927-28 Stanley Cup playoffs. He then purchased the Toronto St. Pats and changed the club's name to the Maple Leafs. By November, 1931, Maple Leaf Gardens was constructed and Smythe became managing director and later president of the Gardens, retiring in 1961 after his teams had won seven Stanley Cups.

Spengler Cup

Early competitive hockey in Europe centered around the Swiss winter resort of Davos. In 1923 a tournament for club teams was inaugurated and a trophy was donated by Dr. Carl Spengler who organized the event with the help of another physician, Dr. Paul Muller. The Oxford University hockey club was the first winner in 1923, and tournaments have been held regularly since then. Unlike most European hockey tournaments which were abandoned during the early 1940s, Spengler Cup matches were held throughout the War years of 1941-45, but were limited to Swiss teams. Played every year at Christmas week, the Spengler Cup has recently welcomed North American teams, and in 1984 a team of Canadian collegians and pros playing in Europe became the first North American club to claim the trophy. In 1988 the U.S. Selects won, while the 1989 winner was Moscow Spartak. Dr. Spengler died in 1937.

Stanley, Allan

b. Timmins, Ontario, 1 March 1928.
Hall of Fame: 1981

During his 21-year NHL career as a defenseman, Stanley's play was often eclipsed by that of some of the game.s all-times greats – including Doug Harvey, Red Kelly, Tim Horton and Harry Howell. Yet he was one of the most durable of players, playing 1,244 regular-season and 109 playoff games. Stanley was a three-time second team all-star, and played on four Stanley Cup winners with the Toronto Maple Leafs. Stanley broke into the NHL with the New York Rangers in 1948. He later played for the Chicago Blackhawks, Boston Bruins, and Maple Leafs before concluding his career with the Philadelphia Flyers in 1968-69.

Stanley, Barney

b. Paisley, Ontario, 1 January 1893; d. 16 May 1971. Hall of Fame: 1961

In a 15-year professional career, Stanley played every position except goaltender.Despite his tenure in the game, his only Stanley Cup win came in 1915, his first year as a pro when he was a member of the Vancouver Millionaires. He remained with the Millionaires through the 1918-19 season, and then played a season with the Edmonton Eskimos – an amateur club which he also coached. He returned to the pro ranks in 1920 as player and coach of the Calgary Tigers, and assumed similar duties with the Regina Capitals in 1922. He coached and managed the Chicago Blackhawks in 1927-28, played the following season with the Minneapolis Millers, and returned to coaching with the Edmonton Pooler juniors for three years.

Stanley Cup

The Stanley Cup, the oldest trophy competed for by professional athletes in North America, was donated by Frederick Arthur, Lord Stanley of Preston, Earl of Derby and Governor-General of Canada in 1893. Lord Stanley purchased a silver bowl for 10 guineas ($50) for presentation to the amateur hockey champions of Canada. In its earliest days it was a challenge trophy and often was defended several times a year. Since 1910, when the National Hockey Association took possession of the trophy, the Cup has been the symbol of professional hockey supremacy. It has been competed for only by NHL teams since 1926 and has been under the exclusive control of the NHL since 1946. The trophy itself has undergone numerous modifications and has the names of players and executives on Cup-winning teams engraved upon it. It is one of the most impressive cups in sport.

Lord Stanley of Preston's sons were hockey players and fans, and it was their enthusiasm for the game that prompted him to donate the now-famous trophy.

Stanley, Lord of Preston

b. England, 1841; d. 14 July 1908.
Hall of Fame: Builder, 1945

Lord Stanley of Preston, G.C.B., was Governor-General of Canada from 1888 to 1893. During his final year of office, he donated a trophy to be awarded to the championship hockey club of Canada. This came to be known as the Stanley Cup, and originally cost the equivalent of $50. Until 1906, only amateur clubs played for the Stanley Cup but by 1910, it became symbolic of professional hockey supremacy. When the Western Canada League disbanded in 1926, it became the NHL's playoff championship trophy.

The original Stanley Cup as it looked when it was donated by Lord Stanley of Preston. This original bowl sat on the modern trophy until it was replaced in 1967, although this fact was not disclosed until 1970.

Stanley Cup Winners

Season	Champions
1989-90	Edmonton Oilers
1988-89	Calgary Flames
1987-88	Edmonton Oilers
1986-87	Edmonton Oilers
1985-86	Montreal Canadiens
1984-85	Edmonton Oilers
1983-84	Edmonton Oilers
1982-83	New York Islanders
1981-82	New York Islanders
1980-81	New York Islanders
1979-80	New York Islanders
1978-79	Montreal Canadiens
1977-78	Montreal Canadiens
1976-77	Montreal Canadiens
1975-76	Montreal Canadiens
1974-75	Philadelphia Flyers
1973-74	Philadelphia Flyers
1972-73	Montreal Canadiens
1971-72	Boston Bruins
1970-71	Montreal Canadiens
1969-70	Boston Bruins
1968-69	Montreal Canadiens
1967-68	Montreal Canadiens
1966-67	Toronto Maple Leafs
1965-66	Montreal Canadiens
1964-65	Montreal Canadiens
1963-64	Toronto Maple Leafs
1962-63	Toronto Maple Leafs
1961-62	Toronto Maple Leafs
1960-61	Chicago Black Hawks
1959-60	Montreal Canadiens
1958-59	Montreal Canadiens
1957-58	Montreal Canadiens
1956-57	Montreal Canadiens
1955-56	Montreal Canadiens
1954-55	Detroit Red Wings
1953-54	Detroit Red Wings
1952-53	Montreal Canadiens
1951-52	Detroit Red Wings
1950-51	Toronto Maple Leafs
1949-50	Detroit Red Wings
1948-49	Toronto Maple Leafs
1947-48	Toronto Maple Leafs
1946-47	Toronto Maple Leafs
1945-46	Montreal Canadiens
1944-45	Toronto Maple Leafs
1943-44	Montreal Canadiens
1942-43	Detroit Red Wings
1941-42	Toronto Maple Leafs
1940-41	Boston Bruins
1939-40	New York Rangers
1938-39	Boston Bruins
1937-38	Chicago Black Hawks
1936-37	Detroit Red Wings
1935-36	Detroit Red Wings
1934-35	Montreal Maroons
1933-34	Chicago Black Hawks
1932-33	New York Rangers
1931-32	Toronto Maple Leafs
1930-31	Montreal Canadiens
1929-30	Montreal Canadiens
1928-29	Boston Bruins
1927-28	New York Rangers
1926-27	Ottawa Senators
1925-26	Montreal Maroons
1924-25	Victoria Cougars
1923-24	Montreal Canadiens
1922-23	Ottawa Senators
1921-22	Toronto St. Pats
1920-21	Ottawa Senators
1919-20	Ottawa Senators
1918-19	No decision.*
1917-18	Toronto Arenas

Stanley Cup Winners prior to formation of NHL in 1917

Season	Champion
1916-17	Seattle Metropolitans
1915-16	Montreal Canadiens
1914-15	Vancouver Millionaires
1913-14	Toronto Blueshirts
1912-13	Quebec Bulldogs
1911-12	Quebec Bulldogs
1910-11	Ottawa Senators
1909-10	Montreal Wanderers
1908-09	Ottowa Senators
1907-08	Montreal Wanderers
1906-07	Montreal Wanderers (March)
1906-07	Kenora Thistles (January)
1905-06	Montreal Wanderers
1905-06	Ottawa Silver Seven
1904-05	Ottawa Silver Seven
1903-04	Ottawa Silver Seven
1902-03	Ottawa Silver Seven
1902-03	Montreal A.A.A.
1901-02	Montreal A.A.A.
1901-02	Winnipeg Victorias
1900-01	Winnipeg Victorias
1899-1900	Montreal Shamrocks
1898-99	Montreal Shamrocks
1898-99	Montreal Victorias
1897-98	Montreal Victorias
1896-97	Montreal Victorias
1895-96	Montreal Victorias
1895-96	Montreal Victorias
1894-95	Montreal Victorias
1893-94	Montreal A.A.A.
1892-93	Montreal A.A.A.

*In the spring of 1919 the Montreal Canadiens travelled to Seattle to meet Seattle, PCHL champions. After five games had been played – teams were tied at 2 wins and 1 tie – the series was called off by the local Department of Health because of the influenza epidemic and the death from influenza of Joe Hall.

Stastny, Peter

b. Bratislava, Czechoslovakia, 18 September 1956.

One of five hockey playing brothers and the most famous of three who would defect from Czechoslovakia in order to play with the Quebec Nordiques of the NHL. Though he didn.t learn to skate until he was 11, Peter Stastny took to the game and became a member of the world champion Czechoslovakian national teams in 1976 and 1977. Along with his younger brother Anton, he defected in the summer of 1980 and was followed by his older brother Marian less than a year later. Peter was an instant success in the NHL, winning the Calder Trophy as rookie of the year in 1980-81. On six occasions he has finished in the top ten in NHL scoring. A career highlight occurred on May 2, 1985, when he scored a series-winning goal in overtime against archrival Montreal in the seventh and final game

of the Adams Division final. The Nordiques' all-time leader in career assists and points, Stastny was traded to New Jersey in March 1990.

Stewart, Black Jack

b. Pilot Mound, Manitoba, 6 May 1917; d. 25 May 1983. Hall of Fame: 1964

Stewart played junior hockey in Portage la Prairie, Manitoba, for two seasons before signing a pro contract with the Detroit Red Wings in 1938. The Wings sent him to Pittsburgh but recalled him for 33 games that season, and he quickly established himself as a great defenseman. A regular with Detroit through 1949-50, the Wings dealt him to Chicago – where he finished his playing career at the end of the 1952-53 season. He played on two Stanley Cup winners with Detroit, and was a five-time NHL all-star. After leaving the professional game, Stewart coached and managed the Chatham Maroons of

the OHA senior league. He later coached Pittsburgh of the American Hockey League, retiring from hockey in 1963.

Stewart, Nels (Old Poison)

b. Montreal, Quebec, 29 December 1902; d. 21 August 1957. Hall of Fame: 1962

Center Nels Stewart's deadly accurate shot earned him his nickname from goalies around the NHL. A burly 200-pounder, 'Old Poison' collected 324 goals and 191 assists in 653 league games. He was the first player to score more than 300 goals in the NHL, and was the league's all-time goal-scoring leader until surpassed by Maurice Richard. Stewart joined the Montreal Maroons for the 1925-26 season, scoring 34 goals. His seasonal best was 39 goals in 1929-30. Later traded to Boston and the New York Americans, he retired in 1939-40 as a two-time winner of the Hart Trophy. He won one Stanley Cup.

Team Sweden in action during the 1987 Canada Cup. Sweden has been the most successful hockey nation in western Europe, sending more players to the NHL and winning more IIHF World Championship titles than any European country other than the Soviet Union.

Stick Handling

A player adept at moving the puck with his stick, as well as sending and receiving passes is said to be a good stickhandler. In the early days of the game, rules limiting forward passing made stickhandling a vital skill.

Storey, Red

b. Barrie, Ontario, 5 March 1918.
Hall of Fame: Referee, 1967

Red Storey was a standout football player until a knee injury ended his career in 1940. He is famous for coming off the bench to score three touchdowns for the Toronto Argonauts in the final 13 minutes of the 1938 Grey Cup championship game. He stayed in sports as an official, working both football and lacrosse, but it was for his work as an NHL referee from 1951 to 1959 that he was best known. One of the most colorful officials in the game, Storey says his biggest thrill was "just being involved with a great bunch of guys."

Stuart, Bruce

b. Ottawa, Ontario, 1882; d. 28 October 1961.
Hall of Fame: 1961

Stuart played for the Montreal Wanderers when they won the Cup in 1908, and for the Ottawa Senators when they won Cups in 1909 and 1911. He was an all-around forward, although he excelled as a rover. He joined the Ottawa Senators in 1898, and played with them for two seasons before joining the Quebec Bulldogs. In his three Cup victories, Stuart scored 17 goals in seven games. In 45 scheduled games during his career, Stuart scored 63 goals – once scoring six in a game.

Stuart, Hod

b. Ottawa, Ontario, 1879; d 23 June 1907.
Hall of Fame: 1945

Rated one of the best defenseman of all time, Stuart rose through the minor ranks of Ottawa. He broke into big-league hockey with the Ottawa Senators in 1899 and moved to the Quebec Bulldogs in 1900. After the 1901-02 season, he moved to Calumet, Michigan, of the International Pro League where he also acted as captain and manager. He later joined the Montreal Wanderers, winning the Stanley Cup in 1907.

Super Series

As relations between the NHL and Soviet Hockey Federation warmed in the 1970s and 1980s, more and more exchanges between NHL clubs and Soviet teams took place. Super Series was the name given to mid-season visits by Soviet clubs to play NHL opponents. In 1989-90 the Super Series encompassed 21 games with each NHL team playing one of four Soviet opponents. The NHL lost 9-11, with one tie.

Sutherland, James

b. Kingston, Ontario, 10 October 1870; d. 30 September 1955. Hall of Fame: Builder, 1947

Often referred to as the Father of Hockey, Captain James T. Sutherland made Kingston, Ontario, a famous hockey center during the years prior to World War I. He coached the Kingston Frontenac Juniors and rose through district and provincial executive ranks to become president of the OHA in 1915. He served two years in that office and later, after returning from overseas service in World War I, moved on to become president of the Canadian Amateur Hockey Association in 1919.

Sutter, Brian

b. Viking, Alberta, 7 October 1956.

Hardworking leftwinger Brian Sutter joined St. Louis in 1976-77 and spent his entire career skating for the Blues. He retired after the 1987-88 season to become the Blues' coach and proved himself to be as effective behind the bench as he had been on the ice. At his peak as a player, Sutter teamed with Wayne Babych and Bernie Federko to form an excellent attacking line. Sutter scored 41 goals and had 39 assists for 80 points in 1978-79. In 1982-83 he scored 46 goals and had 30 assists for 76 points. A leader and team captain, Sutter was the eldest of six brothers who all played in the NHL. Injuries hampered his career in its later stages, hastening his move to coaching.

Sutter Family

At one point during the 1980s, the Sutter family of Viking, Alberta, had no less than six brothers playing in the NHL as eldest brother Brian was joined by Darryl, Duane, Brent and twins Rich and Ron. Brian was the first of the brothers to make it big in the NHL, signing on with the St. Louis Blues in 1976-77. He remained with the club until the conclusion of the 1987-88 season whereupon he became the St. Louis coach. Darryl became a member of the Chicago Blackhawks in 1979-80 and after his NHL career turned to minor-league coaching. Duane Sutter, in his rookie NHL season with the Islanders in 1979-80, helped the Isles to their first of four straight Stanley Cups. Duane was later traded to the Chicago Blackhawks and remained with them through the 1989-90 campaign. Brent was also an Islander, joining the team in 1981. The twins, Rich and Ron, hoped to be NHL teammates. But Rich was drafted in 1982 by the Pittsburgh Penguins while Ron was picked by the Philadelphia Flyers. Ron remained a member of the Philadelphia team through the 1980s and into the new decade whereas Rich was first traded to the Vancouver Canucks and then to the St. Louis Blues. The Sutters' trademark has always been hustle and tough play. Their tenacity was summed up by the nicknames of Duane and Brent when they were teammates on the Islanders: Duane was 'Dog' and Brent was 'Pup'.

Sweden

Swedish hockey is among the best in Europe. The country's national team won the World Championship in 1953, 1957, 1962 and 1987. The Swedes also reached the finals of the Canada Cup in 1981 and 1984 and won the World Junior tournament in 1981. Beginning in the mid-1970s, Swedish players began to make their marks in the NHL with 155 drafted since 1974. Borje Salming and Inge Hammarstrom joined the Toronto Maple Leafs in 1974 and were soon followed by players like Kent Nilsson, Mats Naslund, Kjell Samuelsson and Patrik Sundstrom. The elite division of the Swedish hockey league consists of 12 teams playing a 40-game schedule.

Tarasov, Anatoli

b. Soviet Union, 1918.
Hall of Fame: Builder, 1974

Anatoli Tarasov coached the Soviet Union's national team to nine straight world amateur championships and three consecutive Olympic titles before retiring in 1972. In the late 1940s and early 1950s he played for Soviet teams that rapidly improved in interhational competition. As a coach, he converted many aspects of North American hockey to his own use. He also stressed off-ice conditioning for his players and, in 1987, served as a coaching consultant to the Vancouver Canucks.

Taylor, Fred (Cyclone)

b. Tara, Ontario, 23 June 1883; d. 9 June 1979.
Hall of Fame: 1947

Taylor was a brilliant player who starred at defense, center and rover. His furious end-to-end rushes earned him his nickname. He first

FRED TAYLOR

Fred "Cyclone" Taylor in the uniform of the Renfrew Millionaires. Taylor's name is associated with one of the great myths from the early days of hockey; his brash prediction that he would skate backwards and score against his old Ottawa teammates. Opinion is divided on whether Cyclone actually accomplished this feat, but one thing is clear: it put his name in hockey folklore forever.

Tiny Thompson led all NHL goaltenders in goals against average four times in the 1930s. He won a Stanley Cup with Boston in 1929.

attracted attention while playing in Listowel, Ontario, and turned pro with Houghton, Michigan, in 1906. He spent two-year hitches with Ottawa and Renfrew and then joined Vancouver in 1912-13, remaining there until retirement in 1920-21. Cyclone collected 194 goals in 186 league games, winning two consecutive scoring titles while with Vancouver. He earned Stanley Cups with Ottawa and Vancouver. In 1960 at age 83, he participated in the sod-turning ceremony for the first Hockey Hall of Fame building in Toronto.

Team Canada '72

One of the most unusual and famous hockey teams of all time was the one selected in 1972 to take on the Soviet Nationals in what was considered to be hockey's summit series. The series, which began with four games in Canada and concluded with four more in the Soviet Union, marked the first time an NHL squad had taken on the Soviets top stars in a truly formal competition that resembled a playoff series. Team Canada was managed by a group including Alan Eagleson, head of the National Hockey League Players' Association, Harry Sinden and John Ferguson. The team began practising during the summer of 1972 in preparation for the September series. Players on Team Canada included Phil Esposito, Brad Park, Frank Mahovlich, Ken Dryden, Tony Esposito, Paul Henderson, Serge Savard, Yvan Cournoyer and Rod Gilbert. Soviet stars included Valeri Kharlamov, Alexander Yakushev, Boris Mikhailov and Vladislav Tretiak. Initial predictions had the NHL winning easily, but the strength of the Soviets was severely underestimated. Team Canada was shocked and defeated in its opening game at the Montreal Forum and trailed the Soviets when the series transferred to Russia by two games to one with one tie. Despite losing the first game played in Moscow, Sinden and Ferguson rallied the Canadians and they came from behind to win the series by winning the last three games. Paul Henderson had the winning goal in all three contests including the tie-breaker with 34 seconds to go in game eight.

Television

Hockey's TV roots go back to the very earliest days of the medium when experiments were attempted with various sports. Like other major sports, hockey did not appear regularly on television until after World War II, but the first telecast of an NHL game took place on February 25, 1940, when the Montreal Canadiens and New York Rangers played at Madison Square Garden. The game was shown on experimental station W2XBS, which is now WNBC-TV. The

Rangers won 6-2 with approximately 300 people watching the game on television. Once the new medium was refined following the conclusion of World War II, television began zeroing in on sporting events and, in the late 1940s, hockey once again appeared on the screen. The pioneer announcers were Win Elliot, who handled play-by-play for New York Rangers' games on station WPIX-TV, along with Bud Palmer, a former basketball star who turned announcer. In Canada, televised hockey began in the 1952-53 season. NHL hockey appeared on U.S. network TV in the 1970s and became a popular attraction on local, regional and national cable systems in the 1980s. The sport returned to network TV in the U.S. in 1990 when NBC Sports telecast the NHL all-star game from Pittsburgh.

Thompson, Cecil (Tiny)

b. Sandon, British Columbia, 31 May 1903;
d. 9 February 1981. Hall of Fame: 1959.
Tiny Thompson won the Vezina Trophy as the NHL top goaltender in 1929-30, 1932-33, 1935-36 and 1937-38. He joined Boston in 1928-29 and played 10 seasons with the Bruins before finishing his NHL career with two years in Detroit. His lifetime goals-against per game average was 2.27 in the regular season and a remarkable 2.00 in the playoffs. He was also a four-time NHL all-star.

Timeouts

In NHL games, each team is allowed one timeout of 30 seconds in regulation time. This timeout must be taken during a normal stoppage in play. All players on the ice at the time a timeout is called are allowed to come to their respective benches.

Toronto Arenas

Toronto hockey franchise, founded in 1917 as a charter member of the National Hockey League. The Arenas, built from the remains of the NHA's Toronto Blueshirts, defeated the Montreal Canadiens in the first NHL playoff series, earning the right to meet the Vancouver Millionaires in the Stanley Cup finals. The Arenas downed the Millionaires in a closely fought five-game series to become the first NHL team to capture the Stanley Cup. In 1918-19, the Arenas dropped to last place and were re-organized as the Toronto St. Patricks for the following season.

Toronto Maple Leafs

In 1926, a group of Toronto businessmen brought together by Conn Smythe purchased the financially ailing Toronto St. Patricks franchise for

$160,000. The club was renamed the Maple Leafs and changed its colors to blue and white. Smythe acquired defenseman Frank 'King' Clancy from Ottawa in 1931 and Clancy would be a key component in increasing fan interest as the Leafs' won their first Stanley Cup in 1932. They lost their next six Stanley Cup final series appearances before defeating the Detroit Red Wings in 1942. They won the Cup in 1945 and then went on to become the first NHL club to win the Cup three consecutive years with victories in 1947, 1948 and 1949. Bill Barilko scored the Cup-winning goal in overtime in 1951 but tragically died in a plane crash that summer. The club won four Stanley Cups in the 1960's with gifted players like Johnny Bower, Tim Horton, George Armstrong, Frank Mahovlich and Dave Keon. In 1967, Toronto won an upset Cup victory over Montreal, the last time that a Maple Leaf team has won the NHL's most coveted prize. The years since have produced some bright memories for Toronto fans including Darryl Sittler's 10-point night in 1976, Lanny McDonald's overtime goal against the New York Islanders in the seventh and deciding game of the 1978 quarterfinals, and numerous bone-crushing bodychecks by Wendel Clark. An era ended in April 1990 with the death of owner Harold Ballard.

CUMULATIVE RECORD	GP	Won	Lost	Tied	Pct
Regular Season	4432	1904	1875	653	.503
Playoffs	396	185	207	4	.472
Series: 88 W47 L41					
TOTALS	4828	2089	2082	657	.501

Toronto St. Patricks

National Hockey League franchise, formerly called the Arenas, that played in the NHL from 1919 to 1926. The St. Pats won the Stanley Cup in 1922 with a roster featuring many of the same players who won the Cup when the team was known as the Arenas. The team missed the playoffs on four other occasions and was in serious financial trouble when Conn Smythe bought the franchise in 1926 and changed its name to the Toronto Maple Leafs.

Torrey, Bill

b. Montreal, Quebec, 23 June 1944.
Bill Torrey attended St. Lawrence University in Canton, N.Y. where he played varsity hockey and graduated in 1957. He was with the Pittsburgh Hornets of the AHL from 1960 to 1965 as director of public relations and, later, business manager. In September of 1968 he became executive vice-president of the Oakland Seals. In February of 1972, Torrey was appointed general manager of the New York Islanders for their inaugural season in the NHL. In 1972-73 and 1973-74 the Islanders finished last in the East

Division but, in 1974-75 they were a better-than-.500 team and continued to climb through patience, scouting, astute drafting and judicious trading. Torrey was the primary architect of a steady improvement that took the team to the top of the NHL with four consecutive Stanley Cups from 1980 through 1983. In 1988-89 the Islanders finished under .500 and out of the playoffs for the first time since the early years and Torrey, still identified by his trademark bowtie, began a rebuilding process.

Trail Smoke Eaters

Senior amateur hockey team from the town of Trail, B.C., (population 12,000) and the last team to win the World Championship for Canada. Trail won its first Allan Cup in 1937-38 and brought home the World title for Canada the following winter. In 1960, they lost the Allan Cup finals to the Chatham Maroons, but were chosen by the CAHA to represent Canada at the 1961 World Tournament. The 18 players on the team, almost all of whom worked for the Cominco Mining Company, went undefeated through the Championships, whipping the favored Soviet Nationals 5-1 in the final game and winning the World title for Canada. The Smoke Eaters won their second Allan Cup in 1962 and again represented Canada at the World title matches, but this time finished a distant fourth. They were the last senior team to skate for Canada at the International level. In 1984 the team folded operations because, as Seth Martin, goalie on the 1961 team and manager of the 1984 team put it, "Nobody came to the games anymore."

Training Camp

Each year, prior to the start of the regular season, teams conduct training camps that allow players to improve their physical conditioning and enable coaches to assess new players who are trying out for a position on a team.

Tretiak, Vladislav

b. Dmitrovo, Soviet Union, 25 April 1952.
Hall of Fame: 1989
Vladislav Tretiak gained a worldwide following for his superb play in the nets for both the Soviet Nationals and the Central Red Army club of Moscow. He joined Red Army's senior roster at age 17 and immediately established himself as the top goaltender in the Soviet Union. He was a Soviet league all-star for 14 consecutive seasons beginning in 1971 and was chosen outstanding player in the country on five occasions. With Tretiak in goal, the powerful Red Army team won its league championship 13 times. Beginning in 1972, his play against the best shooters of

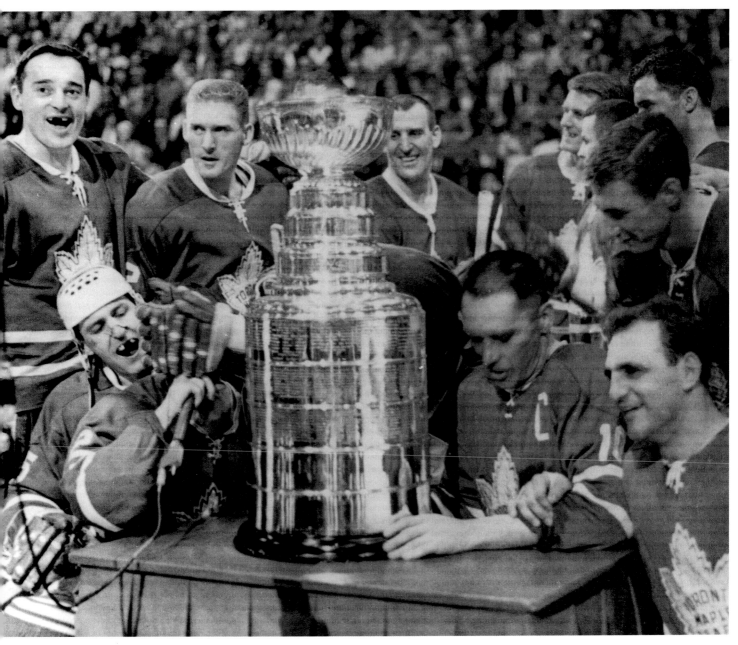

the NHL changed North American perceptions of the strength of the Soviet game. Backstopped by Tretiak, the Soviet Nationals could unleash their high-pressure, swirling offensive attack secure in the knowledge that the big save would be made in their end of the rink. In Olympic and IIHF championship play, Tretiak was part of three gold medal wins and 10 world championships before retiring in 1985.

Trihey, Harry

b. 25 December 1877; d. 9 December 1942.
Hall of Fame: 1950

Center Harry Trihey starred in hockey, lacrosse and football. He was a smart stickhandler and was the first to utilize a three-man line, leaving the rover free to roam; he also encouraged defensemen to carry the puck. On February 4, 1899, he scored 10 goals when the Shamrocks downed Quebec 13-4. He was captain of the Shamrocks when they won the Stanley Cup in 1898-99 and 1899-1900, after earlier starring at McGill University. After retiring as a player, Trihey became secretary-treasurer of the Canadian Amateur Hockey League and, later, league president. He eventually became an advisor to the Montreal Wanderers, and refereed many league and Stanley Cup games.

Tripping

When a player trips his opponent with his stick, or any part of his body (e.g. hand, arm, foot, etc.), he is assessed a minor penalty for tripping. If a player has a clear breakaway to the net (beyond the center redline) and is tripped from behind, preventing a reasonable scoring opportunity, a penalty shot is awarded to the player fouled.

Trottier, Bryan

b. Val Marie, Saskatchewan, 17 July 1956.

One of the game's all-time top centers, Bryan Trottier led the New York Islanders to a four-Cup dynasty that began in 1980. Rookie of the year in the 1975-76 season, Trottier won the Calder Trophy with 95 points. He broke 100 points in 1977-78 with 46 goals and 77 assists and was a first all-star selection. He upped this total to 134, winning the Ross and Hart Trophies the following season. In 1979-80, the Islanders' first Cup-winning season, he had 29 playoff points and won the Conn Smythe Trophy as playoff MVP. The line of right wing Mike Bossy and left wing John Tonelli, centered by Trottier was responsible for scoring more than 1,200 goals in less than eight regular seasons. He continued to excel for the Islanders in both the regular season and playoffs. He was named Budweiser/NHL Man of the Year in 1988 and in 1989-90 scored his 500th NHL goal.

Turnbull, Ian

b. Montreal, Quebec, December 22, 1953.

A defenseman with a scoring touch, Ian Turnbull played 10 seasons in the NHL with Toronto, Los Angeles and Pittsburgh beginning in 1973-74. He scored 123 goals and had 317 assists in 617 games with 753 penalty minutes. He holds the record for most points by a Leaf defenseman with 79 in 1976-77. In that same season he set a league record for goals by a defenseman in a single game when he scored five times against Detroit in Maple Leaf Gardens.

Tutt, William Thayer

b. Coronado, California, 2 March 1912.
Hall of Fame: Builder, 1978

William Thayer Tutt became active in the Amateur Hockey Association of the U.S. through his acquaintance with Walter Brown of Boston. When the NCAA sought a site for its first national collegiate championship tournament, Tutt offered his family-owned arena in Colorado Springs, subsidizing the tournament until the event was able to pay its own way. He also financed the first series in the U.S. against visiting Soviet teams in 1959, hosted the IIHF world championships in 1962 and served as IIHF president from 1966 to 1969. In 1972, he succeeded Tommy Lockhart as president of AHAUS.

The Vancouver Canucks have an emerging star in Trevor Linden who was selected to the NHL all-rookie team in 1989.

Udvari, Frank

b. Yugoslavia, 2 January 1924.
Hall of Fame: Referee, 1973

Despite the many physical risks of his business, Frank Udvari missed only two officiating assign-

ments in 15 years. He refereed 718 regular-season and 70 playoff games in the NHL, beginning with 12 matches in the 1951-52 season. He remained in the NHL as a referee through 1965-66, recognized as the best man on staff for a number of seasons. He was appointed supervisor of NHL officials in 1966.

Ullman, Norm

b. Provost, Alberta, 26 December 1935.
Hall of Fame: 1982
Ullman broke into the NHL with Detroit in 1955, and spent the next 20 years plying his craft at

center ice for the Red Wings and Toronto Maple Leafs. In his 20 NHL seasons, Norm scored 490 goals and assisted on 739 others. He scored at least 20 goals in 16 seasons, and led the league with 42 goals in 1964-65. He was a two-time all-star, moving to the Leafs in 1967-68, along with Paul Henderson and Floyd Smith, in a trade for Frank Mahovlich, Pete Stemkowski, Garry Unger and the rights to Carl Brewer. Following his NHL years, Ullman moved to the WHA for two seasons before retiring in 1977. Upon retirement, Ullman was in NHL's all-time top 10 in both goals and assists.

United States Hockey Hall of Fame

Located in Eveleth, Minnesota, the United States Hockey Hall of Fame is dedicated to players, coaches, administrators and referees who have made significant contributions to hockey in the United States. Opened on June 21, 1973, the Hall of Fame has 70 enshrinees. The U.S. Hockey Hall of Fame closed its doors in 1989 due to financial difficulties.

Vachon, Rogie

b. Palmarolle, Quebec, 8 September 1945.
Injuries to the Montreal Canadiens' Gump Worsley gave Rogie Vachon his first chance in the NHL. He shared the Vezina Trophy with Gump in 1967-68 and played on Cup winners in 1968, 1969 and 1971. He joined the Los Angeles Kings in 1971-72, and was selected to the second all-star team in 1974-75. He was outstanding in the nets for Team Canada at the 1976 Canada Cup. Vachon left the Kings after the 1977-78 season. Very popular with the fans – his number 30 is the only Kings' jersey that is retired – he finished his playing career with Detroit and Boston. In 16 seasons he was 355-291-115 with 51 shutouts and a 2.99 average. In 46 playoff games he was 23-23 with a 2.77 average. Vachon returned to Los Angeles in 1982-83 to work with the Kings' young goalies. He was named general manager in January of 1984.

Vaive, Rick

b. Ottawa, Ontario, 14 May 1959.
Rick Vaive was one of the Baby Bulls of Birmingham, signed as a teenaged professional in the WHA. He joined Vancouver of the NHL in in 1979-80 but was traded to Toronto before the

season was out. In 1981-82 he scored 54 goals as a Leaf and went on to top 50 goals in each of the next two seasons as well. A tough but respected player, Vaive became Toronto's team captain. He was traded to Chicago in September of 1987, playing two seasons for the Blackhawks before being traded to Buffalo. As a Sabre, Vaive scored 19 goals and 13 assists for 32 points in just 28 games. He scored his 400th NHL goal late in 1989.

Vanbiesbrouck, John

b. Detroit, Michigan, 4 September 1963.
Drafted by the New York Rangers in 1981, John Vanbiesbrouck did his junior goaltending for Sault Ste. Marie of the OHL from 1980-81 through 1982-83, although he came up to win a game for the Rangers at age 18 in the 1981-82 season. 'Beezer,' as he is nicknamed, became a Ranger regular in 1984-85 and established himself as

Rick Vaive, as this photo illustrates, can always be found in the center of the action. Vaive has made a career of standing in the slot area and became only the 29th NHLer to score 400 goals in December of 1989.

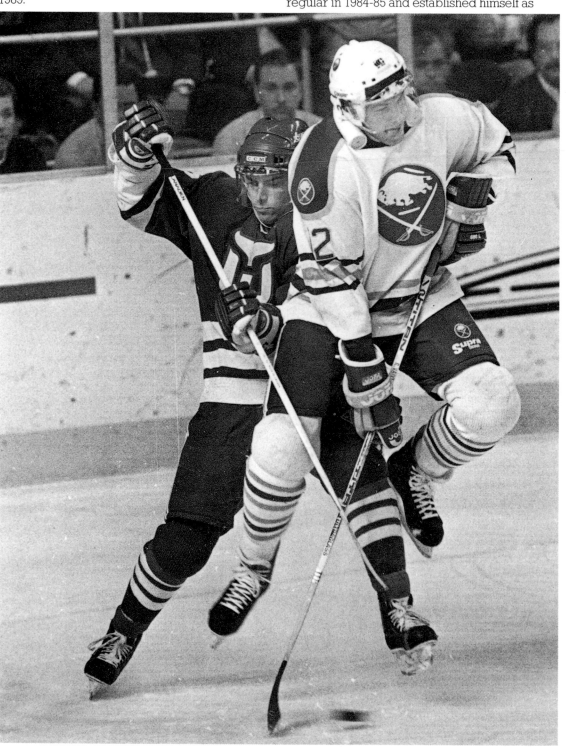

their premier goalie and one of the best in the league, winning 119 and tying 24 through the end of the 1988-89 season. In his best year (1985-86), he was a first team all-star; won the Vezina Trophy and had 31 wins, the most in Rangers' history. He had an average of 3.24 in 24 playoff games that spring as the Rangers went to the Conference finals. A severe wrist injury sustained in a household accident in June of 1988, threatened to hamper his career, but microsurgery enabled him to start the 1988-89 season and he won 28 games in helping the Rangers make the playoffs.

Vancouver Canucks

The Vancouver Canucks joined the NHL in 1970-71 as part of a two-team mini-expansion with the Buffalo Sabres. Despite Vancouver's location on Canada's west coast, the new team played in the NHL's East Division. The club was enthusiastically supported at the gate, but remained at or near the bottom of the standings until 1974-75, the first year of the NHL's four-division setup, when the Canucks finished first in the Smythe Division. Vancouver's best playoff showing came in 1981-82. The Canucks defeated Calgary, Los Angeles and Chicago in the first three rounds of the playoffs. Led by coach Roger Neilson, forward Tiger Williams and goaltender Richard Brodeur, the Canucks were the underdog heroes of the NHL. Swept by the Islanders in the finals, the Canucks struggled through the 1980s until the hiring of general manager Pat Quinn director of hockey operations Brian Burke and coach Bob McCammon. Led by sensational rookie Trevor Linden, in the 1989 playoffs the Canucks extended the highly-favored Calgary Flames to seven games before losing in double-overtime.

CUMULATIVE RECORD	GP	Won	Lost	Tied	Pct
Regular Season	1592	538	812	242	.414
Playoffs	52	19	33	0	.365
Series: 13 W3 L10					
TOTALS	1644	557	845	242	.412

Vancouver Millionaires

The Vancouver Millionaires were the PCHA entry operated by Frank Patrick. The team was organized by Patrick in 1911, and included some eastern stars (Cyclone Taylor, Jack McDonald, Didre Pitre) who were enticed by high salaries and friendly weather. The team won its first and last Stanley Cup in 1915, when it defeated the Ottawa Senators three games to none. The Vancouver team made the finals on five other occasions, but was turned away each time. In 1923, the Vancouver team changed its name to the Maroons, and played under that name until folding following the 1926 season. Outstanding

contributors to the team include: Lloyd Cook, Hughie Lehman, Mickey MacKay and Frank Nighbor.

Vezina, Georges

b. Chicoutimi, Quebec, January 1887;
d. 24 March 1926. Hall of Fame: 1945

Georges Vezina is one of the most renowned goaltenders in the history of the NHL. He was unflappable, earning the nickname of the 'Chicoutimi Cucumber.' He never missed a game throughout a 15-year career that began with with the Montreal Canadiens in 1910-11. His 3.45 goals-against per game average is remarkable when one considers that until 1922, goalies were not allowed to drop to their knees to stop the puck. Vezina played on five league champions and two Stanley Cup winners. His consecutive games string was broken on November 28, 1925, when severe chest pains forced him to leave the ice. This was the first indication of tuberculosis which claimed him in March of 1926. His name is perpetuated by the trophy presented annually to the NHL's top goaltender.

Voss, Carl

b. Chelsea, Massachusetts, 6 January 1907.
Hall of Fame: Builder, 1974

Carl Voss was the NHL's first rookie of the year in 1933, but made his mark in hockey through his ceaseless efforts to develop and improve the skills of referees and linesmen. After his playing career, he was president of the U.S. Hockey League and, in 1950, was named the first referee-in-chief of the NHL. As hockey developed he also became referee-in-chief of minor pro leagues and conducted hundreds of officiating schools and was one of hockey's most effective and enthusiastic ambassadors.

Waghorne, Fred

b. Tunbridge Wells, England, 1866; d. 1956.
Hall of Fame: Builder, 1961

In 50 years of officiating, Fred Waghorne was responsible for several important innovations including dropping the puck on faceoffs instead of placing it on the ice between the stick blades of the players. He also implemented the use of a whistle rather than a handbell to stop play.

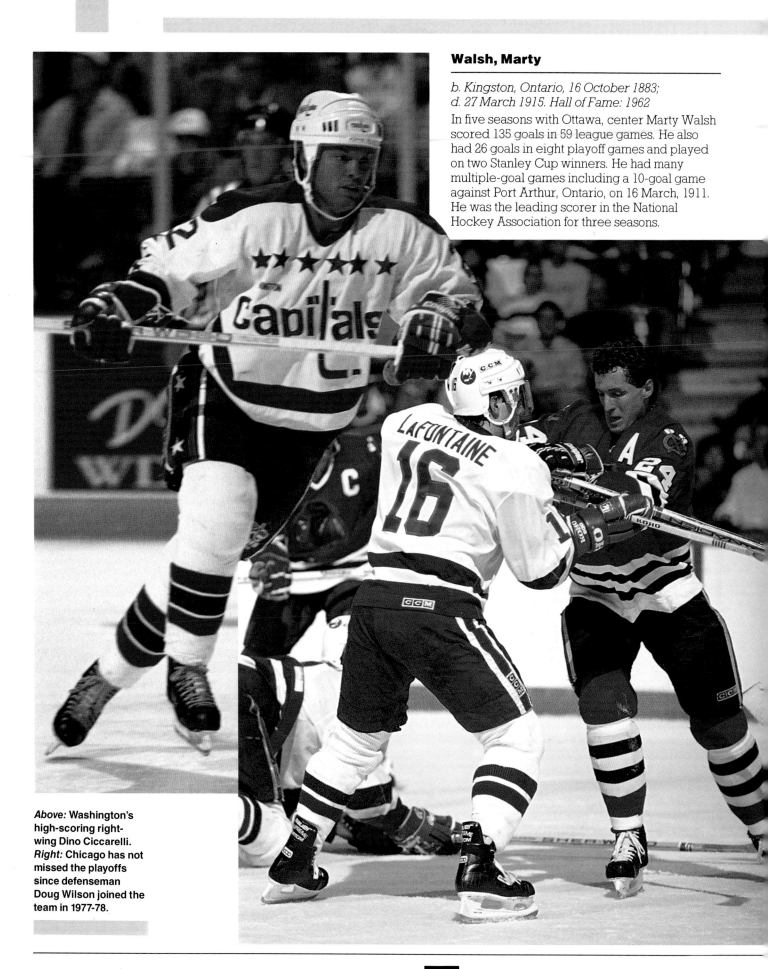

Walsh, Marty

b. Kingston, Ontario, 16 October 1883;
d. 27 March 1915. Hall of Fame: 1962

In five seasons with Ottawa, center Marty Walsh scored 135 goals in 59 league games. He also had 26 goals in eight playoff games and played on two Stanley Cup winners. He had many multiple-goal games including a 10-goal game against Port Arthur, Ontario, on 16 March, 1911. He was the leading scorer in the National Hockey Association for three seasons.

Above: Washington's high-scoring right-wing Dino Ciccarelli.
Right: Chicago has not missed the playoffs since defenseman Doug Wilson joined the team in 1977-78.

Washington Capitals

The Washington Capitals joined the NHL as an expansion franchise in 1974, posting a lowly 8-67-5 record in their inaugural season. The Caps missed the playoffs for eight consecutive seasons, being eliminated on the final night of the season in 1979-80 and 1980-81. They finally made post-season play under coach Bryan Murray in 1982-83, finishing with 94 points, and went on to record three seasons above the 100-point plateau. But despite these impressive results, the Caps were unable to get out of Patrick Division during the playoffs. After a slow start in 1989-90, Bryan Murray was replaced by his brother Terry, the first brother-for-brother coaching change in the NHL and led the Caps to the Wales Conference finals in 1990.

CUMULATIVE RECORD	GP	Won	Lost	Tied	Pct
Regular Season	1280	499	607	174	.458
Playoffs	68	32	36	0	.471
Series: 13 W5 L8					
TOTALS	1348	531	643	174	.458

Watson, Harry (Moose)

b. St. John's, Newfoundland, 14 July 1898;
d. 11 September 1957. Hall of Fame: 1962

Considered one of the greatest all-around forwards in the history of hockey, Watson played for the Toronto Dentals in 1919, moving over to the Toronto Granites the following year. The Granites won the Allan Cup in 1922 and 1923, adding the Olympic championship in 1924. Watson was an outstanding player for that Olympic squad, scoring 13 of his 30 goals in one game against Czechoslovakia. Regarded as the best amateur center in Canada at the time, Watson was offered a $30,000 contract to play the 1925-26 season for the Montreal Maroons. He retired in 1925, but came back as both player and coach in 1931 to win the Allan Cup with the Toronto National Sea Fleas.

Webster, Tom

b. Kirkland Lake, Ontario, 4 October 1948.

In the prime of his career, Tom Webster was one of the speediest and hardest shooting rightwingers in the NHL and WHA. He broke into the NHL in 1968-69 with the Boston Bruins but reached his peak in 1970-71 when he scored 30 goals and 37 assists for 67 points in a Detroit uniform. He later moved on to the California Seals but in 1972-73, the first year of the WHA, joined the New England Whalers and scored 103 points in 77 games, helping the Whalers to the new league's first title. He remained in the WHA until 1979-80 when he returned to the NHL, playing one game for the Red Wings. Webster eventually moved into coaching, taking over the New York Rangers in 1986-87. Webster was considered a bright prospect but an ear ailment aggravated by flying sidelined him several times and finally forced him to relinquish the position. He returned to coaching junior hockey in Windsor and rejoined the NHL as coach of the Los Angeles Kings in 1989-90.

Weiland, Cooney

b. Egmondville, Ontario, 5 November 1904;
d. July 1985. Hall of Fame: 1971

Weiland played 11 seasons in the NHL with Boston, Detroit and the old Ottawa Senators. He was a member of two Stanley Cup champions with the Bruins of 1928-29 and 1938-39 – his first and last NHL seasons. He totalled 173 goals and 160 assists in 509 games. His best season saw him score 43 goals in 44 games in 1929-30. He was voted a second team all-star in 1935. A slick stickhandler, Weiland came to the Bruins from Minneapolis. After retiring as a player, he coached the Bruins beginning in 1939-40. He was behind the bench when the club won its

third Stanley Cup – and last until 1969-70 – in 1940-41. After leaving the Bruins, he coached at Hershey and New Haven of the American Hockey League. He was later named coach of the Harvard University Crimson, a position he held until his retirement in 1971.

West Germany

Germany became the sixth member nation of the International Ice Hockey Federation when it joined on September 19, 1909. Following World War II, Germany was denied participation in world or Olympic tournaments but by 1951, the Federal Republic of Germany was reinstated as an IIHF member. Though never a gold medalist in world or Olympic competition, the nation won silver medals as Germany in 1930 and as West Germany in 1953. Today, the West German national team is a constant threat at world tournaments though they have not won a medal since the bronze at the 1976 Olympics. The first division of the country's Bundesliga consists of nine clubs which play a 32-game regular-season schedule.

Western Canada Hockey League (1922-25)

Professional hockey league formed in the fall of 1921. Franchises were awarded to the cities of Calgary, Edmonton, Regina and Saskatoon, and it was decided that the league champion would play the PCHA champion to determine which club would challenge for the Stanley Cup. Regina won the first WCHL championship, but lost to Vancouver in the series to ascertain the western Cup challenger. For the next two seasons, both the PCHA and the WCHL sent challengers east to play for the Stanley Cup. In 1925, the rival PCHA folded and two teams, Vancouver and Victoria, joined the WCHL, bringing the league's membership to six teams.

Western Hockey League (1926)

After financial problems forced the Regina Capitals to relocate in Portland, Oregon, WCHL officials dropped 'Canada' from the league title. The new Western Hockey League remained a six-team operation but it was clear the league's survival was in jeopardy. At the conclusion of the 1925-26 season, the WHL folded with most of the players being sold to teams in the NHL, which was planning extensive expansion into the United States. Professional hockey did not return to the west coast of Canada and the United States until 1948.

Westwick, Harry (Rat)

*b. Ottawa, Ontario, 23 April 1876; d. 3 April 1957.
Hall of Fame: 1962*

His elusive style and comparatively small physique earned Westwick his nickname during his early days with the Ottawa Senators. He started his career as a goaltender, but was soon converted to rover. He graduated to the Senators in 1895, winning three straight Stanley Cups starting in 1902-03. Westwick had his most productive season in 1904-05, scoring 24 goals in 13 games. Following his retirement as a player, he refereed briefly in the National Hockey Association.

Whitby Dunlops

Senior hockey team best remembered for winning the World Championship in 1958. The 'Dunnies', as they were called, were also the first team to beat a Soviet national team on Canadian ice. Whitby – a small town east of Toronto – turned the trick at Maple Leaf Gardens on November 22, 1957, defeating the touring Russians 7-2. The team was born when the Bowmanville Truckmen relocated to Whitby for the 1955-56 season. With the Dunlop Tire Company providing sponsorship, the Dunlops were formed. With such talent as Harry Sinden, Sid Smith, Roy Edwards and Wren Blair on board, they won the Allan Cup in 1957 and were invited to represent Canada at the 1958 World Championships. Canada had not defeated the Soviets in international play since 1955, and the whole country paid particular attention to the 1958 tournament. Canada and Russia, both undefeated going into the final contest, were tied late in the game when the 'Dunnies' scored two goals 30 seconds apart to earn a 4-2 victory and bring the World title back to Canada.

Williams, Dave 'Tiger'

b. Weyburn, Saskatchewan, 3 February 1954.
The NHL's all-time penalty-minute leader with 3,966 in 962 games, leftwinger Tiger Williams played 13 seasons with Toronto, Vancouver, Detroit, Los Angeles and Hartford. Put in other ways, he spent just over 2¾ days, 66 complete games, or about 7% of his whole career in penalty time. Despite his extensive time in the penalty box, Williams' hockey skills were considerable. A colorful character whose comments enlivened many sportswriters' columns, he scored 241 goals and had 277 assists, adding 12 goals and 23 assists in the playoffs. His best scoring year was with Vancouver in 1980-81 when he had 35 goals and 27 assists.

Wilson, Doug

b. Ottawa, Ontario, 5 July 1957.
Doug Wilson has been an all-star wherever he has played, beginning with the Ottawa 67s of the OHL. He was a first team all-star in 1976-77, moving up to the Chicago Blackhawks the following season where he commenced to establish himself as a fine, two-way defenseman with a devastating shot from the point. The highest-scoring defenseman in Chicago history,

Right: Dave Ellett, all-star blueliner of the Winnipeg Jets, played a vital role in the club's dramatic improvement in 1989–90. The Jets improved by 21 points over their 1988–89 finish and moved up to third place in the NHL's tough Smythe Division. The Jets led Edmonton 3-1 in games in the first round of the 1990 playoffs before the Oilers came back to win the series.

he went 39-46-85 in 1981-82, winning the Norris Trophy and a position on the first all-star team. He played for Team Canada in 1984, and was voted a second all-star in 1984-85. Wilson rebounded from a shoulder injury that limited him to 27 games in 1987-88 to score 62 points the following season. His totals through 1988-89 are 191-475-666 plus 14-47-61 in the playoffs.

Winnipeg Jets

One of 12 teams to begin play in the inaugural season of the World Hockey Association in 1972-73, Winnipeg would be instrumental in giving the new league credibility by signing superstar Bobby Hull to a contract totalling $2,750,000 in 1972. The Jets would later acquire

Swedes Ulf Nilsson and Anders Hedberg as linemates for Hull and the trio immediately became the league's top line. The Jets used a style that emphasized skating, passing and team play during those WHA years, winning the Avco Cup in 1976, 1977 and 1979. One of four teams to be accepted into the NHL in 1979, the Jets set an NHL went 30 consecutive games without a win in 1980-81. The selection of Dale Hawerchuk in the 1981 Entry Draft proved to be the turning point for the franchise as the Jets have made the playoffs every year but one since 1981-82.

Vancouver Blazers do battle with the Jersey Knights during the 1973-74 WHA season. The Blazers, who relocated to Vancouver from Philadelphia, moved on to become the Calgary Cowboys. In total, 28 different teams skated in the WHA in the league's seven year existence.

CUMULATIVE RECORD	GP	Won	Lost	Tied	Pct
Regular Season (NHL)	880	331	432	117	.443
Playoffs	43	12	31	0	.279
Series: 10 W2 L8					
TOTALS	923	343	463	117	.435

Winnipeg Victorias

The Victorias of Winnipeg challenged for the Stanley Cup on eight occasions between 1896 and 1903. On three of these outings they were victorious (February 1896, 1901 and January 1902). Playing in the Manitoba Hockey League, this team dressed in scarlet uniforms, and are credited with two innovations: in 1896, George Merritt appeared in his goalkeeper's crease wearing cricket pads for protection, and in 1901 they introduced tube skates to Stanley Cup play. The captain and driving force behind the team was Dan Bain, who had with him such notables as Merritt, Fred Scanlon, Jack Armitage and Jack Marshall.

Wirtz, Arthur

b. Chicago, Illinois, 23 January 1901; d. 21 July 1983. Hall of Fame: Builder, 1971

Arthur Wirtz joined forces in 1931 with James Norris, Sr., acquiring the Detroit Red Wings hockey club and Olympia Stadium. Later, along with James Norris, Sr. and James D. Norris, Wirtz acquired control of the Chicago Stadium Corporation, Madison Square Garden, St. Louis Arena and other facilities. In 1954, two years after Norris, Sr.'s death, Wirtz and James D. Norris bought the Chicago Blackhawks, and divested themselves of their hockey interests in Detroit. They invested heavily in rebuilding the Chicago organization, turning it from a perennial last-place finisher to one of the most successful clubs in the NHL. As well, Wirtz was primarily responsible for persuading the NHL to include St. Louis in its 1967 expansion plans.

Wirtz, Bill

b. Chicago, Illinois, 5 October 1929. Hall of Fame: Builder, 1976

When Bill Wirtz's father Arthur and James D. Norris acquired the Chicago Blackhawks in 1952, Bill became a part of the organization. He became a vice-president in 1953 and, in 1966, joined the NHL Board of Governors and became club president. Under new ownership, the Blackhawks enjoyed a resurgence, winning the Stanley Cup in 1961 and the league title in 1966. In the early 1970s, Wirtz's efforts to make expansion a success were recognized by his peers who elected him chairman of the NHL's Board of Governors.

Women's Hockey

The growth of organized women's hockey through the 1970s and 1980s culminated in the staging of the first IIHF-sanctioned Women's World Championship tournament in Ottawa,

Ontario, in March of 1990. Eight nations competed in this event: Canada, Finland, Japan, Norway, Sweden, Switzerland, West Germany and the U.S.

World Championships (IIHF)

The IIHF held sanctioned European championships as early as 1910, but the first World Championship did not take place until 1920 in Antwerp, Belgium. Other early host cities included Stockholm, St. Moritz, Chamonix, Milan, Davos, Vienna, Budapest and Zurich. The IIHF regrouped after World War II and tournaments were resumed in 1949. Under the direction of IIHF executive Bunny Ahearne, the World Championships grew into a major sports event held each April. As part of improved relations between the NHL and the IIHF, Canadian NHLers eliminated from early rounds of the NHL playoffs were added to the roster of Canada's entry at the championships beginning in 1977.

Roy Worters relaxes in the net for the New York Americans. One of 'Shrimp's' greatest performances came in a losing cause during the 1928–29 playoffs when the Americans met the Rangers in a two-game total-goal series. The Americans, who scored only 53 goals in the entire season, couldn't buy a postseason marker. Worters was outstanding, but the Rangers finally won the series 1-0 after an overtime ie in the second game.

World Hockey Association (WHA) (1972-1979)

The World Hockey Association was the first league to attempt to compete with the NHL since the demise of the Western League in 1926. Formally organized on November 1, 1971, play began in the 1972-73 season with 12 franchises: Alberta Oilers, Chicago Cougars, Cleveland Crusaders, Houston Aeros, Los Angeles Sharks, New York Raiders, Minnesota Fighting Saints, New England Whalers, Ottawa Nationals, Philadelphia Blazers, Quebec Nordiques and Winnipeg Jets. The new league operated without a reserve clause in its player contracts, effectively guaranteeing an open market for players. More than 70 NHLers eventually jumped to the WHA, including Bobby Hull, Bernie Parent, Johnnie McKenzie, Ted Green, J.C. Tremblay and Derek Sanderson. Gordie Howe came out of retirement to join his two sons in Houston and the Winnipeg Jets built a team around Bobby Hull and as many

as 11 Scandinavian players. The WHA lasted seven seasons through numerous franchise shifts and closures. At the end of 1978-79, six franchises remained in operation. Four of these – Edmonton, Quebec, Winnipeg and New England (Hartford) – were admitted to the NHL to begin play the following season. The addition of these clubs to the NHL brought the established league up to the 21-team configuration that was maintained into the 1990s.

World Junior Championships

Beginning in 1977, this IIHF event brought together the best junior hockey players in the world in a format similar to the IIHF World Championships. The 1990 tournament was held in Helsinki, Finland, with Canada winning the gold medal. The World Juniors have become a showcase event for players of junior age from Europe and North America to be evaluated by NHL scouts.

Worsley, Lorne (Gump)

b. Montreal, Quebec, 14 May 1929.
Hall of Fame: 1980

Gump Worsley played goal for the New York
Rangers, Montreal Canadiens and Minnesota
North Stars with minor league stops in New
Haven, St. Paul, Saskatoon, Vancouver, Providence, Springfield and Quebec. He was the
NHL's top rookie in 1953 with New York, and
played 10 seasons for the Rangers before being
traded to Montreal. With the Canadiens' strong
defense in front of him, he was part of four
Stanley Cup champions in 1965, 1966, 1968 and
1969 and twice shared the Vezina Trophy with
other Montreal netminders. His NHL career
goals-against per game average was 2.91 with 43
shutouts in 860 regular-season matches.

Worters, Roy

b. Toronto, Ontario, 19 October 1900;
d. 7 November 1957. Hall of Fame: 1959

In 1928-29, Roy Worters registered a 1.21 goals-against per game average and became the first netminder to win the Hart Trophy as the NHL's MVP. Worters was only 5-3 and seldom weighed more than 130 pounds, earning him the nickname 'Shrimp', but he starred in the NHL for 12 seasons with the Pittsburgh Pirates and New York Americans. He won the Vezina Trophy in 1930-31 and was a two-time all-star, averaging 2.36 goals-against in 488 league games. He is considered to be the first goaltender to use the backs of his gloved hands to divert shots to the corners of the rink.

★★★ Ⓨ ★★★

Yzerman, Steve

b. Cranbrook, British Columbia, 9 May 1965.

Few players in the post-World War II era have had as much impact on their teams as Steve Yzerman. Selected fourth overall by the Detroit

Overleaf: **John A. Ziegler, Jr., the president of the National Hockey League. Under his leadership, the NHL has experienced unprecedented growth, is poised to expand in the 1990's.**

Below: **The invention of the Zamboni has been as important to the modern age of hockey as the center red-line and the slapshot. Not only did Zambonis do a better job than any earlier method of maintaining the ice surface, they also provided NHL publicity directors with early opportunities for advertising and promotion.**

continued and in 1988-89, he played so well that he was favorably compared with Wayne Gretzky and Mario Lemieux. He had 65 goals and 90 assists for 155 points and led all NHLers in even-strength goals. He was a finalist for the Hart Trophy and won the Lester B. Pearson Award as MVP selected by his fellow players. Not only a superb scorer, Yzerman had become the unquestioned leader of the Detroit hockey club and its most prominent performer since the days of Gordie Howe.

Zamboni

The Zamboni is a four-wheel drive vehicle that scrapes and floods the ice surface before each period of a hockey game. Invented by Frank J. Zamboni, the machine grew out of experiments with a tractor pulling a sled to reduce the resurfacing time at Iceland, the rink Zamboni had built in Paramount, California. In 1949 the first one-driver Zamboni made its appearance. Today it is possible for one man to lay down a fresh sheet of ice in ten minutes. Before the Zamboni, six men needed 90 minutes to do the job. The Zamboni takes the snow off the rink's surface, at the same time giving it a fresh coating. Improved ice quality as a result of resurfacing between periods has added greatly to the speed and finesse of modern hockey. Zamboni also invented machines to service artificial turf. The Astro Zamboni sucks up water from the carpet of a baseball or football field.

Ziegler, John A. Jr.

b. Grosse Pointe, Michigan, 9 February 1934. Hall of Fame: Builder, 1987

John Ziegler began to do legal work for the Detroit Red Wings and Bruce Norris in 1959 and, in 1966, joined the NHL Board of Governors as an alternate governor for the Red Wings. He worked on league committees and various aspects of litigation and was elected president of the NHL in September, 1977. As president, he lead the league to an accommodation with the rival WHA which resulted in the expansion of the NHL to encompass Edmonton, Hartford, Quebec and Winnipeg in 1979. Ziegler also forged a unique working relationship with the NHL Players' Association, maintaining labor peace while significantly amending the bargaining agreement between the league and its players.

Red Wings in 1983, Yzerman tallied 39 goals with 48 assists for 87 points in his rookie season. He cracked 100 points in 1986-87, scoring 50 goals with 52 assists in 64 games. His improvement